# Mystics and Heretics in Italy at the End of the Middle Ages

Émile Gebhart

Translated by
Edward Maslin Hulme

Routledge Revivals
Routledge
Taylor & Francis Group

First published in 1928
by George Allen & Unwin Ltd

This edition first published in 2015 by Routledge
2 Park Square, Milton Park, Abingdon, Oxon, OX14 4RN
and by Routledge
711 Third Avenue, New York, NY 10017

*Routledge is an imprint of the Taylor & Francis Group, an informa business*



**Publisher's Note**

The publisher has gone to great lengths to ensure the quality of this reprint but points out that some imperfections in the original copies may be apparent.

**Disclaimer**

The publisher has made every effort to trace copyright holders and welcomes correspondence from those they have been unable to contact.

A Library of Congress record exists under LC control number: 22023140

ISBN 13: 978-1-138-18166-3 (hbk)
ISBN 13: 978-1-315-64682-4 (ebk)
ISBN 13: 978-1-138-18169-4 (pbk)

NICHOLAS-ÉMILE GEBHART
1839-1908

*Routledge Revivals*

# Mystics and Heretics in Italy at the End of the Middle Ages

Originally published in 1922, this translation of French historian Émile Gebhart's work by Hulme gives a detailed religious history of Italy in the middle ages clearly demonstrating Gebhart's expertise in this area. Poetry, art and politics all centred around religion in the period studied and Gebhart identifies three key areas to be discussed; the Church in Rome, Christian concern and rationalism or secular independence whilst also focussing on famous heretics of the period including Arnold of Brescia and Francis of Assisi. This title will be of interest to students of History.

# MYSTICS & HERETICS IN ITALY

## AT THE END OF THE MIDDLE AGES

BY

ÉMILE GEBHART

TRANSLATED, WITH AN INTRODUCTION, BY

EDWARD MASLIN HULME

LONDON: GEORGE ALLEN & UNWIN LTD

RUSKIN HOUSE, 40 MUSEUM STREET W.C. 1

*This translation*
*First published in 1922*

# CONTENTS

TO

THE MEMORY OF

MY MOTHER

ANNIE LOUISE HULME

THIS VERSION OF "L'ITALIE MYSTIQUE"

A BOOK THAT REVEALS THE SPIRIT OF AN AGE

IS DEDICATED

Youth fades, love droops, the leaves of friendship fall.
A mother's secret hope outlives them all.

# INTRODUCTION

ALTHOUGH the French historian and man of letters who is the subject of this brief sketch lived almost exactly the traditionally allotted term of three score years and ten, the frost of age had failed to chill the fires of his youth ; his poet's heart still beat high within his breast ; his enthusiasms had lost nothing of their old intensity ; his interests were ever widening and deepening ; and his sympathies, more inclusive than ever with the passing of the years, had but mellowed in the autumnal glow. To have devoted half a century to the writing and teaching of history (for though he sat in a chair of literature he emphasized the historical aspect of his subject), to have written many exquisite historical sketches, one ambitious historical novel impregnated with the authentic spirit of its time, and at least two important historical works unsurpassed in insight and synthetic power in their respective fields, and, in addition, to have created in the minds of many students an understanding of the significance of two great periods in the story of the human past, and to have enkindled in their hearts a deep and abiding love for those times, for the noble men who lived in them, and for the beauty of the art that still gives voice to their ideals, to have done all this, and without stain in the doing, is surely an enviable accomplishment and one well worthy of commemoration. Yet thus far only one of his books has been done into English, and that a minor one ; in no paper published in the English-speaking world did his death evoke more than a brief paragraph ;

and in his own country he seems to be generally underrated as a writer of mere exquisite miniatures rather than esteemed as a scholar of insight and learning as well as of grace.

Nicholas-Émile Gebhart was born in 1839 at Nancy, the old capital of Lorraine, which at that time was not as prosperous and animated as it afterwards came to be, but which could nevertheless boast a grace now vanished. The men of Lorraine, so one of their number has said, have three ruling passions—the army, art, and the forest. Gebhart and his two brothers, although of Alsatian parentage, personified these three passions. The eldest was a soldier and rose to the rank of general; the youngest became a commissioner of forests; and the second was the man of letters whose life we are to narrate and whose work we are to estimate.

The sensitive and imaginative boy proved to be an excellent pupil in the public school at Nancy, and among the prizes he won was a copy of the *Journey from Paris to Jerusalem*. No other writer made a deeper impression upon French literature in the nineteenth century than Chateaubriand. His extraordinary faculty for the description of nature, his exquisite sense of style, his impassioned eloquence, the richness of his imagination, the ardour and the violence of his passions, his *sombre fidélité pour les causes tombées,* and, above all else, the touch of Celtic magic that distinguishes so many of his pages, enchanted the child Gebhart and induced him to dream, beneath the pale sky of his northern town, of the olive and the oleander, of purple seas and purple mountains, of distant lands where the temples are fallen and where the silence of the long summer days is broken only by the hum of the insects. The passion he conceived for Chateaubriand never left him. And, as was the case with little Pierre in *Le Lys Rouge,* from these school days dated a taste for sonorous Latin and elegant French which he never lost despite the example, and, indeed, if not even the counsel, of many of his more famous contemporaries. In due time he continued his studies at Nancy under the newly-established Faculty of Letters, of which five of the professors had been members of the French School at Athens. When he received the degree of Bachelor of Letters his father, who was himself a provincial magistrate, sent him to Paris to study law. There he became a lawyer, and, although it is not recorded that he ever pleaded a case, he long maintained a nominal connection with the profession.

But even while preparing for his degree in law, young Gebhart did not neglect letters. He frequented the Sorbonne and was in particular attracted by the lectures of M. Saint-Marc Giradin. One day, in speaking of La Fontaine, the famous professor vigorously denounced the idle and improvident grasshopper. The next week he read a letter of protest, received, he explained, since the last lecture, which, pleading the cause of the light-hearted insect, was signed "A Grasshopper of the Latin Quarter." So delighted were the auditors with the cleverness of the reply that they requested the name of the author. Thus did Gebhart enjoy the intoxication of a first literary triumph. Strange that a defender of *la cigale* should be found in a youth whose race has always been noted for its ant-like industry!

Gebhart was not yet twenty-one when he sustained his two theses for the doctorate of letters. In the first one, *De varia Ulyssis apud veteres poetas persona*, he reviewed the various characters lent to Ulysses by the poets of antiquity. The second, *Histoire du sentiment poétique de la nature dans l'antiquité Grèque et Romaine*, based upon his own reading of the classical authors and upon lectures to which he had listened in the Sorbonne and the Collège de France, was a larger theme. It betrays the immaturity of its author, of course, but scattered throughout its paragraphs are quotations from Chateaubriand and Goethe that reveal something of the intense longing that possessed him for the classical countries. Fate was kind to him. He was appointed to teach logic in the public school at Nice, the gateway to the land of his heart's desire.

The thoughts of the new school teacher were not always confined to his half-empty classroom. They often followed the sails that winged their way over the blue sea and disappeared in the east. Fortunately the new charter of the French School at Athens rendered it no longer necessary that the candidates should be men distinguished for scholarly research. Gebhart received an appointment without opposition. To Athens, by way of Italy, he accordingly went.

For the first time he saw Florence, suave and austere, whose soul is revealed in the work of Frà Angelico and Dante, in that of Donatello and Michelangelo, her severe grandeur always penetrated with grace, her exalted mysticism never unregardful of the daily and common life of man. To Siena he went also, the winsome city, seated aloft upon her hills, her walls and towers the colour of the rose, whose beauty is matched only by the memories that surge within the brain. " There is a soul in the charming body of the old city ", he wrote a generation later, " a memory universally present that unceasingly carries the thoughts of the living back to distant times ; an angelic vision ever hovers in the pleasant atmosphere of Siena. There Saint Catherine will always be queen." He entered Rome by coach and put up at the Villa Medici, from whose windows he could see the Eternal City spread before him. He told at a later day with how keen a pang he saw the ancient ruins despoiled of their mantle of clematis and the river no longer running between reeds and willows but canalized with granite walls. On he went through Naples and Pompeii to Palermo, that city which, with its plain, the Golden Shell, lies so picturesquely within half-encircling heights and fronts upon a gently curving bay. A place of thronging memories, indeed! Phenician, Greek, Roman, Carthaginian, Saracen, Norman, Angevin, and Aragonese has each contributed to its story. In its cathedral, eloquent with echoes of the past, Gebhart stood before the tomb of Frederic II, Saint Catherine at Siena and the Emperor Frederic at Palermo; the most fragrant flower of mysticism and the pioneer of rationalism; the sweetest exponent of religious rapture and the forerunner of the Renaissance! What greater antithesis could there be? Yet to each was the young student attracted, and of each was he to write with insight, sympathy, and charm. His imagination had been stimulated by the Middle Ages. Let him now follow Ulysses over the violet sea and make his way to Greece, there to "learn the art of tempering the imagination by reason and of wedding sentiment with judgment".

The great memories of Greece were vividly revived and the fascination of that marvellous civilization came over him with increased intensity. Four years (1861–1865) he resided there. The time was not spent in archæological research. For such work Gebhart had little capacity and less taste. Something had to be done, of course, to discharge the debt contracted when he entered the School at Athens. So he set to work upon a book having for its subject Praxiteles. Clearly he cannot be counted among the few sons of fame who win their kingdom in a single night. The book is not a scholarly work. The archæologists gave it a harsh reception. Yet in it one catches a glimpse of the later writer, who reveals to us the significance of art as an expression of the spirit of the time that witnessed its birth, the nation in which it was born, and, above all else, of the personality of the artist who created it. And though it has many of the faults it has also many of the engaging qualities of youth, exuberance, obvious delight in the exercise of talent, in a word the *fougue de vingt ans*. While in Greece he wandered from place to place—Peloponnesus, the Ionian Isles, Beyrouth, Jerusalem, Memphis, Constantinople. With Renan he stood before the Parthenon. From his window in Athens he often looked upon Hymettus with its violet tones, upon the azure gulf, and upon the Acropolis. At times his eyes were filled with tears, for nature had bestowed upon the young humanist the gift of reverie. So the old enchantment came upon him ; the miracle of Greece was renewed.

Upon leaving the School at Athens a place was found for Gebhart in his native town. He was appointed assistant professor of foreign literature in the Faculty of Letters at Nancy. There, in the town that was the scene of his first successes, that was always dear to him above all others, he taught for fourteen years. His very first lecture was a general survey of the Renaissance in Italy. Thenceforth his public life was made up of two activities, that of lecturing and that of writing. In 1880 he began his work as a professor of foreign literature at the Sorbonne, where he continued to lecture until 1906, two years before his death. The record of the subjects of his courses in the first three years, 1880–1883, is lost and it seems impossible to find it ; but we have that of the remaining twenty-three years. The large preponderance of his courses was devoted to the literature and the civilization of the Renaissance in Italy. Occasionally he gave courses devoted to the Spanish theatre of the Renaissance period and to *Don Quixote* and its sources. Only once did he deal with a more recent subject, and that was in 1885–1886, when he gave a course of lectures on the poetry of Leopardi.

In 1895 Gebhart accepted the seat, left vacant by the death of Constant Martha, in the section of the Academy of Moral and Political Science that is concerned with morals. And in 1904 he was elected to take the place in the French Academy that had belonged to Octave Gréard.

What manner of teacher was Gebhart? That is a question which can be answered only by those who were his auditors. Let our first witness be M. Henry Bordeaux. "M. Gebhart speaks better than he writes. When he teaches he throws his whole being into his lesson. He explains clearly and his improvizations are always methodical. He seems ever to be pursuing his subject at random, and always finds himself travelling on the right road. He has a wonderful faculty of pausing at the right moment, so that one is tempted to ask, as children do, 'And what happened then?' Then he unfolds learnedly and slowly the sinuosities of his narrative, preferring to the stronger emotions those that are tender. He combines a modicum of irony with the most exalted sentiments; an irony akin to good nature; an irony that conceals a taste for credulity, a taste disciplined by intelligence." We may summon, too, President Poincaré, likewise a native of Lorraine, who took the seat in the French Academy left vacant by the death of Gebhart. "He began his lessons in a serious tone, laying stress upon the words and emphasising the syllables. But this solemn commencement was succeeded very quickly by a freer manner, made up of witty good nature and roguish familiarity. At times, when he had taken pains to arrange his subject well and to elaborate its form, he offered his delighted audience a foretaste of the best chapters of his coming works; and sometimes, when he gave himself up to his inspiration, he carried the minds of his auditors through a labyrinth of readings and quotations, varied with ingenious comments." Finally, we may repeat the words of M. René Doumic. "Gebhart's was one of the most complex characters imaginable; even for those who came most closely into contact with him and lived longest upon familiar terms with him, he never ceased to be in a certain undefinable way an enigma. As to the rest, his colleagues, his pupils, and men of the world, who gradually, from being strangers to him, became his friends, these are the stages they passed through and the series of discoveries they made, which made their delight all the greater when they really knew him. The first sight of him was disconcerting enough : a head quite round in shape, cheeks and neck fat and puffy ; one would have sworn he was some Rabelaisian canon or monk. Only the small, lively and mobile eye, that was wont suddenly to light up, betrayed the mind that watched beneath this sleepy appearance, a mind that was curious, observant and amused with the things of life. . . . It was quite impossible not to conceive an affection for him. None of those who have spoken of him since his recent death have been able to remember him without emotion. In the French Academy, where he was almost a new-comer, he had at once made himself loved : the last time he appeared there, bearing upon his face those signs that cannot be mistaken, every heart was touched with grief."

Gebhart spoke little of himself ; and, with the exception of the quality of his prose, was content always to adopt a tone of careless irony about his own achievements. His character, despite what has been said of the undefinable and enigmatic element in it, was essentially simple, clear-cut, and masculine. He had the distinction that comes from personality and intellect rather than from the accidents of a career. Courtesy, like a subtle fragrance, interpenetrated all that he did or said. His life was not one of incident, but rather one of thought. Outwardly it is lacking in variety. Like most teachers he did not make history himself, but he instilled into his students and readers the spirit that directs the course of history. He lives not so much by virtue of action as by virtue of the thought, and still more by virtue of the sentiment, he aroused and developed in others. For his thoughts dwell in the mind as well as in the memory, and his emotion is contagious and passes into deeds. The way to understand him, then, is not to attempt a record of his daily life, but to study his writings ; for in them we shall find his most vivid experiences, his deepest feelings, and his most pregnant thought ; in them his inward and spiritual life stands revealed.

The first of Gebhart's books to attract serious attention was his study of *Rabelais,* published in 1877, and issued in 1895 in a revised form. His five previous publications may be passed over lightly as *souvenirs d'enfance.* M. Poincaré does not think very highly of this book. " After the recent progress in Rabelaisian studies," he says, " one cannot dream of remarking any great degree of erudition in Gebhart's work. Let us not require of the author either new researches in the biography of Rabelais, or learned dissertations upon the authenticity of the fifth book. Instead of pursuing truth along precipitous paths, Gebhart tries to attract it into spacious alleys bordered by beds of roses. Yet the portrait he presents to us, if not very deeply thought out, is exceedingly life-like and placed in a good light. Here is the mediæval man, recognizable by the turn of his satire and the freshness of his Gallic intellect ; and here is the first French representative of the new age, revealed by his intellectual richness, his critical sense, his intoxication with life, and his worship of science." It is quite true, as M. Poincaré observes, that Gebhart was not an authority in the field of Rabelaisian studies. His book is not a contribution to our knowledge of the subject. Yet something less than justice has been done to it in the remarks we have repeated. Gebhart's study of Rabelais is careful and accurate, and it is distinguished by insight (particularly the chapter on Rabelais' religion) and sympathy, by sound judgment and breadth of view, qualities not possessed by every grubber of facts, and qualities without which facts would be comparatively meaningless. Biography makes exceptional demands upon sympathy and judgment, and in these qualities few of Gebhart's contemporaries excelled him. He displayed but a slight disposition to participate in the work of delving into dusty archives, and he had never a very sedulous regard for the "petty decalogue of mode." But there is an ampler air and a broader outlook upon humanity in his books than are to be found in those of many of his better known and more highly estimated contemporaries. And if Bolingbroke was right when he declared genius to be "great coolness of judgment united to great warmth of imagination," then something more than talent may be claimed for Gebhart upon the warrant of this his first important book.

In 1879 there came from Gebhart's pen a much more important book, *The Origins of the Renaissance in Italy,* a book crowned by the French Academy. This and *Mystic Italy* are the two books by which he must be judged as a historian. It is an attempt to discover the remote origins of the Renaissance, to ascertain why that movement began in Italy and not in France, and then to analyse, in the early writings and works of art, the genius of Italy in the period of the Renaissance. It is a masterly work and one of absorbing interest. There is, of course, the perennial interest of the Renaissance itself; but what attracts us most is the skill and the charm with which the Renaissance, in its beginnings and its early stage, has been revealed. It is not an exaggeration to say that to the study of this period, and this people whom he loved, he brought the eye of a painter, the touch of a pianist, the heart of a poet, and the mind of a philosopher. All the essential factors that denied to France the high privilege of becoming the birthplace of the new movement and bestowed it upon Italy are segregated from their accompanying and inconsequential circumstances with unfailing insight and analytical power, and are then grouped into a most illuminating synthesis. His inductions are made from a wide range of facts, so that when he begins to subsume the characteristics of the Italian people and the life of the period with which he is dealing his conclusions are accepted with confidence. And this has been done without overloading the book with details. So many historians of to-day give the public too much of their material. It is true they sift and arrange, but as the interest of their work grows, so also grows in them, apparently, an irresistible desire to permit their readers to share in the preparation of materials, and to give them, therefore, not results but processes. To do away with unnecessary and oftentimes tiresome detail, to abstract unessentials for some great end, to leave out for the sake of revealing what was hidden or only dimly discernible—these are the necessities alike of great art and of great history, which is so largely an art. If this book proves nothing else it proves that its author had the shaping touch. But the book reveals beyond all doubt that its author penetrated into the genius of Italy and the spirit of the Renaissance as few others had succeeded in doing, and this is in itself sufficient to establish Gebhart's claim to the title of historian. For surely it is a delicate task to comment upon a national psychology and the psychology of an era alien to one's own. On so slippery a path even the surest-footed may occasionally stumble and fall. The historian of a country or a period not his own, if he be not content with a chronicle of external and easily apprehended facts, is likely to miss an occasional nuance of vital importance. And it is just this difficult work of intellectual and spiritual diagnosis with which our author is always primarily concerned. It may be added, furthermore, that not the least of the merits of this book, and of every other book that Gebhart wrote, is the delicacy of feeling and the skill which, while retaining the impression of a comprehensive and accurate study of its subject, have suppressed all parade of learning and sifted and sublimated the residuum of research in the crucible of a reconstructive imagination.

The third of Gebhart's important historical works is the one here done into English, *Mystic Italy,* published in 1890, which by many is regarded as his masterpiece. It is a study of the religious history of Italy from the heart of the Middle Ages to the dawn of the Renaissance. It deals with the transition from the age of faith to the age of reason. Stimulating and suggestive studies of Italian thought and life in those centuries had been made by Michelet, Ozanam, Renan, Thode, Müller, and Schmidt; but it remained for Gebhart to group the results of the researches of these men and his own studies into a revealing synthesis, rendered attractive not only by the interest of its theme but also by his rich and romantic yet always direct and lucid style, by his extraordinary sense of the picturesque, by the unfailing charm that comes from his enthusiasm, by his true insight, his poetic sensibility to emotional experience, and by the fragrant sentiment that exhales from so many of his pages.

The scalpel of Gebhart's analysis was employed with skill. With a delicate hand he has disentangled the threads of Italian life throughout the twelfth and thirteenth centuries and revealed their strange interconnections. The springs of action are all exposed. It would seem, as we have already said, that a foreign observer, and especially one writing at so distant a day, could not perceive every subtle current in the stream of national progress; but that which mere analytical skill would have failed to lay bare was disclosed by Gebhart's unusual power of divination, of intuitive insight, the faculty that enables those who possess it to apprehend the subtle essence of an alien personality, or period, or nationality.

In *Mystic Italy* our author leads us upon what the

French call a *promenade à travers les ages.* But he is no mere showman content to point out the external and obvious things of an historical pageant. What an illustrious roll of diverse personalities it is that he has given us ; no mere harlequinade of marionettes, but men who represent the mingling currents in the religious life of Italy and who live for us once again after the lapse of many centuries ! Arnold of Brescia, who met so pitiful a death on the banks of the Tiber ; the abbot Joachim of Flora, a restless soul who traversed Christendom for more than three-score years seeking for truth, and who gave as his final injunction to the world the old truth that " the letter killeth, but the spirit giveth life " ; Frederic II, whose intellectual initiations constituted of themselves a Renaissance pathetically premature ; Francis of Assisi, the Spouse of Poverty, whose brave and kindly eyes pierced the wrappings with which the ages had ever more thickly veiled Jesus of Nazareth from the sight of men ; John of Parma, successor of the Seraphic Father, counsellor of moderation in the quarrel between the strict and the easy-going Franciscans, illustrious in his day for learning and for saintliness, who devoted himself to the memory of Francis with the tenderness that John had displayed for the memory of Jesus ; Frà Salimbene, the itinerant, timid, and egotistic friar, a joyous representative of the second generation of the Franciscans, whose *Chronicle* is so interesting a history of its period ; Jacopone da Todi, the singular poet, the " jongleur of God ", who protested against the secular interests of Boniface VIII, and who in consequence was chained to the wall in the dark and narrow prison of Palestrina ; Giotto, true son of Francis, whose frescoes still tell their stories of that gracious and comely spirit on the walls of the church in Assisi ; and, finally, Dante, whose personal religion flowed from the Franciscan fountain : *Iddio non vuole religioso di noi se non il cuore.*

Every thought of all their thinking sways the world for good
or ill,
Every pulse of all their life-blood beats across the ages still.

The power that enabled Gebhart to reveal to us all these various personalities and to lay bare for us the hidden penetralia of their remote period was not, as we have already said, a thing of the intellect alone ; for the soul of a single person or of a people can never be explained by the unaided process of scientific rule. It was created in large part by those qualities of insight and imagination that enable a writer to re-think himself into a society other than his own and so to reconstruct a vanished world that it acquires reality for a later age. These indispensable qualities of the historian were Gebhart's in abundant measure.

But it is by its sweeping synthesis, as well as by its power of analysis and insight, that *Mystic Italy* appeals to all who would rightly understand the life of the peninsula from the rise of the communes to the appearance of Petrarch. Its generalizations arrange all the facts disclosed by its analysis and reveal to us their significance in masterly fashion. In dealing with form, the Aristotelian canon lays its first emphasis not upon finish of detail but upon architectonics. Judged by this canon of classic art the book is a noteworthy achievement. Without this power of synthesis Gebhart's explorations in the dim regions in which thought and emotion are generated by elusive and impalpable causes, his studies of the interior life and its laws, his concern with the spiritual dynamics of humanity that were his passion, would all have been left comparatively meaningless to us. Fortunately our author possessed not only the power of seizing upon spiritual significances but also of arranging and unfolding them in orderly and illuminating form. The gift of wide perspective was his. The events of two hundred years are brought within easy view of the reader ; and the book has that unity that comes only from a logical organon historically defensible, justified by the facts with which it deals. "The book throughout is a model of composition," says M. René Doumic; "the historian has been captivated by his subject: he has tasted that sublime joy of pursuing an idea in its development through time and in its individual expressions."

*The Origins of the Renaissance in Italy* and *Mystic Italy*—these, as we have said, are the two books by which Gebhart's name as a historian must live or die. There are, however, other works that deserve notice; the two books that deal respectively with *Botticelli* and *Michelangelo,* appreciating the dreamy mysticism of the one and penetrating to the tortured soul of the other; and then there are the essays and sketches in which appear a long pageant of historical and fictional personages, which reveal a remarkable facility for exploring old chronicles for their buried riches, for understanding and recreating the past. Gebhart was always travelling up and down the centuries with a mind prepared like a sensitised plate for impressions, ever on the watch for the picturesque. That he wrote many polished and pregnant essays and so many brief and beautiful sketches is, perhaps, the reason why he came to be generally regarded as a miniaturist rather than as a historian, an artist whose *genre* was not great but who may be thought to have been great in his *genre,* a mere purveyor of "dainties that are bred in a book."

> This craft of thine, the mart to suit,
> Is too refined, remote, minute;
> These small conceptions can but fail;
> 'Twere best to work on larger scale.

But several of these essays have notable historic value, and nearly all the sketches are steeped in the spirit of the time and make an undiminished appeal by means of their picturesque character. This last fact in itself speaks eloquently of their enduring worth ; for few things go out of fashion so quickly, so soon become stale, flat and unprofitable, as the picturesque element in historical writing when it has been laid on as a veneer, instead of having had its origin in the nature of the subject and in the temperament of the writer, when it is gilt and not gold. Aye, even when it be pure gold, the flight of years often steals from picturesque history an absolute quality it once possessed and that won for it a meed of popularity at the moment of its publication. The flight of time, then, is an exacting test ; and the fact that, after a generation, Gebhart's picturesque sketches have not been left pale and bloodless is proof not to be passed unnoticed of their vitality and staying power. In all these briefer products of his pen, as in his larger works, his main interest is in the currents of intellectual and spiritual change. The observation, the thought, and the emotion, of these miniatures are entirely his own ; they possess the quality the French call *vecu* ; the personal note is everywhere, though linked, as it must ever be in work that is to count, with the note of the universal. And quite as much as his larger books they bear witness to the perfection and the consecration of his work.

There remains Gebhart's one historical novel, published in 1893, *Around a Tiara*. To write a successful historical novel is no easy task. It requires for its subject-matter a wealth of learning, for its movement a well-devised plot ; and then, in order to make it live, it must have insight, imagination, and the dramatic sense. Mere erudition amassed from books will not suffice. Learning that has not been assimilated will be found, indeed, to weigh upon the wings of fancy, to check the flight of imagination. Not in the seclusion of a library shall one prepare himself fully to realize and adequately to represent a vanished age. These things require a knowledge not only of books but of men ; and lacking this knowledge a writer shall give us not men but the phantoms of men, incapable of moving us either to love or to hate. For the springs of action to-day are much the same as they were yesterday. "The eternal life of man," says Robert Louis Stevenson, "spent under sun and rain, and in rude physical effort, lies upon one side scarce changed since the beginning." *Autour d'une Tiare* follows the plan approved by the best masters of historical romance in that the leading rôles are assigned to imaginary characters, whereas the real historical characters, though exercising a profound influence upon the fortunes of the principal *dramatis personæ,* are relegated to the rank of minor figures and are permitted to cross and recross the stage only at intervals. Thus a constant demand is made upon the imagination, and only occasionally is there a dependence upon the mere recital of historic fact. It deals with Italy in the late years of the eleventh century and interweaves a somewhat idyllic love story with the austere and tragic history of the pope of Canossa. The great defect of the novel is that it is not an organic whole. Various scenes, the incantation at the beginning, for example, and the interview at Canossa, stand out by themselves more or less detached from the current of the story and give to the book its fragmentary character. And it is not only entire scenes that give the impression of lacking organic relation to the whole ; many a sentence proudly isolates itself from its neighbours. Then, too, most of the characters are mere types, not quivering figures with the blood in them, and often the only motive for their entrances and exits is the medium they offer to the author of completing his picture of Italian society under the great pope. Gebhart did not see his fictitious characters with such clearness that they pressed upon upon him for representation ; and, in a work of this kind, no truth to history will atone for the absence of the vital spirit. Yet if the book fails, on the whole, as an historical romance, it succeeds as a history ; for it gives us a faithful picture of Rome in the eleventh century, an admirable portrait of Gregory, and a vivid idea of the character of the Papacy at the time of its great struggle with the Empire.

Such, briefly, is the story of Gebhart's work as a teacher and writer of history. The present writer cannot hope to have succeeded in conveying to his readers anything more than a suggestion of Gebhart's charm and ability, as a lecturer, and scarcely more than a suggestion of his grace and power as a writer. He never heard Gebhart's voice ; and he realizes keenly his limitations as a translator. It is not the easiest task in the world to translate one of Gebhart's books. It was Shelley who said that "It were as wise to cast a violet into a crucible in order to discover the formal principle of its colour and odour as seek to transfer from one language into another the creations of a poet." And that Gebhart was a poet, yet a poet in whom the historian was not lost, is beyond denial. There is no English for Ronsard's *Mignonne, allons voir si la rose* ; nor for his *Quand vous serez bien vielle, au soir, à la chandelle* ; and there does not seem to be an equivalent in English for many passages in Gebhart's subtle and musical prose, every line of which has been as delicately pondered as though it were poetry. But this brief estimate of his life and work, and still more the translated book to which it is prefixed, may serve to indicate that Gebhart has a genuine claim to be considered as one of the notable historians of our time. I do not mean to place his accomplishment upon a level with that of Von Ranke or even of Taine. He would not gain by any such appreciation as that ; and I feel sure he would have been the first to have disliked and disclaimed it. No one knew his limitations better than did he himself. But his claim to be considered as a noteworthy historian is justified by the catholicity of his distinguished and delicate mind, by the fairness of his judgment, by the logic of his exposition, by the swiftness and the sureness of his intuition, and by the indefinable quality of charm with which all that he has written is interpenetrated. It is quite easy to name historians who possessed a greater range of knowledge, and others who have done more creative work with the original sources of history, but it would be difficult to name one whose knowledge was more subtle and more idiomatic. "The original merit of the man and writer," says M. René Doumic, "is that he succeeded in combining in so happy a harmony those qualities which in others are too often mutually exclusive: imagination with knowledge, irony with good sense, and attachment to tradition with complete liberty."

# FOREWORD

I HAVE attempted to study the religious history of Italy during the Middle Ages. Religion was at that time the chief product of the Italian genius. Poetry, art and politics, which from the thirteenth century onwards made Italy the principal centre of western civilization, received a constant and very noble inspiration from the religious sentiment. The particular manner in which Italy early conceived the idea of the kingdom of God and the way that leads to it ; the astonishing freedom of thought with which she treated dogma and discipline ; the serenity which she succeeded in preserving in face of the great mystery of life and death ; the art wherewith she reconciled faith and rationalism ; her slender aptitude for formal heresy and the boldness of her mystic imagination ; the impetus of love which often carried her to the loftiest Christian ideal ; finally the anguish she felt at times in her relations with the Church of Rome, and the right she allowed herself of denouncing its weaknesses without pity, of stigmatizing its deeds of violence, and of thwarting its ambitions—such was the original religion of Italy, the religion of Pietro Damiano, Arnold of Brescia, Joachim of Flora, Francis of Assisi, John of Parma, Frà Salimbene, Catherine of Siena, Savonarola, and Contarini. It was also the religion of Dante and Petrarch, of Giotto, Frà Angelico and Raphael, and of Olimpia Morata, Vittoria Colonna, and Michelangelo. Of the two dates which mark the beginning and the end of this form of Christianity, the first is very undecided, by reason of the scarcity of documents and the harshness of the times, but undoubtedly Gregory the Great (590-604) nursed it in his heart, and

Gregory VII (1073-1085) would have eagerly embraced it if the fatality of the temporal and feudal interests into which the Empire and the Holy See were plunged had not carried him away from it and kept him on that battle-field where he struggled for liberty, and on which he died doubting the existence of justice in the world. Down to the thirteenth century Italian Christianity had harbingers, prophets and martyrs ; it did not attain to the full consciousness of its genius until the time when the glad tidings of Assisi were proclaimed in the valleys of Umbria. From the time of Francis onwards it illumined every great soul and penetrated to the inmost recesses of the Italian character. But the date of its end is well known. The Council of Trent, aided by the Inquisition, imposed upon Christendom a moral rule, a devotion and a religious method of an absolute uniformity, at the same time that, repairing the breaches made in the pontifical power by the councils of the fifteenth century, it assigned to the Church of Rome an uncontrolled and unlimited disciplinary authority over the episcopate, the monastic orders, the secular clergy, and the simple believer. On that day was fulfilled the saying of the Gospel, "There shall be one fold and one shepherd." Roman Catholicism was in fact instituted and almost immediately strengthened by the religious police of the Society of Jesus and the political sympathies of the old European system. It was a great creation, which long charmed the world by the pomp of its worship, the heroism of its missionaries, the virtues of its preachers and the elegance of its literary education. But this magnificent edifice gives a similar impression to that produced by St. Peter's at Rome There the implacable regularity of the plan, the unvarying flood of light which descends from the dome, the sumptuous adornments, arrest the soaring flight of personal piety ; in that inflexible order of all the lines there is no room left for that freedom of fancy whereby in former days men conjured up at will the vision of things divine. Where are the churches of olden days, which the humble entered familiarly as the Father's house, and whose walls covered with paintings presented to them in so simple and artless a fashion a free interpretation of liturgical texts? There, seated in the shadow of the little chapels, the Christian was wont lovingly to meditate upon Paradise: he listened far less to the distant psalmody of the priest than to the joyous song of his own heart. Here, should the soul, weary of the splendours of the great temple and its worship, essay to take its flight heavenward, it beats its wings against the immense shining cupola; the sacred bird will fall back again on the marble slabs of the altar.

The reforming work of the Council of Trent, the effects of which were long attenuated in France by the political tradition and by Jansenism, was not slow in producing an extraordinary result in Italy. The religious sentiment had owed its life so far in that land to freedom, individual faith, and love. On the day when, contrary to the prophecies of the abbot Joachim and the expectation of John of Parma, the age of servitude returned once more and put an end to the age of filial obedience, when the age of thorns delayed the coming of the age of lilies, men's consciences fell into a state of indifference, powerless to receive a new form of Christianity or to welcome it with fervour. They accepted its outward practices, sought no spiritual nourishment in it, and quietly closed their minds alike to enthusiasm and fanaticism. The less cultured transformed the ardour of the old faith into superstitions of an entirely pagan sort; the more lettered took their religion as a ceremonial incumbent upon well-educated persons and prudent citizens. It is easy to perceive the cause of this religious sterility. If Italy, unlike Spain, refused to hand herself over to the Council of Trent and to enclose the whole of her moral life in a narrow and austere Catholicism, analogous to the religion of the Spaniards, it was because a long rationalistic education, carried at times to the limits of scepticism, had accustomed her to a free intellectual life. Classical culture, which was never entirely destroyed even in the darkest ages, continual intercourse with certain of the ancient moralists, and a very lively sense of reality, had saved the Italians from the excesses of scholasticism. Their neighbourhood to dissident religions, the Greeks and the Arabs, had preserved them from religious egotism. Tolerance led them to adopt a very liberal interpretation of orthodoxy : the story of *The Three Rings* was in the *Novellino* long before the time of Boccaccio. They early learnt to reason without syllogisms upon the soul, its destiny and its duties ; to see this it is only necessary to recall the writings of Brunetto Latini, Dante's *Convito*, and the letters of Petrarch. The Italians were, in fact, the first men in Christendom to look nature in the face and to study her methodically. The decisive moment of this intellectual development was the reign of Frederic II (1212–1250), his troubadours, physicians, inams, and alchemists. But the first essays in free thought and reasoned doubt go back further still. The wandering students of the *Carmina Burana*, and the so-called heretics whose memory disturbed Villani, belong to the twelfth century. Observe that there was never any serious conflict between the religion of the Italians and their rationalistic thought. The thirteenth century was able, without any historical scandal, to couple Francis of Assisi with Frederic II. Where the spirit alone gives life to souls and the letter counts for little the faithful is able to ascribe to the supernatural whatever part he pleases, and he always does so. He believes that God is not a very severe creditor and that He lavishes His blessings on men of goodwill. But where the letter has killed what the sixteenth century called "profound faith," the Christian can choose only between an unreserved abdication of his reason and the discreet incredulity of devout politicians, between the painful piety of the simple, who submerge their whole life in the supernatural, and amiable piety of men of the world who make the supernatural subservient to the fair fame and elegance of their life. Italy had passed through too long a period of rational culture to be lulled to sleep in a kind of religious infancy. Deprived of freedom to believe, she unconsciously retained of her freedom of thought that measure of scepticism which, while permitting the external observance of religious rites, preserves men from mystic passion. But that form of Christianity which is no longer sustained by political interest, and whose mysteries and discipline have no more meaning for the crowd, slowly dies out, like a lamp lost in the depths of the sanctuary.

Thus, in this history of Italian religion, we can distinguish three chief elements, or, if you prefer it, three leading actors in the drama: (1) the Church of Rome; (2) the Christian conscience; and (3) rationalism, ironic unbelief or free investigation, the spirit of secular independence, lay resistance, or scientific indifference. I purpose in this book to describe the heroic period of that history. The first attempts at heresy or schism, Arnold of Brescia, Joachim of Flora, Francis of Assisi and his religious creation. Frederic II and the civilization of southern Italy, the revival of Joachimism in the institutions of Assisi, the militant work of the Holy See between the times of Innocent III (1198–1216) and Boniface VIII (1294-1303), will occupy our attenton one after another. At the same time I shall indicate what part Italian faith played in the renovation of the arts and poetry, and what beam, sent forth by the great Christians of the twelfth and thirteenth centuries, rested on the cradle of Nicholas and John of Pisa, Giotto, Jacopone of Todi, and Dante.

# MYSTICS AND HERETICS IN ITALY

## CHAPTER I

## THE RELIGIOUS AND MORAL CONDITION OF ITALY BEFORE THE TIME OF JOACHIM OF FLORA

### I

THE words of Jesus "My kingdom is not of this world", the promise of an entirely ideal religion, had been impossible of fulfilment in the catastrophe of the barbarian inundation. Life was then so hard that the Church was compelled to take part in worldly things. Until the time of the Carolingians it was the last remaining organized society and the last tradition of government; and so it opened its gates, as a refuge of peace, not only to souls possessed by the desire of eternal salvation, but to the nations terrified by the violent results of conquest. The more utter the ruin of all civilization, the more necessary and the more important appeared the temporal rôle played by the Church. In Italy and at Rome the political work of the bishop and pontiff was really, in its origin, a work of charity. Beneath the shelter of the Holy See, enveloped by barbarism, Christianity restored to civil society the springs of life that had been lost since the fall of the Roman Empire.

Gregory the Great was the incarnation of that apostolic period of the Church and the Papacy. He came upon the scene at the bitterest moment of the invasions. Alaric and Attila had passed like a hurricane over Italy. The Ostrogoths had very quickly assimilated the Roman civilization. But when the Lombards arrived it was believed the end of all things was at hand. The terror of the Lombard barbarism is still visible in Paul the Deacon, who lived in the eighth century, and who belonged to their race. These rude heathens, with their green-tinted hair, erected their tents everywhere, as far as the Straits of Messina, leaving here and there a few wrecks of old Italy still floating, Ravenna, more Byzantine than Italian, Naples, soon to enter into alliance with the Saracens, and lastly Rome, where a monk buried in his cell on the Cælian Mount was the last hope of Latin Christendom. The Benedictines of Monte Cassino fled to Rome. All Italy turned to Gregory, asking him to save her, and he did so. He was a man of letters, of patrician family, very gentle and pure ; by the culture of his mind and the nobility of his race he represented all the memories of a vanished world, and by his monastic austerity all the promises of the future. He was, above all things, an apostle. While treating with the Byzantines, the Franks, and the Goths of Spain, he was at the same time converting the Anglo-Saxons and evangelizing the Lombards. He saw them bow beneath his pastoral staff. A great peril was thus averted, and Italy henceforth sheltered from pagan or Arian contagion. Nevertheless, Gregory pined away in melancholy. He had accepted with terror the charge of the pontificate. He had a presentiment that the Church, once launched upon the seas of worldly things, would soon depart from its primitive mission. He died in affliction at the thought of the tragic times that awaited his successors.

The Christian republic had been set up with pope Gregory as its centre. At Rome he had been the supreme bishop, but not the chief of a state. The apostolic age of the Holy See, however, was about to close. The Carolingian donation made of the pope an Italian seigneur, and the feudal system made the bishops counts and barons. The Church thus became a secular power, superior to all the rest by the action it exercised upon men's consciences, weaker than the rest because the hereditary system never perpetuated the power in a single family. The irony of history obliged the vicars of God to enter upon a political and military existence, while refusing them the vital principles of every government, blood succession, the authority of ancestral tradition, security for the morrow, the right to undivided command over a whole hierarchy, and the uncontested possession of a territory. From the eleventh to the thirteenth century the Church struggled against the absurd reality of its temporal conditions. The quiet theorists who, from John of Salisbury and St. Thomas to Dante, Marsilio of Padua and William of Ockam, reasoned upon the pre-eminence of emperor or pope, upon the two luminaries and the two swords, did not keep sufficiently in view those surprising conditions that were too strong for a saint and man of genius like Gregory VII. They did not understand that, in the feudal state of the world, secular greatness was the Church's guarantee of religious integrity. Outside Rome the Church found the Empire overshadowing all Christendom ; the emperor, king of the Romans or patrician, with his juridical claims upon the Eternal City ; the feudal system that, embracing the episcopate and the monastic orders, compelled the bishops and abbots to fidelity towards the secular suzerains and the empire as the foundation of the European compact. Thus the feudal law put the episcopate into the emperor's hands and in part removed it from the pope's authority. In Italy the Church had to do with the advocates of national independence who forced it to choose between the Empire and the restoration of the Italian kingdom ; it came into conflict with the Lombard or Tuscan episcopate, closely related by feudal ties to the Germanic Cæsar ; with the Greeks, attached to Byzantium by the bond of schism ; with the Normans, who made mock of the Holy Father and humiliated him with their protection. At Rome, lastly, the Church was in the den of lions, betrayed by the cardinals of the factions opposed to the reigning pope, done violence to by the counts of Tusculum who sold the Holy See by auction, pillaged by the barons of the Campagna, enslaved by the patrician families, again and again dispossessed by the senate of the Capitol, outraged by the people who drove the popes from the city with showers of stones, threatened by the republican tribunes who wished to despoil it of its feudal rights. Add to all these the Saracens, who came up the Tiber, burnt St. Peter's, and laid waste the patrimony ; the Germans, who at each imperial coronation made the streets run with blood ; the feudal bandits, who carried off Gregory VII one Christmas night from the altar of Santa Maria Maggiore and abducted Gelasius II (1118–1119) when sitting in full conclave ; and, finally, the robbers, disguised as priests and monks, who roamed in troops round the church of St. John Lateran and seized the apostolic treasure. Ascend this scale of miseries in the contrary direction. From the populace of the *monti*, the patricians who encamped in the theatre of Marcellus or the Coliseum, and the savage barons of Latium to the emperor himself, through the whole of feudal society runs the thread of the Church's temporal necessities and anguish. If the pope were not master in his own house and his basilicas, if the Roman commune rose against him, if the patrimony was taken from him and the barons denied him as their suzerain, he lost rank in the Italian feudal system, in the political and social order of the world ; he was a bishop deprived of his see, and nothing more. Ten times in the course of a century he was obliged to hide himself in the castle of St. Angelo and to appeal to the emperor for succour, or to flee with some faithful clerics to the Alps and wait for the emperor's coming. It was always the great lay suzerain of the West who said the last word in the ecclesiastical crisis that began in some brawl at a street corner in Rome.

But in all this it was not merely a question of temporal interests. Undoubtedly in the unity of a Holy Empire similar to that of Rome under Trajan, under a wise master of the civilized world, the Church and the pope would have enjoyed religious liberty ; they would have been able to abdicate all secular ambition, remain pure from all contact with earthly things, and think only of the governance of souls ; that, in his *De Monarchia*, was the dream of Dante. But in the feudal condition of Italy and Europe, and in the communal state of Rome during the Middle Ages, every temporal failure of the Church and the Holy See was necessarily a religious failure. Every time the pope was less powerful than the commune, the nobles, or the people, the rebellious cardinals or the emperor opposed an antipope to him. Once there was seen on the same day one pontiff at the Vatican, another at Santa Maria Maggiore, and a third at St. John Lateran. Gregory VII had an antipope at Tivoli, facing his metropolis—Clement III (1187–1191), who survived him. In the twelfth century Anacletus II (1130–1138) and Innocent II (1130–1143) were elected in two neighbouring conclaves at the same hour by two rival factions of the Sacred College ; Bernard of Clairvaux had to decide for Christendom which was its real pastor. If the antipope did not arise from a popular upheaval or a feudal intrigue, the Empire and the Germanic church took it upon themselves to proclaim him. In reality the most dangerous usurpations of the spiritual power came from the emperor. If he opposed the Germanic church to the Italian, the imperial council to the pontifical ; if he addressed, as Charles the Great did, encyclicals to the bishops, abbots, clergy and faithful ; if a mystic dreamer, Otto III, "Servant of the servants of God," or politicians, such as Henry III and Henry V, appointed or deposed popes, and, strong in the holy unction that had touched their foreheads, spoke and acted as the visible vicar of Christ, did not the emperor thereby assume to himself the supreme religious power? In the troublous times of Christendom did he not appear between the Byzantine emperor, chief of a schismatic church, and the Roman pontiff, ever followed by the shadow of an antipope, as the lawful ruler of men's souls and their universal pastor?

## II

Thus condemned to keep its rank in the temporal hierarchy and to reign in order to avoid destruction, the Church passionately clung to a strip of territory ; it made the prestige given to it by the faith of the bygone centuries subservient to its secular domination ; it employed an unscrupulous diplomacy and pitiless mercenaries, and was all the more haughty in proportion as it felt its weakness ; it was passionately fond of riches and set up a usurer's office hard by the altar of the living God. Simony was at that time the most efficacious means of government at Rome, just as was nepotism at a later date when the Church was faced by princely Italy. Everything was sold in the pontifical market : red hats and mitres, forgiveness of sins, the removal of excommunications, suzerainties, the right of conquest by land and sea, relics of saints, the imperial crown, the Roman tiara, and the gate of Paradise. So irresistible was the current that carried the Church towards the good things of the world that Gregory VII, who had once entered Rome with bare feet and head, was tormented more ardently than any other by secular ambitions ; he attempted to assign to the Holy See, by Matilda's donation, not only the *allodia* of his friend between the Po and the Liris, but all the great imperial fiefs of Tuscany, and then Spoleto, Camerino, Mantua, Modena, Brescia, and Parma. The ambition of Alexander VI (1492–1503) was to be more modest.

We meet here not only the abandonment of the rôle of the apostolic Papacy, but also a serious corruption of doctrine and discipline. All the virtues that Jesus had exalted were disdained ; the poor, the peaceable and the simple, were no longer the elect of the Church ; all that Jesus had disdained and stigmatized, the love of gain, harshness towards the humble, the unbridled pursuit of the goods of this world, the possession of land and power, were raised to the rank of beatitudes and took the place of the charity and renunciation of the first Christian community. It seems as though the Middle Ages had closed the Gospel for ever. Primitive Christianity, which was derived from Paul and rested upon justification by faith, had no meaning from this time forward ; idealism retired from the sanctuary ; narrow religion, the religion of works, was set up in its place. Between God and the faithful was set the Church, which hides God from the faithful. Feudal practices invaded the religious life. The Church in those days needed devoted servants, vigorous arms, generous friends ; legions of mystics were not worth in its eyes a single well-armed vassal or a good condottiere ; the treasure of St. Peter was something more precious in its eyes than the purity of men's souls. In that rude combat it carried on against Rome and Italy and Europe, the passive discipline of Christendom was its strongest defence. It exacted obedience by terror ; it curbed men's wills by the observance and rigours of devotion. It struck at the impious emperor and at intractable kingdoms and cities with the anathema and interdict, thus rendering the conscience of peoples uneasy, and shaking the loyalty of subjects. To the middle classes, the serfs, and all the humble folk who are consoled by the divine promises for the miseries of life, it gave the priest, ever at hand and ever needed, because of the sacraments, alms-giving, prayer, pilgrimages, fasting, the fear of judgment and the apprehension of purgatory. Thus it had a hold upon all Christians and summoned them in long processions to Rome to kneel at the tomb of the apostles, and to Jerusalem, to kneel at the sepulchre of Christ. And for three days of victory, which compensated for ten centuries of humiliation, the pontiff of this Church had the joy of seeing at his feet the emperor, that is to say, the feudal world, kneeling before him in the snow, a suppliant, smitten to the ground under the ban of excommunication. But he had forgotten the words of the scriptural saying, *Beati misericordes, quoniam ipsi misericordiam consequentur*.

The Church of Rome was henceforth obliged to prove that it was right and the Gospel wrong and to justify its policy by the excellence of its morality. In order to reassure Christians and confirm the sacerdotal system of Christianity, it would have needed a pure clergy and impeccable pontiffs. But at that time the pastors were the scandal of the flock. Read the decisions of ten councils against the married clergy and the *Liber Gomorrhianus* of Pietro Damiano. The story of the popes, from the ninth to the thirteenth century, staggers belief. The follies of Caligula, the ferocity of Nero, the lust of Heliogabalus, appear in the world once more. In the tenth century the counts of Tusculum abandoned the Holy See to courtesans and ruffians. John XII (955–964), pope at seventeen years of age, installed his harem in the Lateran and ordained a deacon in a stable. Boniface VII (984–985), overthrown after being pontiff for forty-two days, fled to

Constantinople with the treasure of the Church. He returned on the death of Otto II, starved his successor John XIV (983–984), to death in the wells of St. Angelo, and put out the eyes of his cardinals. Benedict IX (1033–1056), pope when only twelve years old, led a life so horrible that the captains of Rome tried to strangle him at the altar. He escaped, sold the tiara, asked a girl in marriage, returned to Rome, which was occupied by two antipopes, was again driven out, had the German pope, Clement II (1046–1047), poisoned, mounted for a third time the chair of St. Peter, and then disappeared for ever and shut himself up like a wild beast in the forests of Tusculum.

Astounding tragedies were enacted again and again before the eyes of the faithful. Pope Formosus (891–896), taken from his tomb and clad once more in cope and mitre, was duly tried and condemned for heresy; the fingers that had given the papal blessing were cut off, and his body was dragged through the city and thrown into the Tiber. Some days later he returned in triumph to the mortuary crypt of the popes, and the statues of the saints were believed to have bowed their heads as he passed. The bloody corpse of Boniface VII was kicked by the people from street to street as far as the statue of Marcus Aurelius. On every road in Italy for two centuries processions of exiled popes passed and repassed, Gregory VII, surrounded by the Norman chivalry, Pascal II (1099–1118), prisoner of Henry V. Gelasius II and the Sacred College fled by way of the Tiber on two galleys pursued by the German archers along the banks of the river. A storm prevented the ships from putting out to sea. The cardinal of Altri lifted the pope on his shoulders and carried him through the fields by night to a castle in the neighbourhood; at break of day Gelasius embarked again and escaped to Gaeta; he returned to Rome on foot, begging the hospitality of the barons, and one evening knocked at the door of one of his partisans in the city. But the German antipope was on the alert. On the day of St. Praxides the pope was officiating in the church of that name; the Frangipani burst in, hurling stones and shooting arrows towards the choir. Gelasius escaped by way of the sacristy, hastened across Rome with his stole on, followed by a cleric bearing the cross, took refuge in the Campagna, and in the evening we find him alone, seated on the ground, near the church of St. Paul outside the walls. He was weeping like a child, and women were weeping around him. *O vos omnes, qui transitis per hanc viam, attendite et considerate si est dolor sicut dolor meus!*

This Papacy, either demoniacal or profoundly miserable, this Church, soiled by all manner of crimes and overwhelmed by the brutality of the age, became the horror and torment of Christendom. Some of the protests made against it have come down to us; as the year 1000 approached there was a cry of pain from a monk of Mount Soracte, and a cry of anger uttered at the synod of Rheims by a bishop of Orleans. Glaber thus concludes his chronicle of the pontificate of Benedict IX: *Horrori est quippe referre turpitudo illius conversationis et vitæ.* In the eleventh century Pietro Damiano, in a letter to the bishop of Fermo, deplores the fact that the Church has the temporal sword at its disposal; he regrets the times when Ambrose and Gregory appeased the pagans and barbarians by gentleness. The popular conscience, which saw the hand of God in all the crises of history as well as in all the disturbing phenomena of nature, silently condemned the Church of Rome. If God permitted such catastrophes, it was because he had abandoned the shepherds of Christendom to the malice of Satan. The terror of the antichrist from that time forward seized upon the imagination of the Italians. A bishop of Florence, Raineri, announced from the pulpit that he had already been born and would soon appear. From century to century, till the time of Savonarola, this anxiety constantly reappeared and even manifested itself in works of art. The sick souls of men sought eagerly on every side to recover the true way of salvation. (1)

## III

Some of them, the noblest, took refuge in the monastic life. Thus, while escaping from the world in which the secular Church had lost itself, they thought they remained faithful to Christianity. Monasticism, in the century of horrible disorders which Benedict of Nursia witnessed, had been a port of refuge ; but it could receive only a very insignificant part of Christendom. It rested, in fact, upon the idea that the civil life is pernicious and that the isolation of the faithful in the solitude of a cell is the best preparation for the death of saints. Bruno, in the eleventh century, founded the Chartreuse upon the same idea. *O beata solitudo! O sola beatitudo* ! The cloisters, buried in the shadows of the forests or lost on the mountain tops, never seemed to be far enough removed from the towns and the commerce of men. In order to conform to the word of God, and to taste in its fulness the sweetness of God, it was necessary first of all to purify oneself from all pride, all love, and all earthly memories. Absolute detachment from all that is not Jesus is the most frequent precept of that book of the *Imitation* which, towards the end of the Middle Ages, summed up, as in a melancholy testament, the discouragement and sadness of these friends of solitude. "*Claude super te ostium tuum*. Shut thy door behind thee and call to thee Jesus, thy well-beloved ; live with Him in thy cell, for nowhere else wilt thou find peace so profound." So the monk said good-bye to the world, or, rather, he despised and feared it. Even on the threshold of the convent he put a trembling foot in the diabolic region, full of snares and mortal seductions. The monk of Novalese, on Mount Cenis, was persuaded that the demon roamed unceasingly over the mountain, in the form of serpents or buffoons. (2) He returned in haste to his brethren, and in the night all sorts of childish or terrible visions disturbed his slumber. The Benedictine rule, a fairly mild monastic rule, had reserved its severest prescriptions for the relations of the monks with the outside world. Fear of the world was so decidedly the principle of all wisdom that the Sicilian abbots at an early date had translated into the vulgar tongue, as a breviary useful to the less cultured of their brethren, the *Mirror of Monks,* written in the eleventh century by Arnoulf of Beauvais, a regular manual of monastic discipline. The monk, it is there written, ought not to concern himself with political events, or wars, or factions, or the joys and vanities of the earth, or strangers, or even his own relatives. His countenance should be neither sad nor smiling ; he should merely preserve the cold serenity of a man who has already half laid himself down in the peace of his tomb. "Let the monk," says the author of the *Mirror,* in conclusion, "be like Melchisedech, without father, without mother, without any relatives. Let him call no one father or mother on earth. Let him look upon himself as alone and upon God as his Father. Amen. Praise to Jesus Christ. Amen." (3)

Undoubtedly in that lively Italian society that was soon, by means of the communal revolution, to shake off the triple feudal, pontifical, and imperial yoke, monasticism had nothing to say, nothing to offer. The serf, the artizan, the citizen, the petty country nobleman, saw in these pious solitaries bent over their missal neither allies against Rome, consolers for evil days, nor charitable messengers of the divine word. If the monks had found God for themselves they either could not or dared not bring Him to the crowds and stretch out a helping hand to their brothers of the outside world in order to lead them back to the Heavenly Father. They kept themselves too far from humanity. Their voices were uplifted in nocturnal psalmody beneath the Romanic arches of their churches, but no longer descended to the ears of the living.

And again the ideal conception of the first Benedictine monasticism was every day being contradicted by reality in the strangest way. The monks had necessarily entered, like the secular church, into the feudal system. The abbots became counts on the same ground as did the bishops. The Italian abbeys were moreover constrained, more than any other in Europe, to adopt the military life. After the Hungarians and Arabs, the bishops and the barons and the emperors pillaged them and burnt them without mercy. Subiaco, the first refuge of Benedict, had to defend itself several times against the bishops of Tivoli and the counts of Sabinum or the district of Preneste. Monte Cassino and the Cave of Salerno were Benedictine strongholds that kept a look-out from the summit of their rocks by turns for the Saracens, the Roman barons, the Norman adventurers, and the Suabian princes. In 1192 Monte Cassino took the part of Henry VI against the pope, and all its monks found themselves excommunicated. The possession of power very soon spoilt the monks, and riches corrupted them more shockingly than they had corrupted the lay seigneurs. At the very time of the Cluny reform, that arrested the ruin of Benedict's order, the monks of Farfa in Sabinum, one of the most opulent feudal monasteries in Italy, poisoned their abbot, sacked the convent and lived the joyous life of bandits. Later on they welcomed Henry IV and supported him, in spite of the anathema of Gregory VII. All the efforts of popes and abbots to restore the rule in its primitive purity, to bring back the monks to perpetual prayer, manual labour and abstinence, failed owing to the temporal conditions of monasticism.

It was then that delicate souls, enamoured of silence, sought better retreats for the life contemplative outside the monastic institution. In the tenth and eleventh centuries the *pineta* of Ravenna, the solitudes of Gubbio, Vallombrosa, the Sila Mountains of Calabria, and Monte Gargano, the Athos of the west, were peopled with hermits. They were still there at the end of the thirteenth century. True fathers of the desert, they sang psalms, fasted, and disciplined their bodies. Several, such as Romuald, the founder of the Camaldules, and Nil, the Greek hegoumenos of Calabria and first abbot of Grotta-Ferrata (1002), enjoyed great renown throughout the whole world. (4) Some, such as Pietro Damiano, Dominico of Sora, and Bruno of Segni, returned at times to the secular Church to purify and direct it. Christendom admired them for their extraordinary acts of penance, their renunciation of all earthly consolation, and the long ecstasies during which the secrets of God were revealed to them ; the masters of feudal society, the pope and emperor, venerated them, while they feared them at the same time for the very grandeur of their sanctity and the gift of prophecy that was attributed to them. Otto said to his barons as they came down from Nil's hermitage in the mountains of Calabria : " These men are truly citizens of heaven—they live in tents as strangers upon earth." They had, in fact, set themselves free, as far as the present life is concerned, from the human community. Their social activity was even more insignificant than that of the monks. Neither the hermits nor the monks could therefore regenerate Christendom. They were powerless to reform, even for a few days, ecclesiastical society. Should a monk of Cluny, Gregory VII (1073–1085), or an abbot of Monte Cassino, Victor III (1086–1087), mount the papal throne and require of the clergy the austerity and obedience of the cloister, this attempt at religious renovation lasted but the time of a single pontificate. In no part of the west was this eclipse of the apostolic work more obvious than in Italy. It was among the Italians that the preaching of the Crusades awoke fewest echoes. Whilst Europe was rising at the call of popes and monks, the great maritime cities, Venice, Genoa, Pisa, and Amalfi, while exacting a high price for the help of their fleets, indifferent to the fate of the Holy Sepulchre, sought in the east nothing but the interests of their politics and their trade, and sometimes also relics that might be useful to those politics. (5) Thus, at the very moment when the communal revolution began, the spiritual rôle of the Church seemed to be ended in the peninsula, and Christianity was retiring from the social crisis in which the destiny of the weak and oppressed was at stake.

## IV

Between the appearance of the commune of Brescia, at the end of the tenth century, and the completion of that of Florence, at the end of the twelfth, the towns pulled down the strongholds of their counts and bishops and took possession once more of their civil franchises. They gave back to the children the little fatherland that encircled the municipal campanile; at the time of the great Italian leagues they were to succeed in waking the memory of the greater fatherland that had embraced all Italy. But they were unable to found social peace upon a lasting basis.

The Italian city in fact was a work of liberty and equality in appearance only. The community watched over and fettered the individual, for the franchises of republican association had as their guarantee the abdication of all personal will. The citizen was attached to his city as rigorously as the cultivator to the soil. The anonymous power upon which he was dependent was a narrower constraint than the old feudal pact. The contract that bound the man to his lord rested upon a permanent and reciprocal interest, whilst the arbitrary lordship of the commune, at once irresponsible and changing, modified, twenty times in a century, according to the needs or dangers of the moment, the social agreement and rendered the lot of the individual the more difficult in that it was more uncertain. Here the man was enclosed in some one of the groups whose sum total constituted the communal state ; he belonged for his entire life to a determined class, to a trade, a corporation, a parish, a quarter. His consuls and councils not only assigned him his share of political liberty, but regulated by decree the acts of his private life, prescribing the number of fig and almond trees he might plant in his field, the number of priests and tapers that should attend his funeral, forbade him to enter into taverns reserved for foreigners, to give presents to newly-married couples, to wear jewels or precious stuffs beyond a certain value ; if he was a barber, to shave for more than a penny ; if a ropemaker, to work on wet days ; if a huntsman, to catch quails otherwise than in a snare ; if a fisherman, to sell his fish outside the city ; and if he were a farmer he was commanded to bring to the commune the corn he did not himself consume. Air and sunshine alone seems to have escaped this regulation of individual rights. Exile, either voluntary or compulsory, could alone restore a shadow of independence to the Italian, the lamentable exile of the *fuoruscito,* whom the neighbouring communes could receive only as a vagabond or a suspect, who had no other resource than to enroll himself among the mercenaries of a baron of the highways, the enemy of all communes, and had no other chance of seeing his birthplace again than the hazards of civil war.

Down to the end of the twelfth century the Italian commune was entirely permeated with the aristocratic spirit. Later on it was disturbed almost everywhere by the imperious claims of the democracy and with terror saw passing through its streets and squares the supreme power, from which there was no appeal, that had gradually invaded the communal constitutions, the demagogic *parlamento* set in motion by the tocsin of the public palace. But then, as the thirteenth century waned, the communes, corrupted in their vital principle, degenerated into tyranny. At the time with which we are dealing, however, when the municipal form of government was coming into being, this principle was in its full vigour. The Italian Middle Ages were still too powerfully possessed by the sentiment of the human hierarchy to pass at a leap from the feudal system to pure equality. The communes were set up for the benefit of a nobility of the second rank, which at the beginning of the new order even allowed itself for some time to be ruled by the captains or vicars of the old counts. It was the middle class that formed the Italian city for its own great advantage. At Florence it even succeeded in establishing in its midst the hierarchy of the major and minor arts, of the "fat" and "lean" people. But in all the towns there was set up in a manner more or less rigorous a social system that placed one according to the value of the industry or commerce in which he was engaged and that consequently depended upon wealth. At the top were the notaries, money-changers, physicians, judges, weavers of silk or of velvet or cloth; beneath them were the people of cruder manual occupations, wool-carders and butchers; and lower still came the *minuto popolo,* that had no corporation of its own and was attached to one or other of the major or minor arts, the obscure crowd of the *Ciompi* who went barefoot, the *popolani*, whom Dino Compagni shows us as incessantly insulted and trampled upon by the "great and proud citizens", the plebians of Milan whom a noble could kill at the cost of a few crowns. (6)

As we see, the Italian hive, so ingenious and lively, was by no means equally kind to all the bees. When, in the days of Boniface VIII (1294–1303), the factions of Guelfs and Ghibelins, making use, as engines of war, at once of the hates of families and quarters and the deadly rancour of the wretched against the middle class, had set fire to central Italy, poets and historians had no difficulty in discovering in the social state of their country those two irreconcilable elements, hardness of heart in the great and envy in the humble. "Thy city," says one of the damned to Dante, "is so full of envy that the sack is overflowing." And it is Campagni who tells us that "the weak were too much oppressed by the strong." Later on Giovanni Villani (1275 ?–1348), in his *Chronicle* of the history of Italy, was even to say with regard to the fires that ravaged Florence at the close of the twelfth century: "Our middle class citizens were too fat and lived in repose and pride." Florence was the first city that was able to begin an actual class war, for she was always in advance of the other towns as much in her revolutionary logic as in her civilization. But everywhere else, in the first centuries of the communes, if, to make use of a tragic expression of Dante's, "it came to bloodshed," it was as yet by no means a simple social struggle. The discontent of the nobles and the upper middle class, whose personal liberty was stifled by the municipal government, and the wrath of the *popolani*, for whom the ranks of the privileged classes were closed, were rather manifested in religious uneasiness. Anxiety about divine matters was too strong at that time for men not to expect from God a remedy for the ills that distressed men's souls, and for them not to ask from religion consolation in their earthly life. And as, in this period of social renovation, the Church always continued to be, between the feudal lords whose power was declining and the communes whose power was increasing, an august symbol of immovable authority, it was to the Church that men's consciences long turned, and for a century and a half Italy sought in a freer faith and a more tender charity the liberty and pity refused her by political institutions.

## V

Deprived of all doctrinal method, and greatly troubled in mind, Italy tried during this same period, and without ever attaining satisfaction, several religious creations. Indifference or negation certainly had their adepts soon enough, especially in Lombardy and at Florence. Among the heretics of whom Villani speaks under the dates of 1115 and 1117 we find "an epicurean sect," that is to say, according to the definition of Benvenuto of Imola, referring to the unbelieving Ghibelins of Dante's epoch, men "who assert that the soul perishes with the body." (7) On the other hand we know that Lombardy gave birth to a great number of those *clerici vagantes,* joyous fellows who were to be met with nearly everywhere in Europe at that time. These men's infidelity was of a very original kind, mingled with irony, sensuality, and a real instinct of paganism. They made mock of the Church, parodying the text of the Gospel and singing the mass of the god Bacchus: *Introibo ad altare Bacchi, ad Deum qui lætificat cor hominis.* They were men of letters, precursors of the free-thinkers, who gaily broke away from the scholastic pedantry and the Christian gravity. They disconcerted the Middle Ages, which, although they by no means spared either the secular or the regular clergy, did not approve the mockery of holy things. They were accused of believing "in Juvenal rather than in the prophets,"

*Et pro Marco legunt Flaccum,*
*Pro Paulo Virgilium.*

But these first Tuscan or Lombard sceptics formed only a small group lost in Italian Christendom. It is not possible exactly to measure the scope of their religious indifference. The contagion of it at any rate caused no concern to the faithful at that time. For the negation of the lettered to penetrate to the masses of the people a century had first to see the triumph of a great heresy, or the consummation of a decisive schism, or the development of a philosophical civilization. Free thought, in its modern sense, really began only at the time of Frederic II (1212–1250) and the Averroist propaganda.

For those believing souls, who by no means wished to renounce the hope of Paradise, schism and heresy were a far stronger temptation than mere unbelief. In the middle of the eleventh century there broke out in Lombardy a schismatic revolt of a very remarkable kind, which old historians and the poets, such as Pulci, deceived by the analogy of names, often confounded with the heresy of the Cathari. I am speaking of the Patarins or the *Pataria,* an entirely popular and monastic attempt, that was openly encouraged by Rome, during the period of the reforming popes inspired by Hildebrand. The rivalry of the two leading bishops of Italy, a doctrinal debate between Rome and Milan, was the cause of this religious war that ended in civil strife. The Lombard church had long maintained a schismatic attitude towards the Roman See. It preserved the very peculiar liturgy of the Ambrosian form of worship, *letanias execrandas* writes the deacon Arialdo. (8) The archbishop of Milan had claimed since the time of Charles the Bald the right to dispose of the crown of Italy, a privilege that was taken from him by a constitution of Otto III. *Mediolanensi episcopo papatum ablatum est.* Supported by a rich clergy and by the Lombard episcopate which derived its powers from him alone and which he assembled in council, indifferent to the anathemas of Rome, and covered almost always by the buckler of the Empire, the archbishop of Milan appeared to be the actual pope of northern Italy. He coined money and raised armies. He reigned over that powerful hierarchy of feudal bishops that the Empire had favoured for the past two centuries, in the secular order, with extraordinary privileges, to the detriment even of the lay counts. The commune of Milan, entirely aristocratic in character, resigned itself to the political primacy of its pastor out of fear of the Empire. But it looked with anger upon the scandals of the Ambrosian church, the simony of the superior clergy, the impudence of the married priests, the Nicolaites, who laughed at councils and replied to the decrees of Rome by the words of the apostle : *Qui se non continet, nubat.* The grudges of the lower classes were moreover kept alive by the poor inferior clergy, who, in the presence of the poverty-stricken people, incessantly commented upon the Sermon on the Mount. "Do not forget," Arialdo said to them, "that the Son of Man had not a stone whereon to rest His head. But he said 'Blessed are the poor '. Look now at your priests, with their palaces and castles, their soft raiment, their pride, their lust and idleness !" In the sordid alleys of Milan, to which the degraded trades were consigned as to a ghetto, the booths of the sellers of old iron and rags, the bazaar of the *Pataria,* there thus sprang up an enthusiastic Christianity, quite democratic in character, that waited only for the sound of its bell to assault the patrician and simoniac Milanese Church.

The signal came from Rome, where the future Gregory VII was endeavouring to restore the austerity of monasticism. At Milan the clergy and noble laymen began the revolution. One of these clergy, Anselm of Lucca, became pope in 1061, under the name of Alexander II (1061–1073). The military chief, Erlembaldo, carried a blessed gonfalon to Rome. The legates of the Holy See, Hildebrand and afterwards Pietro

Damiano, came to Milan to break down the resistance of the Ambrosians. The archbishop Guido, a creature of the emperor's, had to proceed to Rome in order to receive the episcopal ring from the hands of his rival. But the people, roused to revolt by their preachers, rose against the Milanese Church and tore the Nicolaites from their altars. The evangelical reform degenerated into democracy. (9) Public worship became impossible at Milan. When once Gregory VII was elected to the pontificate, Erlembaldo instituted a reign of terror in the city. He dared even to forbid the administration of baptism in the metropolitan baptistery. The populace pillaged the houses of the simoniacs, and in Holy Week burnt the two cathedrals and the other churches. The nobles then took up arms and sought out the Patarins. A feudal battle was necessary to settle with these tattered mystics. Erlembaldo fell in the front rank of his men, holding in his arms the papal gonfalon, and at his side fell also the priest Liprando, bearing the cross. The incipient heresy of the vanquished *Pataria* was not slow in disappearing from Lombardy. (10)

This first religious protest, quite local in character, left the field free for the heresy of the Cathari. This latter, at the end of the eleventh century, spread over the whole of upper Italy to within sight of the very walls of Rome. As early as 1035 the sect had appeared in the region of Milan. There it grew in obscurity, favoured by the fermentation of the *Pataria*. It is well known that it was from Lombardy that it later made its way into Waldensian France. In 1125 it was already mistress of Orvieto ; in 1117 and 1150 it was to be found at Florence ; in 1166 at Milan ; and in 1184 at Verona. In 1194 Florence afforded asylum to the heretics of Prato. This new heresy combined, in an extremely confused manner, on the very old foundation of Asiatic Manicheism, the majority of the old heresies, the negation of the eucharist, for example, and the traditional sacrament of baptism. For the

Cathari the primitive Church, anterior to pope Sylvester and Constantine, when it had not yet secured its secular power and was more or less unconcerned with secular things, had alone been pleasing in the sight of God. Of the great hierarchy of the mediæval Church they retained nothing but the bishop and the deacon. They kept the Gospel of John, the feasts of Christmas and Pentecost and some of the sacraments in a very modified form, such as baptism by the laying on of hands, and, finally, the predominant theory of the Holy Spirit. The perfect, the really pure, clad in a sad-coloured garment, had to prepare for death by means of solitary meditation or the fanaticism of a perpetual preaching. They renounced all the good things of the world, condemned themselves to the severest penances, to the insupportable weariness of religious communism, and to the incessant espionage of the secret society. They hastened the hour of death by the tortures of the *Endura*, by horrible fasts, blood-letting or poison. (11) To those of their brethren who had not the vocation to sanctity they accorded a less severe moral system. Many of them were fond of riches and power. They could thus come to an understanding with the political order and fill the magistratures of the cities.

The Cathari were very numerous in Italy throughout the twelfth century; they did not succeed, however, in calling forth a great proselytizing movement in the peninsula. Their doctrines were incoherent; and they were repugnant to the great majority of the Italians owing to their too pronounced character of asceticism and pessimism. Theirs was a gloomy religion and intolerant, according to which all sin was mortal, which condemned joy, believed nature to be corrupted by the operation of Satan, cursed marriage as prolonging humanity's stay in a world of perdition, and by its moral teaching and discipline detached the most ardent of its believers from public life no less than from social life.

The Waldensian heresy came in its turn, in the second half of the twelfth century, and presented itself to the religious uneasiness of Italy. The Waldenses, or Poor People of Lyons, whose founder, Pierre Waldo, an heresiarch forerunner of Francis of Assisi, had voluntarily resigned his wealth in order to be poor among the poor, had only a very mediocre theology ; they referred all Christianity back to the simple text of the Gospel, and did away with the entire clerical hierarchy. They were never weary of repeating that it is better to obey God than man, a good layman than a bad cleric ; that the layman is the equal of the priest for all mystic works, even for the sacrifice of the mass ; thus they escaped the Church and confession, and recovered the liberty of individual religion. The Italian Waldenses separated themselves from the *credo* of the Church in a more radical fashion than their French brethren ; with regard to the profession of absolute poverty, on the other hand, they were more tolerant. They were a community of humble folk who called themselves the "humiliated", who made a practice of begging, and who were despised by the middle classes of the townsfolk. At times they went forth to preach in the public squares and to force open the doors of churches ; at others they fled to the mountain or the forest. When the day of persecution came their leaders went through the villages and towns in order to comfort their co-religionists. They were truly protean, says a document of 1180 ; every morning they changed their dress, being pilgrims, barbers, cordwainers, penitents, as necessity arose. Their goodness of heart was admirable. According to the confession of the Roman inquisitors themselves, the Waldenses had returned to the fraternity of the Gospel. They held out a helping hand to the poor, the infirm, the orphan, the prisoner, the exile. They founded hospitals for travellers and the sick, opened free schools, maintained their students at the University of Paris, and even extended their beneficence to the orthodox. Christian equality seemed thus to have been recovered by dissidents from the orthodox Christianity of the time, to have been resuscitated by the enemies of the Church. (12)

But the ideal of the "humiliated" was very poor and their morality very austere for southern consciences; and their worship, deprived of churches, images, joyous feasts, seemed too gloomy to Italy. Neither the Waldenses nor the Cathari could win over a mobile and refined people, whose sensuous piety required a liturgy calculated to please the eye and the flattering indulgence of the priest for the weakness of the heart. These heresies, too much imbued with rationalism, rendered God in some sort implacable; in vain did they deliver the believer from the shackles of the Church, they could not regain that filial familiarity towards God that marked the apostolic days; they left to man the weariness of the present life, the feeling that all things here below are bad, and that the work of salvation is in very truth too difficult for humble souls.

And that was the most painful wound that the conscience of the time could endure, a conscience that henceforth could not turn towards God without fear. The misery of the Middle Ages continued; the deeds of violence, which the monks and hermits fled to the desert to avoid, never ended. The state of war seemed to be everlasting. Men's minds, dismayed by the tragic spectacle of life, saw in nature herself a deadly enemy; the unexpected phenomena of the heavens conspired with the calamities of the earth against the sons of Adam. The arm of God seemed at that time too heavy, the image of the Redeemer was veiled, there remained in His place only the formidable judge of the Apocalypse. It was in vain that many of the fears of the time proved to be unfounded. The skies were still dark, and the Christian continued to perceive, on a horizon that he believed to be very near, the apparition of the Last Judgment. The law of Christ, so full of hope in the first ages of the Church, had become a symbol of terror. Italy was no less tormented than the rest of Christendom. The works of her first mosaicists bear witness to the religious anguish of the time quite as much as do the disquieting sculptures of the French Romanic churches. I am not speaking of the sombre and awkward mosaics anterior to the close of the eleventh century, such as those of Santa Maria in Navicella at Rome, in which the unskilfulness of the hand may have betrayed the artist's feeling. But in the works that issued from the Byzantine Renaissance called forth by the abbot Didier in the time of Gregory VII terror always dominates. At St. Angelo-in-Formis, near Capua, above the central porch of the church, it is at the very table of the Last Supper, at the moment when He is giving His apostles His flesh and blood, that Jesus rejects with a gesture of malediction the damned at the last day ; on the friezes of the great nave, nailed to the cross, He bends a threatening face to His mother. The Gospel beams of love were therefore extinct. And everywhere from that time forth until the coming of the thirteenth century, in the cathedral of Pisa as in that of Monreale, in the baptistery of Florence as at St. John Lateran, there appears, on the gold of the apses, the solemn Christ, like an eastern despot, His look fixed and hard, the stern God on Whose bosom Christian society no longer dared to rest its head, as the disciple John had done at the Last Supper of Jesus.

## VI

However, in France, at the University of Paris, a great effort had just been attempted for the enfranchisement of the human mind. It was not in vain that Abelard (1079–1142) had endeavoured to reconcile reason with faith, and that in the great University, in the full sunlight, he had long nurtured the youth of Europe upon the doctrine of liberty. The fundamental notion of his philosophy contained the germ of a triple revolution in science, politics, and Christianity. By proving, in opposition to the idealism derived from Scotus Eriugena, that ideas are not entities, but conceptions of the mind, he had staggered the mediæval world. If man's thought is at once the source and the measure of all reality, it is upon thought, and not upon tradition and the syllogisms of the masters that truth rests. Every man bears in himself a marvellous cipher by the aid of which he can translate the laws of nature and the Word of God. Reason is its own authority and its own light. It has therefore the right to investigate everything, to discuss everything, and to judge everything. And Abelard had submitted the whole of Christianity to his criticism. He had compared and checked, the one by the other, natural philosophy, the Jewish faith and the Christian faith. (13) He explained in a way that children and women could understand the mystery of the Trinity ; he did even more : he weakened the notion of mystery, removed the veils of the tabernacle, and invited the Christian to look upon God face to face. "The more we feel God," he said, "the more we love Him, and our intelligence grows with our love. *Cum profectu intelligentiæ caritatis accenditur flamma.*" (14) The distinction between the sons of God and those of the demon, Heloise wrote to him, can be made only by charity, which, according to the apostle, is the fulfilment of the law and the end of the commandments. He had gone back to the Christianity of Paul, and he restored to faith the primacy over works. "The kingdom of God," Heloise said once more, "according to the apostle, is not abstinence from meat or drink ; it is justice, peace and joy in the Holy Spirit." At the same time that he renounced the theology of the contemporaneous Christendom he renounced also its morality. For him virtue, like truth, came forth from the depths of the soul, and the root of sin was to be sought in the inmost recesses of thought. Therefore it is not the act but the culpable intention that makes the fault. Those who crucified Jesus without knowing Him did not commit sin. But who shall weigh the intention, if not the soul itself, which has given birth to it, and which alone can properly understand it? Of what value henceforth are the sentence of the judge, that is to say the priest, and the entirely external practices whereby the Church believes it can vivify the conscience? An act of faith, an impulse of tenderness, can bring the Christian into closer communion with God than penance and ceremonial. And if the master were asked what became of original sin in the logical sequence of his teaching he would say that it is not sin but suffering. Then had the Redemption been a useless sacrifice, and was the Christianity that deemed it to be an essential article of faith no more than a delusion? The redemption, Abelard replied, was an act of pure love. (15)

## VII

Did Arnold of Brescia (?–1155) bring to Italy and Rome these words of Abelard that suddenly burst forth in the shadows of the twelfth century like the initial text of the true eternal Gospel? Thousands of scholastic students, clerics, and monks, who had gathered round the great teacher had returned to their cities with their hearts filled with his teaching; his books passed from hand to hand throughout the peninsula, and were read with avidity by even the bishops and cardinals. Arnold, who was surnamed "Abelard's squire", was able therefore to undertake an apostolate, while remaining faithful to the tradition of his friend. His school was ready waiting for him.

But the apostle was eclipsed behind the tribune. He hastened to the hurly-burly of public contests, and in the religious crisis of his age he did not understand, or would not see, anything but the reformation of the temporal Church. Perhaps, moreover, even the same man and the same city and the same age combined had not sufficient strength to uplift both religious liberty and social liberty simultaneously. This great figure long remained enigmatic, the Middle Ages not having transmitted anything concerning Arnold but a few obscure or prejudiced evidences. His contemporaries, like the cardinal of Aragon, saw in him a dangerous heresiarch, or, like Bernard of Clairvaux (1090–1153), they believed him to be a schismatic ; and yet in matters of faith they could reproach him only with holding a peculiar view of the eucharist, the dogma concerning which had scarcely been determined till the time of Bérenger of Tours (?–1088), and of the baptism of little children, of which, doubtless without immersion, he disapproved. But Otto of Freysingen, who reports this accusation, expresses himself in very vague terms : *non recte dicitur sensisse*. There is nothing in that which justifies the violence of the language used by Bernard against Arnold's "poisonous" teaching, when he calls him "the mortal enemy of the Cross," who has "the head of a dove and the tail of a scorpion." Evidently, upon the question of orthodoxy, *quell' infame*, as Luigi Muratori (1672–1750) says, in his monumental work that deals with a thousand years of Italian history, must have suffered from the ecclesiastical hatred that pursued his master Abelard till the day of his death. Innocent II (1130–1143), at the council of Sens, hurled against both of them a decree of malediction. Arnold at that time held his master's chair at Paris, Abelard having been exiled to Cluny. In this supposed heretic it was certainly the disciple of the school of Sainte-Genevieve that Bernard and the Church wished to stigmatize ; but it was above all else the reformer and the man of action who frightened them, and whom they crushed. Arnold's personal theology did not extend to heresy, and it stopped short upon the edge of schism. At Rome he said not a word either against the universals or against the Trinity, or against the spiritual authority of the Holy See. The Italian of the twelfth century, the child of free Brescia, had but one thought: to found at Rome a communal form of government independent of the pope, and to crown the royalty of the people on the Capitol. What we know of Arnold's speeches shows him to us preaching the evangelical simplicity and poverty of the early Church, denying the right of property to monks and the secular clergy, conferring upon the state, that is to say upon the commune, the goods of the ecclesiastics, exhorting Celestine II (422–432), Lucius II (1144–1145), Eugenius III (1145–1153), and Adrian IV (1154–1159), to renounce the temporal jurisdiction and confine themselves to the white staff of the apostolic popes. He took from the bishops the feudal domain. He forbade them the enjoyment of sumptuous clothes, delicate viands and illicit games. He could appeal to Pietro Damiano, and even to Bernard of Clairvaux himself, in writing to Eugenius III: "Who will grant me before I die to see the Church of God such as it was in the ancient days, when the apostles cast their nets, not to catch gold and silver, but souls?" The demands of Arnold seemed for a moment to be not unlike the views of Bernard, in his book *De Consideratione,* so that the pope raised the ban that had been pronounced against the exile. The tribune established himself for a few days at Viterbo, then went to Rome, perhaps in secret, and waited until the precarious peace concluded between Eugenius and the commune should be broken. In the spring of 1146 the pope fled for the second time from his metropolis, and Arnold's religious theory was disclosed in all its gravity.

It was no longer a question of a moral reform, but of a revolution in the historic tradition of the Church. Bernard consented to relieve the pope of the direct exercise of the temporal power, he was glad to deliver him from the embarrasment of the feudal sovereignty, but he always attributed to him the supreme authority, exercised in the name of God, over all the kings and all the cities of the world. The pope disposes of the two swords: with his own hand he wields the spiritual sword; the emperor and the princes, his vicars, wield the temporal sword as he directs. (17)

Gregory VII having no other kingdom than his basilica—such was the ideal of Bernard. The Papacy of the early centuries deprived of all power and all right over political society—such was the ideal of Arnold of Brescia, and, for some years, that of republican Rome and communal Italy. The wretched Papacy of Eugenius III seemed to Arnold to be unworthy of the obedience of Christians. It is astonishing that he did not then and there consummate the schism by adding a new pontiff to the long list of antipopes. Doubtless he had first of all to solve the problem imposed upon Christendom at the time of the Carolingians: could the Church and its chief pastor, in the present state of the world, renounce the secular power? Thus everything was called into question: ecclesiastical discipline, the feudal situation of the higher clergy, the possession of wealth, and works, the source of that wealth, the œcumenical primacy of the bishop of Rome. It was Christianity itself, as formed by the tempestuous history of the Middle Ages, that had to be refashioned from top to bottom. The citizens of the episcopal cities had certainly been able, without stirring up civil war, to bring about the downfall of their bishops in the political sphere; but at Rome, in order to pull down the pope from his position of temporal lord, the Church herself, absolute mistress of the pontificate by the electoral reform of Nicholas II, had to be dispossessed. The secular allies, the petty Roman nobility and the people, were not sufficiently strong to enable Arnold to finish his work ; he called to his side the lower clergy, who accepted the overthrow of the higher ecclesiastical hierarchy. A sort of fatality then drove Arnold to demagogy. Some years earlier he had raised a revolt against the bishop of Brescia. He renewed against the Roman See the Lombard *Pataria* of the eleventh century. He was condemned, as the Paterins had been, to all the excesses of reformers who claim to regulate civil society upon the pure maxims of the Gospel. Moreover, the internal conditions of Rome rendered the religious revolution still more difficult for him. He was obliged to go beyond the programme of the Italian commune, that in all cases had been set up for the advantage of the middle class and the *popolo grasso*. But Rome, in the twelfth century, had no more a middle class than it had possessed in Cæsar's time, and it was for the household dependents of the monasteries and churches, for the wild *popolani* of the Trastevere, that Abelard's squire called Livy's republic into being. He had been welcomed at Rome by the factions of the nobles, and his first care was to abolish the aristocratic constitution of the commune in favour of a popular senate. Thus at one and the same time he prejudiced the two " great luminaries " : if, by the institution of the democratic city, he robbed the pope of his feudal dignity, he also deprived the emperor of the mystic capital of the empire, and removed the keystone of the arch that upheld the whole political system of Christendom. Abandoned by the barons, his allies of yesterday, and harassed by the brutal mob to whom the demagogic tradition had taught neither fidelity nor respect, Arnold perceived suddenly, beyond the patricians he had deceived and the temporal Church he had denied, the emperor, the greatest the world had seen since

Charlemagne and Otto I, who descended the Alps and marched against him.

So Frederic Barbarossa (1152–1190) and Adrian IV combined their justice and their hatred. The pope demanded the heretic, the apostate cleric ; the emperor claimed the tribune. An interdict closed the churches in Rome. Arnold fled, was taken prisoner in the Val d'Orcia, then rescued by the viscounts of that region, who guarded him in their castles, honouring him as a prophet. Barbarossa besieged the castles and recaptured his victim. Arnold was strangled and then burnt secretly on the banks of the Tiber, in that field of Nero's where, in 1115, Crescentius, a Roman patrician who also had sought to free his native city from the imperial yoke, had shed his blood under Otto III.

## VIII

Arnold's dream had been too vast. He had tasted the honey of the ideal and the reality killed him. From the depths of his cell in the castle of St. Angelo he could send up to heaven the desperate cry of Abelard : *A finibus terræ ad te clamavi, dum anxiaretur cor meum*. Conceive the sadness of the martyr who, in his last hour, comprehends that he has been mistaken, and that he bears testimony by his death to the faith of the past and not that of the future. Not only did he fall for having imprudently attempted at Rome the revolution that had been possible at Milan, Pisa, and Florence, in fact, through all municipal Italy, but for having believed, with the reformers of the last centuries, that Rome and the Holy See were the whole Church, and that the Church was the whole of Christendom. As long as the souls of the Italians had this illusion, they waited in vain for the dawning of the day of God. All essays at religious creations ended in the same disenchantment. Italy, still too young to give herself up to indifference or unbelief, could not deprive herself of a positive faith ; she wished to remain Christian ; Christianity had grown in her arms, and she was attached to it with a sort of maternal tenderness. She also wished to remain Catholic ; the Holy Roman See was in part her work, and she was not forgetful of the great popes under whose mantle her national liberties had at times been sheltered. She felt herself to be united to the Church by the pride of memories and the charm of common sufferings. She departed from the Church's side every morning to seek, somewhat at random, the way, the truth, and the life, and every evening she returned, like a disappointed and weary pilgrim, to the old cradle where her hopes ever rested.

Now this painful period was about to close. Arnold's stake is the last station on the way to Calvary. A breath of new life is already passing over Italy. The Lombard communes are about to receive at Legano the bloody baptism of liberty, and the idea of the historic fatherland is about to re-enter men's consciences. Already the first flowers of art and poetry are budding. The masters of mosaic, the first sculptors, the painters of Athos, have rejuvenated the adornment of churches ; and the white cathedrals, the baptisteries of sculptured marble, the slender campanili, rise triumphantly in Lombardy, in Tuscany, and in the Norman kingdom. Sicily is sending to the peninsula, with the delicate models of Arabic art, a kind of reflection of the sensuous graces of the east. Tomorrow the first troubadours will come from gay Provence by the passes of the Alps, and already the chivalric fables of the France of Roland and the legends of Arthur and Merlin rejoice the hearts of the lords of the valleys of the Po and Adige. In this awakening of public life and intellect we get a glimpse of an approaching religious revival, for the universal joy of Italy would be inexplicable if men's souls were still to languish in the tribulation of the Middle Ages. Beams of the approaching dawn fly from cupola to cupola, from the Palatine chapel of Palermo to San Marco at Venice, and on the mountains of Calabria there rises at last the star of a new Christmas.

## CHAPTER II

# JOACHIM OF FLORA

DANTE has placed in his Paradise, among the great mystics (Anselm, Hugh of Saint Victor and Bonaventura) the Calabrian prophet Joachim of Flora (1132–1202),

*Il calavrese abate Giovacchino,*
*Di spirito profetico dotato.*

A very audacious prophet if we mark the fortune of his dreams and the doctrinal boldness of the disciples, more or less legitimate, who, till the end of the Middle Ages, proclaimed him their master; the most dangerous of heresiarchs, if his authentic works (19) are carried to their logical conclusion, to wit, the downfall of the Church and the Law of the Word; the gentlest of Christians, if we take into account the childish grace of his legend and the act of simple faith that he inscribed at the beginning of the most important of his books, the *Concord of the New and the Old Testament.* He very nearly caused a most serious crisis in the Church, and the latter, after having honoured him in his lifetime, as the authorized interpreter of the *Scriptures*, permitted the Cistercian family in the Neapolitan provinces to venerate him as blessed and to invoke him as a worker of miracles. In the dioceses of Calabria, on his feast day, this anthem, of which Dante's verses seem to be an echo, is still sung: *Beatus Joachim, spiritu dotatus prophetico, decoratus intelligentia, errore procul hæretico, dixit futura ut præsentia.*

Here we have a religious phenomenon containing apparently absolute contradictions. The uncertainty of the Italian conscience in the century of Arnold of Brescia would only half explain it ; the reason for it must be sought further in the secular anxieties of Christianity.

## I

One of the most original and most tenacious ideas of the first Christian society was that nothing, in the religious state of the world, was yet definitive, that revelation had by no means said its last word, that the apostolate and death of Jesus were only a single act in the drama of salvation, and that the consummation of the great mystery must be expected in a future more or less close at hand. More than one word spoken by Jesus, the vague promise of a glorious return of the Son of Man, allusions to some unheard-of catastrophe, kept alive a hope mingled with terror during the evangelical generation. Persons whom no dogma could re-assure, who were as yet disciplined by no ecclesiastical hierarchy, debated upon the future religion, and their curiosity about the unknown was all the more lively because the very free interpretation, inaugurated by Jesus against the Jewish Law and the narrow letter, always continued in existence. Every conscience, at the same time that it endeavoured to read the final secret, freely created its own faith, every Christian was indeed a Christ. The ascendancy of Paul is explained by this doctrine of liberty, and the inspiration of primitive Christianity is manifested in the Second Epistle to the Corinthians : "Ye are the very word and message of Christ ; we are the ministers of the New Testament, not as to the letter, but as to the spirit, for the letter killeth and the spirit giveth life. Where is the Spirit of the Lord, there is liberty."

The *Apocalypse* and the *Fourth Gospel* are throughout animated by this sentiment of divine becoming, of continuous revelation. Both of these books, the first by the remarkable character of its images, the second by the metaphysical obscurity of its language, marvellously favoured the liberty of religious invention proclaimed by Paul. The *Apocalypse* opens up a vision that will long dazzle the Christian imagination, and will seem by its gloomy symbols to justify the miseries of history, while promising the revenge of the saints in the near future. It rests upon the conception of a series of crises that will precede the appearance of the heavenly Jerusalem, and of a progress of supernatural things necessary to the final triumph of the believers in the bosom of God. After horrible convulsions, that will destroy the Roman empire, the earthly reign of the Messiah and his martyrs will begin, perhaps in Palestine, and will last a thousand years ; then Satan, the antichrist, will be let loose, God will be eclipsed, and the Church will be on the point of perishing. God will then reappear upon the scene, the general resurrection and the last judgment will conclude the history of the visible world, and the definitive state, beatitude and eternal peace, will be set up.

But the violent impression caused by the *Apocalypse* upon men's souls was bound to grow weaker. The quite material promises of the millennium were disappointed by the actual events. Had the apostle been mistaken in his calculations ; was the temporal reign of Jesus but an illusion? The *Fourth Gospel*, a work of the Greek mind, permeated throughout by Neo-Platonism, came at the right moment to restore its ideal to disturbed Christendom. With a serenity unknown to the seer of Patmos it renewed the assurance of a superior religion, reserved for a time in the near future. " Woman, believe me, the hour is coming when neither at Jerusalem nor on this mountain shall ye worship the Father ; the hour cometh when the true faithful shall worship the Father in spirit and in truth." But the great originality of the Gospel of John, the precious stone brought by that book to the edifice of Christianity, is the first outline of a transcendant theology and the creation of mysticism by means of that very theology. To the Prophet of Galilee, descended from Abraham, grandson of David, whose carnal genealogy Matthew enumerated and whom the Synoptics followed through the familiar details of His earthly life, there succeeded the Word eternal, the intelligence of God, God himself, clothed in mortal flesh. He revealed Himself in the first chapter as a pure divine essence, then as a phantom of light to John the Baptist on the banks of the Jordan, and the Baptist cried : "Behold the Son of God." In the last lines of the book, after the Passion, he appeared again to His disciples in the misty brightness of early dawn, on the shore of the Lake of Tiberias : in the interval between these two visions, He lived and talked among men, but transfigured by a supernatural radiance and like to an angelic form. He acted only in the name of His Father and for the glory of His Father ; by Him only can men go to the heavenly Father and share in the divine. "I and the Father are one." On the evening of the Last Supper the apostles heard Him murmuring these words : "This is life eternal: to know Thee the only true God and Thy Messiah, Jesus Christ. . . . I pray not for them only, but for all those who shall believe in Me upon their testimony : that they all may be one . . . . that they may be but one in Us." But in order to deserve by profound faith to have communion with God and to live by His breath, it is necessary first of all to accept the Spirit. "It is the Spirit that quickeneth, the flesh availeth nothing." This is indeed the final term of the mystic initiation, for which the earthly mission of Jesus was the preparation. The theory of the Holy Spirit, of which Paul had already caught a glimpse, dominates the whole of the Fourth Gospel. The Holy Spirit, the Paraclete, is a mediator in the same way as the Word who will be sent by the Father in the name of the Word and at His request, who will bear witness for the Son as He had borne witness for the Father, and will live for ever among men. By Him shall be consummated the revelation of the Word, and faith in the promises of the Word shall be confirmed. "He will teach you all things, and shall bring to your remembrance all that I have told you." But the coming of the Spirit is absolutely distinct from that of Jesus. "Lo, I am returning to Him that sent me, and none of you asketh me, Whither goest thou? And because I have told you these things, sorrow hath filled your heart. Verily I say unto you, it is expedient for you that I go away, for if I go not away, the Comforter will not come unto you ; when I go I will send Him unto you." Jesus died. The testament that He had brought into the world was then sealed. With His death began a new religious era. In the securely closed room wherein His disciples were hiding for fear of the Jews, He suddenly glided in like a shadow ; the breath of His lips gently touched their brows, and He said unto them : "Receive ye the Holy Spirit."

But the Spirit will descend only upon souls purified by love. Love is the highest of the virtues and the sign of election. The whole morality of the *Fourth Gospel* is contained in this precept of the Master, incessantly repeated : "Love one another and love Me as I love My Father. Be united to Me by love as I am united to the Father. Attach yourselves to Me as the branches to the stem of the vine. Gather closely round Me as the sheep gather round the good Shepherd." He had pity upon the woman taken in adultery. When Lazarus died He wept and the Jews said : "Behold how He loved him! " From the cross He fixed His eyes upon the beloved disciple to whom he bequeathed the mystic religion of love that he might give it to the world.

The tradition of the first centuries attributed the *Apocalypse* and the *Fourth Gospel* to John. The man of Ephesus was regarded as a prophet who, from the heart of the new Law, had caught a glimpse of the Law of the future. Men's souls could await in peace the manifestations promised by the *Apocalypse* : the religion of the Holy Spirit was set up, consisting wholly of faith, charity, and liberty. For very lofty consciences and tender hearts a sanctuary was prepared, the vestibule to the heavenly Jerusalem : how henceforth could they be affected by the evils of life, the harshness of the age, the errors even or weaknesses of the Church? Christendom in the gloomiest days of the Middle Ages, was to return again and again to these hopes, repeating the words of the Samaritan woman seated at the edge of Jacob's well : "Lord, give me of this water, that I may not thirst again."

## II

The two great paths taken by the intellectual life of the Middle Ages start, the one from Augustine (354–430), the other from John Scotus Eriugena. The former created the doctrinal theology that proceeds from Paul and John. For the interpretation of the Johannine ideas Scotus believed himself to be the faithful follower of his master Augustine. He commented upon the bishop's commentary, added a degree to the precision of his views, detached himself in an almost insensible manner from the orthodox line, and sowed the seeds of heresy in Christendom.

The *City of God* is penetrated with the anguish of the *Apocalypse*. Augustine witnessed the shipwreck of the Roman civilization, the first act in the tragedy announced by John. He did not doubt that the shadow of antichrist was already covering the universe ; he heard from afar the approach of the victorious Christ, he already saw the millennium dawning on the horizon. He scrutinized the obscurities of the Johannine text, invoked the testimony of Paul and Daniel concerning antichrist, and endeavoured to fix the apocalyptic periods by an exact calculation. He asked himself whether the forty-two months that the final assault of Satan upon the Church was to last would be comprised in the thousand years or were in addition to them. Moreover, in order to confirm his expectation, he searched in the *Old Testament* for proof of a succession of epochs of which the eternal sabbath would be the last, that seventh day whereon the Church militant would receive the rewards of its trials. The first epoch extended from Adam to the flood ; the following ones, in their order, are marked by Abraham, David, the captivity, and the birth of Christ. The sixth, which it is impossible to measure, was passing at that very moment ; the seventh would be the day of peace, that should have neither waning nor twilight. This last epoch was to be the day of the Church triumphant, that which John, the greatest of the apostles, the only one who saw God in His essence, had glorified, and of which the earthly Church, represented by Peter, was only the figure. "This last," says Augustine, "is the Church of faith, the other will be the Church of direct contemplation ; the one is in the time of pilgrimage, the other will be in the everlasting habitation ; the one is on the journey, the other will be in the fatherland ; the one is good and still unhappy, the other will be better and blessed." (20)

Did the tenth century expect some great disaster? One comes upon writings of the time that are filled with dark forebodings. To Scotus Eriugena, in the ninth century, the Church seemed to be already tottering, and meditation upon the *Fourth Gospel* showed him, with singular clearness, the past, the present, and the future of religious things. If he reproduced almost exactly the succession of periods, as his master had computed them, he classed them into three great divisions, each one marked by its priesthood, thus giving us to understand that, for the first two, the priest himself, like the doctrine of which he was the guardian, corresponds only to a transitory moment in the divine thought. The first priesthood, that of the *Old Testament,* caught only a glimpse of the truth through the darkness of unintelligible mysteries ; the second priesthood, that of the *New Testament,* shed some rays of truth upon obscure symbols ; the third priesthood, that of the future life, will permit us to see God face to face. To the first corresponds the natural law, to the second the law of grace, the third will be the kingdom of God. The first lifted up corrupt human nature, the second ennobled it by faith and charity and hope, the third will illuminate it by contemplation. The first, figured by the material ark, was given to a carnal people, whom the letter alone could touch ; the second, by the tangible symbols of the sacraments, puts men's souls on the way to the spiritual life, which they will fully taste only in Paradise. Thus the outward signs of the present Church will be dissipated in the light of the future Church. The soul will really possess God only by communion with the Holy Spirit. Scotus Eriugena, in his homily upon the first chapter of John, is not afraid even to assert that the Holy Spirit, in Jesus Christ, under a human form, was the principle of the divine life. The Church of the *New Testament* is therefore only the symbolical image of the eternal Church. And already, in their earthly life, Christians of the contemplative order have penetrated into this superior Church and participate in the ideal spirituality of the heavenly life. (21)

A whole religious evolution was contained in these last views. John Scotus Eriugena combined the two Johannine theories one with the other, the *Apocalypse* and the *Fourth Gospel.* The third revelation, that of the Comforter, was given in advance upon this earth to the purest souls, *in primitiis contemplationis.* The promises of the apostle were not in vain; God opens to the contemplative even here below access to the heavenly Jerusalem, he makes them ascend from the Church of the Word to that of the Spirit. This singular notion is found again at the basis of the doctrinal crises of the Middle Ages, in the heresiarchs who resolutely severed themselves from the Roman creed, as in the dissidents, of a disposition more philosophic than sectarian, who were content with spiritualizing Christianity and freely modifying the old *Credo.* Both alike were persuaded that they had at last embraced the true faith and were walking in the divine path. The Church accused them of apostasy, while they themselves believed they were the privileged interpreters of the Gospel, and that the desertion for which many suffered martydom was but the entry to the kingdom of heaven.

John Scotus Eriugena's doctrine long dwelt in the conscience of the Middle Ages. After more than three centuries it suddenly reappeared, in a very dogmatic form, in the school of Amaury of Chartres, and it frightened the Church. Amaury said: "The Father's power lasted as long as the Mosaic law, and as it is written at the appearance of new things the old will be rejected; all the sacraments of the *Old Testament* were abolished after the coming of Christ, and the new law has remained in vigour until this day. But henceforth the sacraments of the *New Testament* are done with, and the era of the Holy Spirit has begun. . . . The Father was incarnate in Abraham, the Son in Mary, the Holy Spirit incarnates Himself in each one of us every day. The Son has worked hitherto, but the Holy Spirit works from this time forth, and His work will endure till the end of the world." This definite law, according to him, was the *Third Testament.* (22)

All this might have been said by a Joachimite of the group of John of Parma (1209 ?–1289), a disciple of the *Eternal Gospel*. Between Amaury and Joachim of Flora it is impossible to suppose there was any intellectual relation. They both lived in the same age, with a common hope that came to them from the most distant sources of the Christian tradition. We must recall that tradition. We shall then be better able to understand why the dreams of a hermit of Calabria were able to stir the Middle Ages and what secret bonds link the religious revival of Italy to the past of Christianity.

## III

Giovanni dei Gioachini was born about 1132 at Celico, near Cosenza, in Calabria. His father belonged to the noble bourgeoisie of the Norman kingdom. He lived in the time of Arnold of Brescia and Frederic Barbarossa. The Christendom in which he grew up to man's estate was of a very peculiar kind ; men felt themselves freer in it than in any other province in Italy ; narrow communion with Rome seemed less necessary than elsewhere to the salvation of the soul. The inspiration of the hermits of the tenth century, the independence of the disciples of Nilus the Younger, who was so ardent a propagator of the Basilian rule in the southern part of the peninsula, was perpetuated in that region. The masters of the Italian south, the Byzantines and then the Normans, had greatly lightened the papal yoke in spiritual matters that rested upon the necks of their subjects. That alpine country of Calabria, with its wild horizons and its vistas over luminous seas, was favourable to the mystic life. And mysticism took there a singular form : the solitaries, from the mountain tops, looked out upon the two great religions which, outside the Roman faith, divided between them the world as known to the men of the Middle Ages—Islam and the Greek Church. Islam, still very flourishing in Sicily, under the Norman sway, recommended itself by the elegance of Arabic customs, its learned culture and the seriousness of its religious conviction. Between the schismatic community of the Sicilian Greeks and the Latin Church, the monks of the Basilian order, faithful to Rome but keeping their own liturgy and the Greek tongue, were a kind of bond of union connecting the two Christian families. Their convents were numerous in this region. While northern Italy and Rome allowed themselves to be tormented by the anxiety of heresy, Magna Græcia peacefully resumed the tradition of the ancient idealism and, amid the diversity of symbols, theologies and rites, contemplated the pure eternal truth.

Joachim, while quite a child, sought solitude; he passed long hours in prayer, resting on a great rock under the shadow of a vine arbour. At fifteen years of age, after having studied letters at Cosenza, he was admitted into the offices of the royal curia of Calabria. But the serious youth "with the angelic countenance" was very soon weary of the rush of secular life. While writing his diplomas he was dreaming of the distant east, of the marvels of Byzantium, of the tomb of Jesus and the vales of Galilee. His father permitted him to set out, not as a humble pilgrim, but with an escort of friends and servants, like a young prince. He entered Constantinople in the midst of the horrors of the plague, and the sight of human misery disclosed his true vocation to him; he sent back all his companions, with the exception of one only, shaved his head, took a poor tunic and set out on foot towards the Holy Land. Some Saracens fell in with him when he was worn out with fatigue, and, as they were devoid of everything, he gave them his garment. He had fallen ill, and so he stayed some time with these infidels, caressed and entertained by their little ones. At last he reached the Holy City and retired for the space of forty days to a grotto on Mount Tabor. On Easter morning he had a glimpse of the plan of his prophetic work ; henceforth he was to be the apostle of a transfigured Christianity. He went down again towards the inhabited regions of Palestine, and "seeing towns, he wept over them". He returned to Sicily and hid himself in a cavern, near a Greek convent, where he fasted and prayed and wept for the sins of Sicily. Then he returned to Calabria and hid himself among the mountains. But when his companion was arrested for picking a fig in an orchard, Joachim, in order to save his friend, disclosed his identity. His father, who thought he had died in Asia, let him enter, as a simple lay brother, into the Cistercian convent of Sambucina, where he became a porter. He stayed there a year. One day, according to the legend, as he was walking in the garden, meditating upon God, he saw before him a young man of great beauty, holding a jar in his hand. "Joachim," said the unknown, "take and drink this wine, which is delicious." After quenching his thirst, the young monk returned the jar. "O Joachim," said the angel, "if you had drunk it to the last drop no knowledge would have escaped you!"

But Joachim had tasted enough of the mysterious chalice to understand that the hour of his mission was striking. As a simple layman he preached for several years in the region of Renda. He possessed the peculiarly southern art of speaking to the crowd by making the spectacle of nature assist his oratorical action. One day, at a time of disastrous rain, the sky became darkened while he was preaching upon the sins of his auditors ; suddenly the clouds parted and a joyous ray from heaven illumined the church. Joachim paused, saluted the sun, intoned the *Veni Creator*, and went forth with the people to contemplate the country.

Joachim, however, did not advance very far along the apostolic road, which he seemed at that time to be preparing for Francis of Assisi. In 1168 the Church, by obliging him to take orders, brought him back to the traditional discipline ; in the abbey of Corazo, where he prepared for the priesthood, he must have conceived a love for the peace of the cloister, more congenial to his spirit than the labour of preaching. So he enrolled himself among the Cistercians and devoted his time to the determined reading of the *Scriptures*. Towards the year 1178, yielding to the importunities of his brethren, he accepted the dignity of abbot. But the care of temporal concerns troubled him, the quarrels of the monks, the diplomatic relations with the Norman court, the government of a community, seemed like a falling away to his melancholy spirit which, in the twilight of the cell, passed such pleasant hours with Isaiah or John. So he fled from his monastery and went to Rome to beg Lucius III (1181-1185) to relieve him of a charge that prevented him from meditating upon the word of God. The pope gave him back his liberty and Joachim returned to Calabria, hungry for solitude. He retired into the desert of Pietralata, like a hermit of ancient days, ceaselessly pursuing the composition of his three great books, the *Concordance*, the *Commentary upon the Apocalypse*, and the *Psaltery with Ten Chords*. The Holy See encouraged him in his task ; after Lucius III, Urban III (1185–1187) and Clement III (1187–1191) blessed his works, upon the sole condition that they should be approved by the apostolic censorship. Sometimes he went from cloister to cloister, throughout the whole peninsula, closely observing the evils of the Church and the decline of monasticism, speaking of reform to the Benedictine houses, "where the founder's rule is falling into disuse, where abstinence and work are neglected, where wealth and indolence are making men sickly valetudinarians, whose delicate stomachs can digest nothing but milk." (23) Joachim announced the approach of very dark days to Christendom, to princes and republics. Italy was turning with uneasy attention towards this strange person who deciphered the secrets of God from beneath the text of the *Scriptures* and who, by the austerity of his life as well as by his preaching, said very clearly that religious society was by no means in the right path. Disciples came to him from all parts, learned monks, such as Ranieri, from the abbey of the Three Fountains of Formia, great sinners, seeking the appeasement of their consciences, mystics who wished to penetrate in his footsteps into the symbolic obscurity of the sacred books. When the retreat at Pietralata had become no longer suited to his purpose Joachim ascended higher still into the solitudes of Calabria, and, on a plateau of the mountainous forest district of Sila, in the heart of the "very cold Alps", writes his biographer James the Greek, he built for his spiritual sons, like a second John at Patmos, the idealistic church of Flora. He dedicated it to John the Forerunner; and in 1196 Celestine III approved its statutes. There, while the Norman kingdom was falling beneath the blows of Henry VI (1190–1197) of Suabia, and a long cry of horror passed over Magna Græcia, these dreamers heard nought but the murmur of the pine forests and the distant lament of the torrents.

## IV

In the first days of the thirteenth century Joachim, seeing he was coming to the end of his long pilgrimage, put the finishing touches to the books in which his anguish and his hopes were to be perpetuated. He chose a successor in the government of the Order of Flora, and then had himself carried to Pietralata, to the little convent of San Martino, in order there to die. The entire Benedictine family of southern Italy hastened to receive the last prophecies of the old abbot. "He preached to them the way of salvation and announced to them the extermination of the Order and unceasingly repeated to them: 'I leave you this which I would have you ever remember—love one another as our Lord Jesus has loved us.'" Then he blessed them, beginning with those of Corazo, as the eldest of his children, and ending with those of Flora. On March 30, 1202, he expired.

No one in the Italian Church at that time had seemed to be a more faithful follower of Jesus. "He had learned from Christ to be gentle and humble of heart." His simplicity and charity were admirable: he warmed on his bosom the heads of the dying; in the winter that preceded his death, when famine was raging in Calabria and Sicily, he gave his last garments to the poor; he washed with his own hands the floor of the infirmary; he saved the towns from the ferocious brutality of Henry VI. He bent over every bed of suffering, without troubling about the sufferer's religion. One evening, at Treborna, he entered the house of a Greek priest, named Leo, to ask his hospitality. The priest's wife, being ill, threw herself at Joachim's feet and said to him: "Lord, if thou wilt, thou canst heal me." And the holy man, filled with pity, answered her: "Dost thou believe that, by the goodness of God, I can heal thee?" "Yes, lord, I do believe it." Then the servant of Jesus, raising his two hands to God, and then putting them on the brow of the sick woman who asked for healing, after having made the sign of the holy cross, said: "Rise, woman, thy faith and piety have made thee whole." And from that very hour the woman was healed.

Nevertheless it was chiefly as a visionary that Joachim impressed the men of the twelfth century. Brother Luke, who was his secretary and became archbishop of Cosenza, has no doubt whatever that the abbot of Flora lived in a perpetual vision, hearing mysterious words that no other human ear could perceive, conversing with supernatural persons whom his eye alone could behold. "I was seated at his feet, and night and day he dictated, and I wrote, and with me two other monks, Brother John and Brother Nicholas. . . . I served for him at mass, astonished at the way in which he celebrated ; he raised his arms higher than do other priests, blessing the Host with more emotion : he whose face was usually as livid as a dead leaf, during the holy sacrifice had a countenance as radiant as an angel's. . . . I have often seen him weep at that time and in particular at the mass when the passion of Our Lord is read. . . . When he preached before the chapter he looked like an angel sitting above us all ; he began in a low voice that soon resounded like thunder. He passed nights in watching, prayer, reading, and writing. He never slept, 'even in the choir', adds the good monk ; the more he fasted the stronger and more joyous he seemed. Many times I have surprised him on his knees, with hands and eyes raised to heaven, conversing joyously with Jesus, as if he saw Him face to face." At the Passion-tide, writes James the Greek, "he was no longer of this world ; he took part in all the sufferings of the Saviour, and, carried away by the charm of the divine agony, complained of the shortness of those days."

When Joachim was dead his books were opened, and it could be seen with what terrors the soul of the old hermit had been ceaselessly harassed at the time when he was dictating to the novices of the abbey his calculations and dreams. It was nothing to have lived, as he did, with the thought that antichrist was about to appear, or to have hesitated an instant, like a simple scholastic, over the dogma of the Trinity, which he nearly changed into Tritheism, from fear of the Quaternity of Peter Lombard. But he had received from the sacred books themselves a prodigious revelation according to which the secular Church, beneath which Christendom was sheltered, was no more than a tent set up for the night, to be taken down and folded up again the next morning. On the night of Easter in the year 1200, when all was silent, he had perceived the near future of Christianity. He feared to remain silent and dared not to speak. The century was closing in the fear foretold by the ancient Gospel, and Joachim asked himself tremblingly with what pangs the world would have to pay for the birth of the Eternal Gospel.

## V

It is indeed an Eternal Gospel that the Calabrian prophet announces with a perfect consciousness of what he is doing. The Holy Spirit will enter, according to him, into the religion of the faithful as the Father and Son have already done. "He will enter it by His Gospel", is written in the *Psaltery*. And what is this Gospel? That of which John says in the *Apocalypse*: "I saw the angel of God who flew in the midst of the heavens, and the Eternal Gospel was entrusted to him; but what then is this Gospel? That which proceeds from the Gospel of Christ, for the letter killeth and the spirit quickeneth." It will emerge from the recesses of the Christian revelation, as the idea issues from the letter. Joachim writes: "This Gospel was called eternal by John because that which Christ and the apostles gave us is transitory and temporal in that which relates to the mere form of the sacraments, but eternal for the truths which those sacraments signify." The spirit contained in the words of the *New Testament*, by its very opening, will destroy the symbolic text in which it was imprisoned, as the flower in opening breaks the covering of its bud. Joachim thus qualifies this ideal Gospel also as "the spiritual Gospel of Christ", that will shine in its full virtue as the sun, and no longer under a veil, or as the face of Moses in a mist. Very often too he calls it *Evangelium regni*. The gifts of the *Old Testament* were the veil of the letter thrown over the truth ; the *New Testament* delivered to the faithful the good things previously promised, taking away the veil from the face of Moses. When, proceeding from brightness to brightness, we embrace in spirit the divine things, we shall see in His glory the very form of Jesus, and we shall hear on the mount of contemplation the voice of the Father saying : "This is my beloved Son." By the Eternal Gospel alone shall we truly be born in Jesus ; the literal Gospel, entirely temporal in character, will disappear in great part before the revelation of the Spirit, and the faithful will possess a land "flowing with milk and honey."

The progress of the divine in the past, the hierarchy of the first two revelations, are, in Joachim's view, the certain pledge of this definitive crisis in Christendom. The distinction between the three ages or the three religious states of the world is an essential point in the doctrine that he established in his capital work, the *Concordia,* with a remarkable wealth of commentaries, historical parallels and calculations. Concordance is with him the rigorous method of exegesis ; he compares it to a road that leads from the desert to the town, arresting the traveller on summits whence he can look upon the road that lies before him. It measures the first two *Testaments* the one by the other, *quoad numerum, non quoad dignitatem,* the Biblical facts and figures reproduce themselves, in fact, in the Gospel facts and figures. But these last surpass the first in dignity, as John the Baptist surpasses Isaac, as Jesus the man surpasses Jacob. The first religious state, in which men lived after the flesh, extended from Adam to Jesus ; it bore all its fruits from Abraham to Zachariah ; the second, in which men live between the flesh and the spirit, began with Hosea and

Elisha and extends to the time when Joachim is writing ; it has borne all its fruits from Zachariah to Benedict ; the third, that in which men will live after the spirit only, began with Benedict ; it will last till the consummation of the ages. To these three periods, of which the last two are concurrent, by their origin, with the end of the preceding epoch, correspond three orders of persons whom God has charged to manifest the religious life in its highest degree : to the first, the order of husbands, that is to say the patriarchs, then the kings ; to the second the order of clerics, which began with the sacerdotal tribe of Judah and Hosea and produced its greatest figure in Jesus, King and supreme Priest ; to the third the order of monks, of whom the first was Benedict. There had been monks before Benedict, but only with him did monasticism take its true form, "when the Holy Spirit showed his perfect authority." And in the following passage, as stirring as a hymn, Joachim concludes the historic vision of Augustine and Scotus Eriugena : "The first period was that of knowledge, the second that of wisdom, the third will be that of full intelligence. The first was servile obedience, the second filial subjection, the third will be liberty. The first was trial, the second action, the third will be contemplation. The first was fear, the second faith, the third will be love. The first was the age of slaves, the second that of sons, the third will be that of friends. The first was the age of old men, the second that of young people, the third will be that of children. The first passed to the brightness of the stars, the second was the dawn, the third will be full day. The first was winter, the second the beginning of spring, the third will be summer. The first bore thistles, the second roses, the third will bear lilies. The first gave the blade, the second the ear, the third will give the full corn in the ear. The first gave water, the second wine, the third will give oil. The first corresponds to Septuagesima, the second to

Quadragesima, the third will be the festival of Easter. The first age corresponds to the Father, therefore, Who is the author of all things, the second to the Son, Who deigned to wear our clay, the third will be the age of the Holy Ghost, of Whom the apostle said: 'Where is the Spirit of the Lord, there is liberty.'" (24)

In Joachim's view the great day is at hand. He has reckoned between Adam and Jesus forty-two generations of thirty years each, or say 1,260 years. This number ought, according to the *Concordance* of the two *Testaments,* to re-appear for the period that will elapse between the coming of Christ and the blessed era of the Holy Ghost. Then will the year 1260 see the mystery accomplished? Here the prophet hesitates. The last two generations cannot, according to him, be counted. It is with the year 1200 that the religious crisis, therefore, commences. The first half of the thirteenth century will be filled with the drama of the Church. Christendom will be first of all overthrown by antichrist amid horrible tribulation: "Sacrifice and offering will fail, the order of the Church will be destroyed, to such a degree that, in the multitude of the people, there will be no longer any man left who will dare openly to call upon the name of the Lord." At last the trumpet of the archangel will sound, all the mysteries contained in the Scriptures will be accomplished, and "that will be the time of peace and truth for the whole earth." Joachim thinks he can already hear the distant muttering of the storm. He cries to the friends of God to provide for their earthly safety: "If there be any of the family of Lot, let him haste to flee from the walls of Sodom; if there be any of the family of Noah, let him make speed to rejoin those who are within the shelter in the ark." He writes the last lines of the *Concordance* in an access of mortal sadness, he supplicates his reader to pray to God for him. "If the last day finds me still living, may I have the strength to fight the good fight for the faith of Jesus Christ and, in company with those confessors of Jesus who are then living, ascend to the kingdom of heaven. Amen. Amen. Amen."

## VI

To the era of religious truth, according to Joachim, will correspond an evolution in men's consciences, in the Church and in the whole body of Christianity. The Eternal Gospel will be deciphered and understood only by the spiritual intelligence, the mystic intelligence, *misticus intellectus*, the only one that attains to the Holy Ghost. So a wholly mystic and contemplative Church will then be found flourishing, the Church of the monks, "which, freed from the cares of the world, lives by the spirit, occupied only in prayer and psalmody." The order of the monks is fired, like the Holy Spirit of which it is the type, with the love of God, for it could not despise the world and the things that are of the world without the impulse of the same Spirit that carried off Jesus into the desert. (26) The monastic life manifested in the ancient times by Elisha, then by Benedict and the Benedictine houses of which Jacob's ladder was the symbol ; but it has best represented the religion of the Spirit by means of Greek Christendom and the hermits of the desert. The hermit, alone in his rocky cave, the hermit whom the wild bees feed with their honey, such is, for the abbot of Flora, the perfect Christian, he whom the Church of the *New Testament* has known at times. It is to him that the future belongs. It is he who will reconcile, in the transcendent faith of the Spirit, all the great religious families of the human race ; he will be the bond of union between the Church of the west and the Church of the east. His apostolate will cover the whole earth ; he will touch the hearts of the heathen, and he will bring old Israel, weary of long revolt, into the fold of the eternal Church.

Thus Joachim expected not the end but the consummation of Christianity, not the ruin but the exaltation of the Christian Church ; he did not believe that the order of clerics was destined to disappear any more than, under the law of the first *Testament*, the order of Levites had disappeared ; the monks were to place themselves at the head of religious society, as the secular clergy had formerly done, when they took precedence over the laity ; the traditional Gospel would not altogether fall from the hands of the faithful like a book that was thenceforth useless. For the *Eternal Gospel* itself would not be a book replacing either the *Old Testament* or the *New Testament* ; rather would it proceed from both of them as the Holy Ghost proceeds from the Father and the Son ; it would give the final meaning of the anterior revelations ; it would be the intimate communion of souls with the Holy Ghost. And thus would be justified, by the fulfilment of the Johannine promises, the age-long hope of humanity.

The writings of Joachim startled Italy, from Sicily to the Alps. All Christendom, the Holy See and the princes of the west, were, so to speak, dazzled by the vision of the hermit of Flora. This singular figure was destined to leave a long memory and an impression of mystery very likely to increase, in the course of several generations, the reputation of a prophet. Joachim answered the religious needs of his age, but he answered them only in part. At first men would not see the contradictions of his teaching, the deceptive side of his theory. They did not understand the double aspect of a character that turned at once towards the past and towards the future, and entrusted to the mystical tradition of the past the spiritual renovation of the future. Joachim's loftier view, the completion of religion in the bosom of Christianity itself, but a sublimated Christianity, disengaged from the narrow letter, purified by the Spirit—this view was well calculated to rejoice the Italian conscience, which the heretical sects never succeeded in detaching from the old faith. Italy willingly heard the announcement of the fall of the clerical order, the temporal Holy See and the secular Church, whose pastoral function would pass to the contemplative and to the saints, "from one sea unto the other." (27)

Arnold of Brescia's dream would therefore become a reality But Arnold, who was a tribune far more than a mystic and who sought religious liberty in the enfranchisement of civil society, would certainly not have accepted the state of hieratic immobility in which the abbot Joachim wished to fix Christendom. In reality the latter, instead of enlarging the Church in order to embrace the multitude of the faithful in it, closed its naves and left room in it for none but a few saints kneeling under the sanctuary lamp. He exalted monasticism at the very moment when secular Italy had just set up the middle class commune in view of the interests of the age, and was abandoning for ever the conception that the ecclesiastical Middle Ages had had of the social order. The lilies of the field that do not spin could not be the symbolic flower of a world whose activity was penetrating the Mediterranean, Europe and the east. The life contemplative supposes a pre-eminent nobility of soul, a detachment from earthly things, a disdain of action, perfect solitude. It loosens the bonds of the human community and dispenses too easily with charity not to end in egotism. It does not satisfy the divine words repeated by the apostle John : "Love one another." The old *Gospel,* whose text had so long consoled men, was surely richer in hopes than the *Eternal Gospel.* Francis of Assisi, upon reopening the *Testament of Jesus*, was soon to discover the secret that no man before him had suspected. He felt that the salvation of the Christian family, the salvation of pastors and flock alike, would be the work of souls, even of the most obscure, and that Christianity would be transformed on the day that the humblest consciences returned frankly to the virtues of the Gospel age. He wished neither to reform Rome, nor to restore the ancient monasticism, nor to dispossess the bishops and clergy, but simply to arouse the inner man in each Christian, and by a unanimous impulse of the faithful carry the Church along with them. That is why, in his poor chapel at Portiuncula, though not a priest, he was able to celebrate Joachim's Easter and to invite all Christendom to the festival that his forerunner had reserved exclusively for the élite of the monks.

## CHAPTER III

# FRANCIS OF ASSISI AND THE FRANCISCAN APOSTOLATE

JOACHIM of Flora was only just dead, and Italy, thrown back by him into the terrors of the *Apocalypse*, was awaiting the catastrophe of the antichrist. Suddenly on the district of Assisi, Perugia, Gubbio, Orviteo, and Spoleto, there descended a bright beam of sun-shine and as it were the exquisite grace of an April morning. These little towns, that had never been touched by the higher civilization of Florence, Milan, and Venice, and that still formed, in the region of the upper Tiber, around Lake Trasimeno, in the centre of the old Etruscan wilderness of Chiana, an isolated and simple-minded world, were the ideal cradle for a religious renaissance. The Middle Ages had shown themselves particularly rough in their dealings with these districts that the emperors could not effectively protect, and of which the popes had made a fortified region for the defence of the ecclesiastical patrimony. The communal form of government did not there soften, as it did in the large towns, the annoyances of its constitution by the pride it aroused in public life. Peace was precarious in these little places ; the barons and the Church disputed unceasingly the possession of Orvieto, Spoleto, or Narni. The Church was less in evidence there than elsewhere ; the ridge of Cimino seemed to hide Rome from Umbria, the Order of Benedict had placed no considerable monastery in those parts ; the pope was looked upon merely as a somewhat inconvenient feudal master. Thus, at the first appeal of Francis (1182?–1226), thousands of souls expanded. Italy had never heard a more consoling apostle. He did not preach the desperate asceticism of the monks and hermits ; he did not attempt to overthrow the faith, as the missionaries of the Cathari or the Waldenses had done ; he did not threaten men with a crisis in their consciences and with a new interpretation of the Gospel, as did Joachim ; nor did he raise a crusade against the old Church, as Arnold of Brescia had attempted to do. From the very first acts of his vocation there was seen in him a southern, an Italian, a poet, a friend of movement and light, ignorant of sadness, never disturbed by a bitter thought. We must picture him as his first disciples have described him for us, with his delicate and smiling face, his bright red lips, his black and sparkling eyes, his slender figure, his quick step, and not with the emaciated face and mournful expression doubtless invented by Spanish artists. He is undoubtedly the child of a century of action. He believes that all is good here below, society and nature. He seeks intercourse with his like ; for all that lives, even for the humblest beasts, he feels an emotion of tenderness and has a word of blessing. He is at his ease in the paternal hand of God. His heart is too pure to fear the snares of the devil, his faith too childish ever to be discouraged. When quite young he had hoped to achieve great things, and did homage in advance to his own future. When for a whole year he was a prisoner of war at Perugia he astonished his guardians by his unvarying cheerfulness. " What do you think of me? " he used to say to them. " Are you aware that one day the world will adore me? " His friends at that time thought him somewhat mad, and did not understand the meaning of those other words he was fond of repeating : " My body is in captivity, but my mind is free and I am content."

He was born in 1182. He belonged to the privileged class of Assisi, at that time a commune flourishing through its commercial relations with the neighbouring cities. His father, Bernardone, was one of the upper citizens, and used to go as far as France to sell his cloth. As to Francis—in his early youth he made his father's florins spin. He was very joyous, writes Thomas of Celano, his earliest biographer. He used to walk by night in Assisi lighted by torches, surrounded by young people of his own age, clad in fine garments and holding the wand of office in his hand. (28) It was the time when the Provençal civilization was enlivening the Italian cities. The troubadours were giving the peninsula the refined culture of southern France, the taste for love-poetry and brilliant festivals. Francis seems often to have made use of French, that is to say Provençal, as a nobler dialect than that of Umbria. These sons of middle-class fathers, brought up upon French romances, *fabliaux* and *sirventes,* even dreamed of chivalry and great adventures in the Norman bands of Gaultier of Brienne. "I shall be a great baron," he often said to his friends.

A thousand painful impressions, however, the harshness of his father, the selfishness of these laborious citizens, the misery he came upon at every turn, the poor who crowded at the church doors, the lepers who wandered in the fields, the dangerous pilgrims who roamed about the district and who when evening came transformed themselves into robbers, the fugitive serfs who begged "for the love of God", all these sights, renewed day by day, cast a shadow over his pleasures. In the smiling natural surroundings of Assisi, in the heart of the Umbrian plain, everywhere adorned with luxuriant vines, sheltered, as in a cradle, by its mountains, in this land where life, liberty and joy seemed to fall from heaven, man alone appeared to Francis to be wretched and disinherited, compelled by the world to carry on a thankless struggle against his fellows, disdained even by God himself, Whose ways were darkened upon all sides. The Church, tormented by heresy, suffered all kinds of violence from the secular powers. At the end of the twelfth century men had seen Henry, son of Frederic Barbarossa, wrest from the pope all the cities in the region of Orvieto, Perugia and Spoleto. Francis, when quite a child, saw for some time according to the words of a contemporary, the Roman Church "reduced to beggary." The youth fell sick, and when for the first time he looked again upon the hills and fields, he received an impression of great melancholy. He wished to set out for the Neapolitan provinces; but he had singular visions on his way. He replied to God's call: "Lord, what wilt thou have me to do?" The free voice of the personal conscience began to speak in him. He returned to Assisi, and once more took part in the pleasures of his friends for some time. One day, at the close of a feast, in which for the last time he had been crowned prince of the youth, as they were carrying him singing through the streets of the town, Francis stopped suddenly and seemed to be plunged into a profound meditation. "What is the matter?" his companions said to him. "Are you thinking of getting married?" "You are right, I am thinking of betrothing myself to a noble and beautiful bride." The divine voice was at that moment crying to him: "Francis, you must hate and abandon what you have heretofore loved on earth." He set out to Rome, begged at the gate of Peter, then returned to Assisi, where he devoted himself to the lepers, the sight of whom had formerly filled him with horror. The chapel of St. Damiano was falling into ruin; the young man secretly conveyed to Foligno the finest cloth his father had and sold it in order to obtain money to repair the little chapel of God. At this time Bernardone deemed the vocation of his spendthrift son to be dangerous; he summoned him before the consuls ; but Francis refused the communal jurisdiction and appealed from it to the bishop, who was, he said, "the father and the lord of souls."

Thus, for yet a moment longer, he turned towards the Church's past, in order to escape from the grip of the social government whose discipline seemed to him to be too hard for the independence and fraternity of men's souls. Francis might have begged his bishop, on the day when he threw himself at his feet, to confer the priesthood upon him ; he might also have taken refuge in some cloister and have died to the world under the Benedictine robe. But he had a vague feeling that neither the secular Church nor monasticism would any longer favour in their bosom the apostolic idea, that the old form of church government no longer answered the needs of Christendom, and that renovated Italy required, according to the expression consecrated by the language of the Church herself, "a new religion." He was at that time eager above all things for liberty and wished to hasten to God along untrodden paths. In a few hours he renounced the world and his paternal heritage, and, covered with the mantle given him by the bishop, went away to the woods of Assisi, singing French verses. He was stopped by robbers ; he told them, laughing, that he was the herald of a great king. They left him in a ditch full of snow. He went on his way and offered his services as cook to a convent. He passed a month among the lepers of Gubbio, and then begged on the roads that cross the plain of Assisi. His former boon companions railed him mercilessly, and threw mud in his face ; his father and brother turned away at the sight of him. "Of all the griefs that I have had to endure," he said afterwards, "this was the most cruel." He tried to find consolation by begging an old mendicant to accept him as his son. But his apostolic novitiate was by that time accomplished ; by charity and voluntary poverty, by humility and love, this generous soul had found the full liberty and the joy that sustained him till the last day of his mission. He had succeeded in opening the *New Testament* at the page that contains the Sermon on the Mount; he was ready to restore to Italy the smile of pity and the words of enchantment wherewith the Church had formerly lulled Christianity to sleep in its infancy. When he had gathered a few disciples round him he said to them: "Let us go to our Mother, the holy Roman Church, and show the Holy Father what God has begun to do through our work, in order that we may pursue our task according to the good will of the pope." It was the year 1209. The pope was then Innocent III (1198–1216). Francis carried to Rome the sketch of his first rule. (29) The pontifical hierarchy and the young Franciscan society, the historical tradition of the Church and the future of Italian Christendom, were about to meet in the solemn desert of the church of St. John Lateran.

## II

Now at this very time the Roman See presented an appearance of incomparable grandeur. The recent storms through which it had safely passed had carried it to a greater height, perhaps, than it had occupied in the days of Gregory VII (1073–1085). Never had the problem of the double pontifical power, the spiritual and the temporal, seemed more difficult of solution than in the last years of the twelfth century. The Church was actually threatening to fall upon Innocent's head. At Rome the commune, now oligarchic, now democratic, and always hostile, was autonomous and brutal; demagogy, faithful to the memory of Arnold of Brescia, again and again rose on the Capitol; the majority of the nobles entered into compact with the people ; the terrible Orsini had just entered into the history of the Papacy ; everywhere, in the town, at the Coliseum, at the baths of Æmilius Paullus, at the Theatre of Marcellus, at the Quirinal, there rose the towers of the rebellious barons. From the heights of the Lateran, where he lived alone, protected by the Annibaldi, the pope heard night and day the bell of the Capitol ringing for civil war. Round about Rome the barons and the communal senator were masters of the entire country ; farther off the German counts, the emperor's captains, were encamped in all the Church's provinces ; farther off still, in the Two Sicilies, Henry VI had set up the pivot of the empire. To the north of Rome the communes, ill-disposed in Tuscany and doubtful everywhere else, had by the ruin of the feudal episcopate deprived the Holy See of its best resource in Italy : they might any day have ranged themselves upon the side of the emperor against the pope. In the most flourishing half of Italy secret heresy was taking possession of all ranks of society ; in one half of France heresy, upheld by the lords, was strikingly triumphant ; finally at Paris the scholastic heresy of Amaury of Chartres denied the eternity of Christianity. Italian Christendom seemed no longer to be obedient to the voice of its chief pastor. Innocent III, younger and more learned than Gregory VII, and as pure as he, saw clearly what must be done to save the Holy See, the Roman Church, and perhaps the unity of the faith. Before all things it was necessary for him to keep possession of Rome. He began in 1198 by reducing the imperial prefect to submission and imposing the oath of fidelity upon the communal senator. The disorder that followed the death of Henry VI restored him the patrimony of Peter and the old Tuscan fiefs of Matilda ; the interregnum and the competition of Otto IV and Philip of Suabia, owing to the disorganization of the imperial party and the loosening of the bonds that united a large number of towns to the empire, finally permitted him to show himself to the peninsula as leader of the national independence, protector of communes, and, as he wrote eight months after his election, "paternal guardian of Italy."

Thus Innocent founded the tradition that sustained the Papacy until the time of Boniface VIII (1294–1303) and the exile at Avignon. It was a tradition incessantly interrupted by revolts of the barons and the Roman people, long compromised by the desperate efforts of the last Hohenstaufen to make Italy the imperial province *par excellence*, and always revived again by the Holy See which, already attacked in its œcumenical suzerainty and its spiritual prestige, and not yet possessing the ecclesiastical principate of the fifteenth century, could maintain itself at the head of the peninsula only by the moral and political hegemony of the Guelf party. Innocent III devoted himself to this work with a constancy that the misfortunes of his own reign never relaxed. He fled from burning Rome in the spring of 1203, and ten months later re-entered his metropolis, hurled his partisans against the demagogic master of the commune, Giovanni Capocci, and while giving battle in the streets bought over the leaders of the people with gold. This time he obtained all he wished, the right to name and depose the senator or *podestà* to whom the executive power in the city belonged. By this constitution he covered Rome once more with the mantle of the Church. If he had endeavoured to destroy the Roman commune at that time, and to establish the papal monarchy more than a century before the peninsula began to move unanimously towards tyranny, he would, by that dangerous creation, have abdicated the protectorate of the republican towns of Italy and left the Holy See, isolated and undefended, between the empire and the communes. It was not out of humility that he contented himself with this measure of temporal power, seeing that about this time he said to the envoys of Philip Augustus of France (1180–1223): "The Lord called the priests gods; the priesthood is alone a divine institution; the empire is only a thing invented by man." But it was enough for him to be the ecclesiastical overlord of Rome and the patrimony, to group the communes round the pontifical cross, to be without dispute the bishop of Rome, in order to speak to the west as universal bishop, to regulate the integrity of the Catholic faith, to impose upon Paris the decisions of his theologians, and to decree a crusade of inquisitors against southern France. He kept in tutelage, secluded in an Arabian palace at Palermo, the grandson of Barbarossa, the child who, when later on he became emperor, was to be the cause of great tribulation to the Church; with Frederic of Suabia the whole of the Ghibeline party seemed to have been brought into the power of the pope. The double mission of the Holy See in the thirteenth century, the primacy of Italy and the restoration of religious discipline, thus began with the wholly political work of a statesman pope; it could last and grow only by the pursuit of the same policy; and even more than in former times the moral force and mystical ascendency of the Church of Rome had as its first condition an essentially temporal interest.

That is why Innocent and his Sacred College welcomed with sincere astonishment the evangelical dream of those twelve unknown men who came from the heart of Umbria to ask permission from the vicar of God to preach to the simple, to beg for the starving, to console the dying, and to share in the conquest of the world by possessing as their sole fief the little field and ruined chapel of Portiuncula at the foot of the hill of Assisi. They bowed themselves before the pope, repeating the words of Jesus that are in Matthew: "If thou wilt be perfect, go sell all thou hast, give the money to the poor, and thou shalt have treasure in heaven." But the secular Church could not understand at that time that religious things were so far detached from all earthly interests. The pope and cardinals hesitated some days to accept the rule of the new community ; they deemed the profession of poverty and absolute renunciation too hard. Innocent III seems even to have foreseen that a schism would not be slow in dividing the rising order. But a cardinal said in the papal council : " If we reject the request of these men as too difficult, let us take heed lest we gainsay the Gospel of Jesus Christ." So Innocent blessed the founder and his work and sent back these pilgrims, committing them to the grace of God. Then he had a dream, that was long remembered by that age : he saw the basilica of the Lateran heeling over like a vessel struck by the tempest, and the child of Assisi lending his shoulder to support it.

## III

We must consider closely the spiritual life of this apostle who despoiled himself of the things of the world not for his own salvation, like the monks, but for the reformation of all his brethren ; not to find God in the solitude of a cloister, but to seek Him and glorify Him openly in the populous towns, on the mountains and in the valleys. The more he forgot himself, the more he seemed to be master of his will and heart. He had so thoroughly vanquished, by the habit of self-sacrifice, the egotism of the vulgar that suffering and humiliation gave him a very lively pleasure ; the humbler he made himself beneath the hand of God, the stronger and more joyous he showed himself to his disciples. One day he wished Brother Leo, with " his dove-like simplicity ", to overwhelm him with reproaches, and, in order that the essay might the better succeed, he dictated to him with his own lips all manner of terrible words. "O Brother Francis, thou hast done so much evil and committed so many sins in this world that thou art worthy of the nethermost hell." But Leo spoke quite the reverse: "God will bring about so much good by thy means that thou wilt go to Paradise." Then Francis, smiting his breast, said in a loud voice, with many tears and sighs, "O my Lord of heaven and earth, I have committed so many sins against Thee that I am verily worthy of Thy malediction." And Brother Leo made answer: "O Brother Francis, God will make thee such that thou shalt be singularly blessed even among the blessed." One winter evening, as they were both walking in a very biting cold from Perugia to Assisi, Francis, while hastening behind his companion, taught him what "perfect joy" really means. "Brother Leo, sheep of the good God, dost thou know what perfect joy consists in for the Minorites? It is not to edify the world by sanctity, nor to restore sight to the blind, nor to cast out demons, nor to raise those who have been four days dead; neither is it to possess a knowledge of all tongues, sciences and scriptures, nor to prophecy, nor to know the stars and the virtue of plants and of waters, nor is it to preach so well as to convert the infidels." "What, then, father," said Leo, "is perfect joy?" "Well, when we arrive at Santa Maria degli Angeli, drenched with rain, pierced with cold, covered with mud, dying of hunger, we shall knock at the door; the porter will come in a great rage and say: 'Who are you?' 'Two of your brethren', we will reply. 'It is not true', the porter will cry; 'you are two ribalds, two vagabonds who rob the poor of their alms.' And he will leave us without in the rain and cold, and we shall think with humility that this porter knows us well. And if we continue to knock and he drives us away with a stout, knotty stick, crying 'Be off with you, you rogues, go to the hospital; there is no supper or bed for you here'; if he takes us by our cowls and throws

MARRIAGE OF ST. FRANCIS TO POVERTY

*Sassetta, Chantilly*

[*To face* p. 104

us down in the snow, and if we bear all this thinking of the sufferings of the Blessed Jesus, Brother Leo, that verily is perfect joy."

This religious gaiety was one of the forces of the apostolate of Francis. He charmed his brethren, and they in their turn charmed Italy, by the smiling serenity with which they welcomed great misery and the little distresses and humble joys of life. Once upon a time he, being of mean appearance, received only a few crusts of dry bread in a village, while Frà Masseo, who was, the *Fioretti* tells us, "tall and comely in person," was given generous pieces of fresh bread. They spread out their takings on a large white stone, near a clear spring, in the sunshine, and Francis was amazed at the beauty of the feast. "But, father," said Masseo, "we have neither cloth, nor knife, nor plate, nor table, nor house, nor man servant, nor maid servant." "And for what then," replied Francis, "do you take this fine stone, this limpid water, and these pieces of bread?" As he had always a merry heart he did not like to have about him any but good-humoured faces, and did not allow the mournful pre-occupation of *mea culpa* to be brought into the cheerful chapter of his Minorites. He used to say to a novice: "My brother, why this sad face? Hast thou committed some sin? That concerns God and thee alone. Before me and my brethren keep always a look of holy joy; for it is not seemly, when one is in the service of God, to show a gloomy and frowning air." (30) And in the Rule of 1221 he made joy a canonical obligation, together with chastity and obedience. The true Franciscans must always be *guadentes in Domino*, "merry and of good courage." There is no valley of tears in the Holy Land of Umbria.

Yet the Franciscans were very poor; every day they held out their hands at the doors of houses and churches; to shelter them they had but a few huts made of rushes near Assisi. Communal Italy, the

Guelfic Italy of money-changers and lawyers, for whom the florin was a sacred thing and their daily bread, was at once astonished and softened by the sight, so marvellous in her eyes, of hearts so light in men so utterly destitute of all earthly goods. A century later Dante and Giotto were still lauding the marriage of Francis with Poverty, "who, deprived of Christ, her first bridegroom, for more than eleven hundred years, had remained despised and obscure." It was in fact the cardinal virtue of Franciscan Christianity. In the winter of 1209, while mass was being performed, Francis heard a voice saying to him: "Go, carry neither gold, nor silver, nor money in your purse, nor two coats, nor shoes, nor staff." And so he chose the dress of the poorest artizans and fishers, the tunic of coarse cloth, the cowl and rope girdle; he forbade on principle the use of sandals and absolutely prohibited his followers to touch money. "Christ's poor," writes Jacques de Vitry, "carry on their journeys neither wallet, nor provisions, nor shoes, nor purse in their girdle. They have neither convents, nor churches, nor fields, nor vines, nor beasts of burden, nor anything in the world on which to lay their head." Of their breviaries, their poor furniture, their household utensils, they have, according to a brief of Gregory IX (1227–1241), only the use and not the possession. But even in the lifetime of Francis divergences manifested themselves about this fundamental idea; and immediately after his death the Order was destined to split upon it. The mere needs of discipline compelled the immense institution of the Minorites to possess convents more worthy of that name than the huts with which they had at first been content. In the thirteenth and fourteenth centuries the debate upon evangelical poverty, exaggerated by the zeal of some of the brothers who advocated the strict rule, agitated the Church and even drove one part of the Franciscan family to the verge of heresy. But these theological quarrels did not impair in any sensible degree the apostolic work of the Minorites in Italian society. They could redeem by charity what they had gained in temporal riches. The lofty ideal of Francis long continued intact. By Poverty he had found the way back to the spiritual leader, forgotten for ages, who was born in the manger of a village inn, while the foxes had their holes and the birds of the air their nests. He said so himself to Jesus in that splendid prayer: "She was in the cradle, and like a faithful squire remained armed for the great fight You waged for our redemption. In Your Passion she was the only one who did not abandon You. Mary, Your mother, stopped at the foot of the cross, but Poverty, ascending it with You, clasped You firmly in her arms until the last. It was she who lovingly prepared the rough nails that pierced Your feet and hands, and when You were dying of thirst she, like a thoughtful wife, had gall made ready for You. You expired in her ardent embrace; she left You not in death, O Lord Jesus, and would not allow Your body to rest elsewhere than in a borrowed tomb. It was she, finally, who kept You warm deep down in the grave. O most poor Jesus, the grace that I ask of You is to grant me the treasure of most sublime Poverty: permit the distinctive sign of our Order to be this, that it never possesses anything of its own beneath the sun, for the glory of Your name, and that it have no other patrimony than beggary!" (31)

## IV

Here we get a glimpse of the admirable passion to which Francis of Assisi owed all his genius. His heart was fired with love:

*In foco l'amor mi mise,*

"Love put me in the furnace; it put me in the furnace of love", we read in a poem attributed to him by Bernardino of Siena (1380–1444). So violent was his love that he reeled like a drunken man. Jesus, he said, had stolen away his heart. "O gentle Jesus! Embrace me and give me death, my love!" The pathetic God of the *Gospel*, the God in the agony in the garden on Mount Olivet, betrayed by his disciples, sold by an apostle, outraged by his people, scourged and crowned with thorns, the wretched God of Calvary Who, dying on a gibbet, cried in despair that His Father Himself had forsaken Him, Jesus crucified, possessed the soul of Francis. In his retreat on Mount Alvernia, Francis wished to live through the last hours of the Son of Man's life one by one. "O my Lord, I ask of Thee two boons before I die: grant that I may feel in my soul and body all the bitter pangs which Thou hast endured, and in my heart the boundless love that led Thee to bear such sufferings, Thee, Son of God, for us, miserable sinners!" But these ecstasies had nothing in common with the visions of Joachim of Flora. The tears that Francis shed in these hours of rapture were all of tenderness and bliss. An angel appeared to him, holding a violincello, and at the first stroke of the bow Francis swooned with love and saw the azure Paradise open before him lighted with the face of his God. The high rocks of Alvernia sparkled before his eyes with more rubies and sapphires than the triumphant Jerusalem described by John. Jesus embraced the mystic of Assisi with his blood-stained arms, imprinted on his hands, feet and heart, the stigmata of His Passion, and bore him, beside himself with love, to the bosom of the heavenly Father.

But high as his spirit carried him, Francis never lost sight of earth and that suffering humanity whom Jesus comforted, the crowd of the humble and simple whose miseries were beguiled by the Sermon on the Mount. He tended the lepers with his own hands, with the gentleness of a sister of mercy, cleansing the wounds of the soul no less than those of the body. To the thieves whom the warder of one of his convents had driven away he sent the bread and wine intended for his own repast, with words so touching that they hastened to throw themselves at his feet and beg him to admit them into his Order. (32) If, on the day of the general chapter, thousands of pilgrims gathered in the plain of Assisi, there were seen about mid-day coming along the roads that lead to Spoleto, Orvieto, and Perugia processions of mules, horses and waggons laden with provisions, bread, wine, beans and cheese, says the *Fioretti,* "and other good things to eat for the poor of Jesus." One Christmas night, in the valley of Greccia, he invited the peasants and shepherds to bid welcome to Him whom he called "the little child of Bethlehem." At the peaceful hour of midnight the woods were suddenly illumined by the light of torches advancing in haste towards a stable where Francis was waiting, near a manger filled with straw, between the ass and the ox. When all were on their knees, he read, as deacon, on the right side of the manger, as if it were a high altar, the Gospel according to St. Luke ; then he turned towards the faithful kneeling in the shadow, and preached to them the birth of the Saviour. Undoubtedly, at the same hour, there was less faith and love in the basilica of St. John Lateran and under the imperial dome of the Palatine chapel at Palermo. Some thought they saw a child sleeping on the straw of the manger, who seemed gradually to awake and open his arms. It was in fact the God of the poor, roused from a long sleep by Francis, Who once more smiled in man's inmost heart.

## V

And at the same time it was a new religion that the men of goodwill received from Francis of Assisi, as formerly they had received it under the starry sky of Bethlehem. We are in contact with the main feature of the Franciscan work. By love and pity Francis led back Italy to the compact of the *Gospel* ; without theology or scholasticism he restored primitive Christianity ; without heresy or conflict he revived the Church and gave religious liberty to his age. He signed a new concordant between God and Christendom.

Francis reconciled God with man. He brought man into the fold of Him Who said : " Blessed are those who weep ! " He did away with the age-long misunderstanding that had cast a gloom over Christianity. He drove away the old terrors and piercing anguish of the Middle Ages ; he put goodness into God instead of inflexible justice, and he brought back to the Christian's heart the hope of Paradise, filial confidence and peace in this earthly life. It was Jesus Who, in place of the Church, was directly presented to the conscience of men. The true mediator, according to Francis, is Jesus, Who was willing to suffer and to die for the family of Adam, in order to pay their debts ; Jesus is the true priest, the bishop of souls, *episcopus animarum nostrarum,* it is written in the Rule of 1221 ; and Francis adds, with the apostle John : " Ye are all brethren ; call no man father upon earth, for your only father is He Who is in heaven. Take not to yourselves the name of masters, for you have but one master, He who is in heaven." So it is to Him, the Father, Shepherd, Teacher and Supreme Bishop, that men must bring their troubles for alleviation and their wounded souls to be healed. He knows better than any other the needs of His children, for Francis repeated, " it is the eye of God alone that judges the worth of man." Before Him no conscience stands higher than another, for he is the source of all merit for them all with equal goodness. " All virtues and all good things ", it is said in the *Fioretti,* " are of God, and not of the creature; no one ought to glorify himself in His sight, but if any do glorify himself, let it be in the Lord." The rôle of priest became less important from the moment when the faithful communicated spontaneously with God; that of the saint had no longer any *raison d'être,* since the Son freely presented his sufferings and wishes direct to the Father. The intercession of saints in some sort disappeared from the Franciscan Christianity. Mary, the two Johns, and the angels, were the only ones who shared the devotion offered to Jesus. The Christian thus became his own priest, the umpire of his faith, the architect of his own salvation. The religion of works lost all that the religion of the heart had gained. "Flatter not yourselves," he said, "that you can become perfect by doing all that a wicked person can perform: such a one can fast, pray, weep and mortify his body: one thing only is impossible for him, to be faithful to his Lord." (33)

The Franciscan undoubtedly held closely to the Church of Rome, through the integrity of the symbols of faith, the necessity of the sacraments and the authority of the pope and bishops, that Francis solemnly recommended, not, however, without some reservations. The brothers, say the two Rules, will submit to the clergy "in all things appertaining to salvation"; but they add "and in all that is not contrary to our Order." The Franciscans were dispensed from the festivals that might be created by the pope outside the canonical breviary, unless they are expressly imposed upon them. In reality this essentially mystic Christianity took away from the secular Church its ceaseless watch over the spiritual life; it escaped from the ecclesiastical hierarchy and organized itself outside of all traditional discipline. Francis observed literally the fine pontifical formula: *Servus servorum Dei.* He himself and all the chiefs of the Franciscan groups were only the "ministers", the guardians, the watchful servants, of their brothers. The monastic and feudal episcopate of the abbots was unknown in the new institution. The testament of Francis forbade the brothers to solicit any privilege from Rome for preaching or against persecution. The majority of the Franciscans did not take the higher clerical orders; the founder was but a simple deacon; but all of them fulfilled the apostolic office by excellence in preaching. The prayer of Francis ascended as near to God as the liturgical words of the bishop of Rome. The brothers who have duly carried out the evangelical life, says the curious little work upon the "Stigmata", will enter straight into Paradise, those whose zeal has been feeble will languish in Purgatory only as long as Francis himself determines; each year, on the anniversary of his death, the saint descends into Purgatory to take from it the souls of his brothers and sisters of the three Franciscan Orders and those of the other Christians who have loved the penitent of Assisi. It had been revealed to him that Brother Elias of Cortona, his first successor in the generalship, would rebel against the order of the Church and be damned. He contrived that the sentence should be revoked, and that Elias, enlightened in his hour, should die with the pope's pardon, clad in the Franciscan robe.

The way of safety, once so difficult, was, therefore, made smooth, and could be trodden with greater ease. Religious observances were simplified, as if God were content, in exchange for the love of men's souls, with a greater virtue; the duties of piety were made capable of a more elastic interpretation. Francis prayed incessantly, not as an obligation, but because prayer gladdened him; he believed that the silent prayer of the heart is better than that which the lips stammer: *mentaliter potius quam vocaliter*. According to him a simple *Pater*, or a few tears shed upon the Saviour's Passion are the finest of prayers. (34) "Thou dost not know what true prayer is," said Brother Egidio to a novice who refused to go to beg bread for the community upon the pretext that he was occupied with his prayers ; "humble obedience is of more value than the converse of angels." Francis would not have his followers build great churches ; he exhorted them to have only one mass celebrated daily in their chapels ; "if the priests are many, let them be content with assisting at the mass of one of their number ; for God gives His grace abundantly to the absent as well as to those who are present at the altar, provided they are worthy of Him." In default of a priest of the Order, or a secular priest, for the hearing of confession, the Minorites were to kneel provisionally before one of their brothers, *confiteantur fratri suo*, according to the counsel of the apostle James. (35) The externals of worship affected Francis very little ; he would rather despoil the altar of the Virgin of its last ornament than be untrue to the law of poverty by amassing florins for the needs of his Order. An old woman, whose sons had become Minorites, asked alms of him, but there was left in the convent only the *Bible* that was used for singing the office in the choir. "Give her the *Bible*," said the saint ; "God will be better pleased with the good we shall do this poor woman than with our psalmody in the chapel ; she has given her children to the Order, she is entitled to ask anything of us." "Francis," it is related in the *Fioretti*, "was once, at the beginning of his Order, with Brother Leo, in a place where they had no book with which to say the divine office. When the hour of matins came, he said to Brother Leo : 'My very dear friend, we have no breviary wherewith to say matins, but, in order to employ the time in praising God, I will speak and thou shalt answer as I will instruct thee.'" A similar accident had formerly befallen Joachim of Flora, but that perfect monk, instead of cheerfully inventing a very free rendering of matins, being suddenly inspired by the Holy Ghost, recited the canonical office to his fellow-traveller, without forgetting a single verse, to the very last syllable.

"God will have mercy," said Francis, "and not sacrifice." (36) The gloomy austerity of the believer who tortures himself in order to please God had no meaning in the Franciscan form of Christianity. It seemed to be a lack of confidence in God. Francis included all kinds of temperaments in his precepts in order to support human weakness. He permitted his brothers, as Jesus once did with his apostles, to eat and drink whatever their hosts set before them in the course of their journeys. If the feast of Christmas fell upon Friday he forbade the rule of abstinence to be observed. "It is a sin," he said, "to do penance on the day when the Child Jesus was born ; on that day the very walls ought to eat meat." One night one of his friars, worn out by fasting, was taken ill. Francis rose, laid the table and sat down beside the young man, and obliged all the brothers to partake of an extraordinary supper, that the novice might not be humiliated by eating alone. "I tell you of a truth each man ought to take account of his strength and take the nourishment that is necessary to him, in order that the body may render true and loyal service to the spirit. Let us avoid two excesses : we must neither eat too much, for that will harm body and soul, nor fast immoderately, because God prefers works of charity to the external observance of religion." (37) If Brother Sylvester were secretly fond of eating grapes Francis took him to the vineyard, blessed it, and let his friend eat his fill of the delicious fruit. At the general chapter at Assisi, if he heard that a certain number of the Minorites were wearing rings studded with spikes, or that they were wearing metal scapulars, he forbade such painful practices and ordered these instruments of penance to be collected immediately ; more than five thousand of them were gathered and abandoned in the fields. Towards the end of his life,

Francis was conscious of having chastened his body too severely. One night he heard these words: "Francis, there is not in the world a single sinner whom God does not pardon if he returns to Him; but he who kills himself by excess of austerity will find no compassion in eternity." Once even he made confession of this severity towards "his brother ass", that is to say his body. He had at the same period a desire to hear once again the musical airs he had loved in his youth; but he dared not ask that musicians should be summoned. In the night, as suffering kept him awake, he heard the vibration of an invisible lyre whose notes seemed to fall from the stars; the melody came nearer and nearer, ever sweeter, and he fell asleep lulled by the song of angels.

For this tender heart the love of all living things was not merely the effect of an instinctive poetry; Francis believed that in the creature he was embracing God. In the flowers of the field he breathed the odour of the stem of Jesse, whose perfume restores the dead to life. The Umbrian country was for him a veritable earthly Paradise, where he conversed familiarly with the beasts, whom he called brothers and sisters. He greeted all these little creatures, carefully removed the earthworm from the path trodden by the foot of man, and, during the winter, had pots of honey or wine placed for the bees. The sight of a lamb, the symbolic figure of Jesus, always filled him with emotion; in order to redeem one he gave his cloak and cowl to the butcher. And the beasts attached themselves to him, as to a sure friend; he spoke to them with great seriousness, and the legend has no doubt whatever that they answered him according to their ability. A young hare caught in a snare and brought to him leapt into his bosom, then, set at liberty, followed his footsteps, like a dog, to the nearest forest. A grass-hopper chirping on the branch of a fig tree, near his cell, when called by him perched on his hand. "Sing my sister grasshopper, and praise God with thy cry of joy." For a week it came back, at the same hour, to accompany the prayer of Francis with its little canticle. The lamb that had been given him entered the church behind him, stopped at the same altar, and at the moment when the Host was elevated knelt down. In the desert at Alvernia a falcon, his neighbour, woke him every night at the hour of vigil ; when the saint was sick the bird waited till the dawn was whitening the mountains before giving the signal for the office. If a young boy gave him some wild turtle-doves, he tamed them and with his own hands made them nests in the bushes that encircled his community at Assisi. Thomas of Celano relates that one day, as he was preaching to the people in the open country, the swallows made so shrill a noise that he had to stop ; he waited patiently for some time, and then, as they continued to cry their loudest, he said to them : "My dear sisters, it is my turn to speak, for you have cried enough ; listen, therefore, to the word of God and hold your peace until the end of the sermon." They ceased their cries and did not fly away until he had said "Amen". Another time, near Bevagna, he preached expressly for the little birds. "Always praise your Creator wherever you are, for He gives you the air of heaven for your kingdom, the rivers and springs to quench your thirst, the mountains and valleys for a place of refuge, and also gives you warm clothing for yourselves and children". The birds, who covered the earth and trees, joyously fluttered their wings, shook their heads and chirped with pleasure. The saint walked as he spoke and touched them with his robe, and none of them was frightened or took to flight. Then he blessed them with the sign of the cross, and all, ascending straight towards heaven, with a song of triumph, dispersed in the form of a cross towards the four quarters of the horizon.

Francis freely accepted all the caresses of nature without being anxious, like the monks of old, about the seductions that wicked angels might have concealed in them. The invisible world manifested itself to his eyes with a simple grandeur that the troubadours of Provençe, his masters in poetry, had never known; in his Galilee in Umbria at the edge of the limpid lake of Perugia, under the foliage of the oaks of Alvernia, he heard the boundless and eternal murmur of divine life. In his turn he wished to share in the universal choir; in the *Canticle of the Sun* he glorified God for all things excellent and beautiful that His hands had lavished:

*Laudato sia, Dio mio Signore,*
*Con tutte le tue creature!*

The *Alleluia* of Assisi, in which the light of day, the starry sweetness of the southern nights, the warm breath of the wind, the rippling of living waters and the maternal graces of the earth, *nostra madre terra*, beautiful with the green grass, with purple flowers and with fruits, are evoked in turn, bursts forth, like a festival chant, over the cradle of Italian poetry. But it is also the canticle of Franciscan Christianity that will not see any painful contrast between the serenity of nature and the miseries of man, and that makes a sacred thing of suffering itself: "Be praised, O God, for those who pardon in the name of Thy love, for the feeble who endure tribulation! Happy are the unfortunate and the peaceful, for Thou, O Most High, wilt give them a crown!"

*Laudato sia, mio Signore,*
*Per quelli che perdonano per tuo amore*
*Et sosteneno infirmitate et tribulatione;*
*Beati quelli que sostenerano in pace,*
*Che da ti altissimo serano incoranati.*

## VI

Thus about the year 1210 Italy saw a renewal of the enthusiasm of the apostolic times. Men crowded to Francis, whose words consoled and delivered their souls. He shed upon all wounds the balm of the Gospel. To those who bore with impatience the yoke of the communal form of government, he showed the Kingdom of God as the recompense for the injustice and tyranny of their earthly life. He calmed the uneasiness of consciences that, in order to escape from the troubles of the world, had gradually detached themselves from the Church: he bore testimony, by the very example of his own conduct, to the treasures of joy that could yet be reaped without one's ceasing to be a regular Christian. He instituted, not free investigation, but the liberty of love; he lightened the hand of the Church, that pontifical hand that the Middle Ages had made so heavy, and beneath which Latin Christendom was bowed; to the Church itself he brought the strength of the primitive apostolate, he rescued it from the sterile melancholy of the cloister, and from the pride of the feudal episcopate, to throw it, no longer as a haughty mistress, but as a mother of pity, into the midst of populous cities, into the ferment of the communes and among the serfs of the country; he brought it back to its most beautiful memories by restoring to it, as if it were a magic word, the sublime cry of Jesus: *Misereor super turbam*.

There is no doubt that the Franciscan apostolate began by discovering the Gospel afresh. There was no question, in its origins, of a new Order or of an institution rigorously constituted. The first thought of the founder stopped for some years at a free confraternity, whose Rule of 1209 contains the essential features which that of 1221 marked with more precision. The great evangelical virtues are enjoined in it, poverty, humility, charity, and prayer. The practice of these virtues very soon assumed a peculiar aspect ; humility led to the absolute contempt of all things ; humility and poverty led to beggary "for the love of God." Charity was not content with the poor and infirm ; in its solicitude it embraced the leper, the criminal, and the pagan. Two functions were manifested in the early days in a very clear way : preaching and manual labour. This preaching took the form of an active and perpetual message scattered broadcast and destined to travel to the farthest regions of the world. As to work, the wages of which were represented by only the barest necessaries of life, we must observe to what an extent the Franciscans of the first period maintained the common conditions of social life. There was nothing among the brothers that recalled the customary conventual discipline : the Rule of 1221 imposed no extraordinary offices upon the priests ; the offices of the lay members were confined to the recitation of the *Pater*, the *Credo*, the *Miserere*, and the *De Profundis* for the dead. The Franciscan group of 1209 rather resembled the future Third Order than a religious militia. That is why from the very first all classes of Italian society, as much reassured by Francis as they were comforted, were stirred at heart and surrendered themselves to him. The oldest of his disciples was a citizen of Assisi, Bernard of Quintavalle, "one of the noblest, richest, and wisest men in the town", who, touched by the self-denial of the young apostle, distributed all his goods to the widows, orphans, prisoners, pilgrims, and hospitals ; next came a priest, Silvester, who till then had been covetous of money, and who gave himself up to the party of perfect poverty, and was to converse with God "as friend to friend" ; humble folk, such as Leo, Ruffino, Masseo ; a soldier, Angelo ; nobles, such as Egidio, Valentine of Narni ; a canon of the cathedral of Assisi, Pietro Cattani, "jurisconsult and master of laws"; a court poet, Pacifico; two students of Bologna, of whom one was "very learned and a great decretalist", Pellegrino and Rinieri; three highwaymen, "murderous ruffians", says the *Fioretti*. The *modus operandi* of Francis was speech, and never was there more popular preaching. The *Scriptures* formed his whole theology. The development of the *Pater*, the death of the sinner and the tender recital of the Passion, were his favourite subjects. He preached without any oratorical devices; he laughed, wept, and made others weep; he played the character of which he was telling the crowd; he leaped for joy in the pulpit, and bleated like a lamb when he pronounced the name of Bethlehem. One day he preached before pope Honorius III (1124–1130); his sermon had been prepared and learnt by heart. At the very beginning he was troubled, lost his memory and stopped short; then he freely improvised, says Bonaventura, as if the spirit of God spoke by his mouth.

When he entered a town all the inhabitants ran to meet him. At Bologna the great communal square was too small for the concourse of the faithful. When he passed through the country regions, the confraternities of the towns, the corporations and the children, went forth singing to meet him on the way with banners and green branches; the little bells of Umbria rang as though for an Easter mass; men crowded round him to touch the hem of his garment or to cut the cloth of his cowl for relics. At Borgo-San-Donnino he fainted in the arms of his devoted followers, being half stifled; at Gaeta he was compelled to take refuge in a boat, in order to put the sea between him and the multitude; at Rieti the inhabitants in their eagerness trampled down the vineyard of the priest whose hospitality Francis was enjoying; the poor presbyter lamented his lost vintage, but his guest consoled him by promising him a miraculous harvest, and never had the parish priest of Rieti seen a more smiling autumn or his presses better filled.

Francis, as soon as he had had his first brethren blessed by Innocent III, sent his missionaries by two and two throughout Italy, saying to them : *Ite et docete.* "*It is not* only for your own salvation that God has called you in His goodness, it is also for the salvation of the people. Beware of judging and despising the rich who live in luxury and wear sumptuous garments, for God is their Lord as well as ours ; He may call them and justify them. We must honour them as our brothers and masters, since by their aid they help good people. Go then and preach peace to men and repentance for the remission of sins. Some will welcome you with joy and hear you gladly ; others, impious, proud and violent, will blame you and rise up against you. In a short time many nobles and learned men will join you. Be patient in tribulation, fervent in prayer, courageous in work, modest in your discourse, grave in your manner, grateful for the good that is done you, and the kingdom of heaven shall be your reward." (38) At the first general chapter, in 1216, he renewed these precepts of tolerance and charity. "Let peace be even more at the bottom of your hearts than upon your lips. Give no man occasion of wrath or scandal ; bring all men to benignity, concord and union. To heal the wounded, comfort those who weep, and seek the poor sheep who have gone astray, such is your vocation. There are some among men who seem to be devoted to the devil, and who yet will one day be disciples of Jesus."

So the friars went from town to town, from village to village, reading their breviary as they walked ; they entered into houses, and preached familiarly under church porches. This Franciscan world was one of extraordinary activity. The founder permitted no idle or "otiose" person in his Order. "Go, brother fly," he said to a novice who thought of nothing but eating and sleeping in the shade after dinner. "You have lived long enough after the manner of the drones, who make no honey and who devour that of the bees." It was a sight to see Brother Egidio going eight miles from Rome to gather faggots, or to gather nuts in the woods, or to glean wheat, or to carry water in the streets, for the benefit of the poor. Those who were priests confessed the faithful; men loved these errant pastors who disappeared the next day, carrying with them the vexatious secrets of the conscience, and whom they never expected to see again. They composed family quarrels, calmed the hatred of factions, and appeased civil revolts. In 1210 they intervened between the serfs and the barons in the neighbourhood of Assisi, and they made the lords sign a charter of enfranchisement. In 1220, at Bologna, Francis exhorted the communal factions, in vehemently persuasive language, to become reconciled. The fierce wolf of Gubbio, whom he brought back as docile as a sheep, to the mystic city famous for its lovely illuminations of missals, was doubtless, as the pious Ozanam suspects, only a baron, a "Ysengrin" impatient of control, or even "the people of the Middle Ages"; but I should almost be tempted to regret the wolf who so devoutly, according to the legend, put his paw into the saint's hand, swore to keep the peace in the future, and grew to old age a friendly guest at the hearth of the good folk of Gubbio. The *Fioretti* almost gives us to understand that he died in the odour of sanctity.

A very simple organization contributed to the rapid progress of the Order of Minorites. It is not yet found in the Rule of 1209, where the "penitents of the city of Assisi" seem to be confided to the exclusive care of the secular clergy and the bishop. It is manifested, in the Rule of 1221, by the somewhat vague institution of the "ministers", servants and counsellors of their brethren; it takes its final form in the definitive Rule of 1223, that was sanctioned by Honorius III. Here we find a regular constitution of the Order rendered necessary by the needs of discipline. As the brothers did not yet shut themselves up in great monastic houses, as they camped, so to speak, in the heart of Christendom, they multiplied very fast, without any concern for temporal interests, and attracted to themselves those who were charmed by the adventurous liberty of the new apostolate. When they became an army it was very necessary to give them a hierarchy. Francis mapped out western Europe into provinces. The provincial minister watched over the ministers or guardians delegated to govern the convents ; the general minister, whose seat was Assisi, was chosen by the provincials and the guardians at the grand chapter convoked every three years in Umbria on the day of Pentecost ; he could be deposed by the same body. A cardinal was the Order's patron in the councils of the Holy See. The general was the responsible representative to the pope for the entire Order.

The aristocratic titles of abbot and prior disappeared, as well as the spirit of Benedictine monasticism, in which the community, feudally constituted, depended absolutely upon its abbot, and in which the sole federal bond between the different convents was the Rule of Benedict. The new wine, Francis was aware, needed new bottles. So he presented communal Italy of the thirteenth century not with an oligarchy, but with a religious republic that, thanks to the parliament at Assisi, was a very free one internally, that was very strong in its unity in the face of the secular world, and that, owing to the elasticity of its hierarchy, was very independent with regard to Rome. In 1219 Francis offered rigorous confinement with the nuns of Santa Clara to women whose weakness shunned the dangers of the world. These sisters of Santa Clara constituted a Second Order. Then he found a means of animating lay society to its very depths by the genius of his institution. In 1221 he founded the confraternity of the Brothers of Penitence, called the Third Order in 1230, for men and women who continued to live in the ordinary life of the world, at the domestic hearth, for husbands and wives, and even for secular priests. It was at Faenza, and afterwards at Florence, that he set up the first Tertiary associations. The Third Order was open to all, rich and poor, artizan and noble ; it was not regulated at first by a written constitution. The pretended rule of the Tertiaries of 1221 is subsequent to the death of Francis. In 1289 it was altered, in the text that we now possess, by the bull *Supra montem* of Nicholas IV (1288–1292). All the observance prescribed by the founder is confined to the great precepts of Christian faith and charity, enhanced by a serious discipline. The brothers were bound to respect the commandments of God and the Church, to become reconciled to their enemies, to restore ill-gotten gains, to dress simply, to make their wills within three months of their profession, to avoid balls, festivals, theatres, lawsuits, and vain swearing. "They will not wear any offensive arms, unless for the defence of the Roman Church or their country." Until the middle of the thirteenth century the Tertiaries in no way resembled an organized militia ; their lawful heads were the diocesan bishops. Thus the Franciscan community corresponded to the extent of the municipality, but it united classes hitherto divided. The Third Order of a town gathered round the same altar, as round a fraternity table, all those whom the government of the arts and corporations separated from one another. It softened the pride of the rich, raised the humility of the lowly, and animated all hearts with pity. "Invite the poor to your fine house, and to your sumptuous feasts," writes a Florentine notary of the fourteenth century to a merchant of the major arts, "in order that

God may not say to you reproachfully: 'Why hast thou never invited My friends to the house I gave thee?'" (39)

But the affiliation of the Tertiaries went even further than the city walls; it made the same word of command run through the entire peninsula; it strengthened men's consciences in a more intimate union with the Church; it fostered in the souls of the citizens the sentiment of Italian liberty. A letter attributed to the chancellor of Frederic II, Pietro della Vigna, but which probably proceeds from the Ghibeline episcopate, is very significant. "The Franciscans and the Dominicans have risen against us. They have publicly reproved our way of life and our undertakings; they have taken away our rights and reduced us to nothing; and now behold, in order to complete the destruction of our preponderance and to rob us of the affection of the people, they have created two new fraternities, that embrace men and women without distinction. All men are hastening to join them. There is scarcely a man to be found whose name is not enrolled in them." (40) In fact, beyond the boundaries of Italy, from the second half of the century onwards, the Third Order restored in the west, divided as it was by political interests, a religious community independent of any national Church, and similar to that of primitive Christianity. A direct bond attached all the members of the Third Franciscan Order to one another; they formed a league of prayer and peace from one end of Europe to the other. We find, in this connection, a pretty legend in the *Fioretti*, which, though destitute of all historical value, is a kind of touching symbol of this European fraternity. Louis IX (1236–1270) one day knocked at the door of the convent of Perugia, clad as a poor pilgrim, and asked for Brother Egidio. The friend of Francis of Assisi, notified by the porter, at once knew that this obscure passer-by was the king of France. He hastened to the convent door and found the king ; they knelt before each other, and, without uttering a single word, held each other in a long embrace ; then, without breaking the silence, Louis resumed his pilgrimage, and Egidio returned tc his cell. When the brothers reproached Egidio for having said nothing to this extraordinary visitor, he replied simply, "I read his heart and he read mine."

The conversion of heretics does not seem to have interested Francis very much, whether it was that he believed in God's boundless pity for those who dissented from Catholicism, or that he foresaw that the Dominicans, the *Domini canes* as the Middle Ages called them, were sufficient to guard the flock and run after the wandering sheep. He knew nothing of the depths of theology ; he was still more a stranger to the subtleties of the School. He had but small esteem for the profane sciences, letters and books. Perhaps also the exploits of the Inquisition in the south of France, of which the Dominicans had charge, indisposed him to an evangelical mission in which the secular arm intervened so efficaciously, and where the cross was almost invariably accompanied by the sword or firebrand. So he left the Italian heretics to the impetuous preaching of his Portuguese disciple, Antony, formerly an Augustinian canon, who was the first theologian and the first canonist of the Franciscans. The genius of Francis felt more at home in dealing with the heathen. The conversion of distant peoples was one of the great Franciscan works from the thirteenth century onwards ; Brother John de Plano Carpini, who was the provincial of Saxony in 1223, was destined to go, in the name of Innocent IV, as far as the heart of Tartary, thus paving the way for Marco Polo. Francis had inaugurated this apostolate ; in 1219 he was under the walls of Damietta, in the midst of the Christians besieging it, whom the Soldan, encamped on the Nile, was endeavouring to drive out of Egypt. He dreamt of converting the Saracens and presented himself to Malek-al-Kamel, of whom he demanded the ordeal of fire. In company with an imam he was to pass through a blazing fire. No Mohammedan priest had the curiosity to test the miracle, and Francis returned to the camp of the Crusaders, bringing with him, according to Jacques de Vitry, archbishop of Acre, these comforting words from the infidel prince : " Pray for me that God may reveal to me the faith that is most pleasing to Him." He had to content himself with preaching to the Christians, who had great need of an apostle ; but his trouble and his sermons were wasted upon them. The historian of this Crusade has the following to say : " This man who founded the Order of the Minorites, and who was called Brother Francis . . . . came to the army at Damietta and did much good there, and there he remained until the town was taken. Francis saw the evil and the sin that were growing among the men of the army, and it so displeased him that he departed and stayed for a time in Syria, and then returned to his own country." (41)

## VII

Francis found his community flourishing, loved by the Holy See, and confirmed in 1215 by the Lateran Council. He passed seven more years in incessant travel, visiting the Italian provinces of the Order with the joy of the householder who sees the harvest ripening in the field that he has cleared of stones and brambles. In 1222, it is said, he met the emperor Frederic II whose half-Mohammedan court he charmed by his purity and innocence. More and more he secluded himself for weeks at a time in the solitude of his Umbrian mountains, feeling that the end of his pilgrimage was near and that he would soon enter the bosom of God. He was sick, exhausted by penance, scarcely able to stand, greatly distressed by eating, and almost blind. He said to his physician: "It is indifferent to me whether I live or die," and to a brother who thought God too severe towards him: "If I did not know thy simplicity, I should send thee hence, seeing thou dost dare to blame God for the sufferings He sends me." He said to another: "My son, the cruellest martyrdom would be less painful than three days of the suffering that I endure; but I prefer my suffering, since God has been pleased to send it to me."

In the spring of 1221 Brother Elias brought him back with difficulty, and by slow stages, from Siena by way of Cortona to Assisi, where he wished to die. All the inhabitants came outside the walls to meet him. The bishop welcomed him in his house, where he languished for several months. At that time he added a stanza to the *Canticle of the Sun* in honour of his sister, bodily death. The physician, having warned him of the approach of his last hour, he had himself carried in the arms of his brothers to Santa Maria degli Angeli. The procession halted in front of the convent. Francis asked to be put down, with his face towards the town where his cradle had rested; he raised his right hand and several times blessed Assisi, saying: "Be thou blessed of God, holy city, for by thee many souls will be saved, and in thee will dwell many servants of God, and many of thy children will be chosen for the kingdom of everlasting life!" The brothers took him up once more and laid him in the infirmary of Portiuncula. He had himself placed on a bed of cinders, despoiled of his robe. The guardian bade him, in the name of holy obedience, receive as his last alms a borrowed tunic and cowl. Then he opened his arms and blessed the Minorites. Night had already descended upon his eyes; he touched the heads bowed before him, and one after the other each of his sons was named to him; he began with Elias of Cortona and Bernard of Quintavalle. Then he had the *Canticle of the Sun* read to him, as if to bid farewell to the light of heaven and the smile of the earth, and, following that, as though to take leave of Holy Church, the chapter of the Gospel of John that begins with these words: "Before the feast of the Passover, when Jesus knew that His hour was come that He should depart out of this world unto the Father, having loved His own that were in the world, He loved them unto the end." The reader continued until the last verse of the eighteenth chapter and stopped at the Passion. Francis uttered the words of the Psalm: "With my voice I cry unto the Lord; with my voice I pray the Lord." The brothers, kneeling and in tears, surrounded the bed of cinders and prayed in low tones. According to Thomas of Celano and Bonaventura, his last words were these: "I have accomplished that which I had to do; Jesus will teach you what you shall do. Behold, God is calling me. Farewell, my children. Live in the fear of the Lord. Trouble and temptation will come; blessed are they who persevere in the good way! As for me, I am going to God. May He have mercy upon you all!" It was at the beginning of October, in the early evening, an autumn evening in Italy, with its long deep-blue twilight, and in the deep silence of the country, lighted only by the dying beams in the sky, that the Franciscan family waited for the soul of their founder to take its flight. Then there happened a marvellous thing, according to the legend recorded by Bonaventura. A flock of larks, that never chirp except in the sunlight, *Alaudæ aves lucis amicæ*, came and lighted with song on the church of Santa Maria degli Angeli, on the roofs of the cells and in the court-yard of the little convent. Francis drew his last breath, lamented by a choir of birds.

That night the children of Umbria made the valleys and hills resound with glorious canticles, according to the tradition of the primitive Church, that celebrated with joy the death of martyrs and confessors. The next day an immense number of people, carrying branches of olive and lighted tapers, carried Francis, with his white face uncovered, in triumph to the cathedral of Assisi, passing by the convent of St. Damiano, in order that the holy Clara and her nuns might see him a last time through a window of the nunnery. Two years later the old Gregory IX, who had been the friend of Francis and the first protector of the Order in the Sacred College of Innocent III, came to proclaim over his tomb the "Blessing" of the Seraphic Father—the first essential step in the process of canonization. In 1230 the body of the saint was lowered into a subterranean chapel of the gloomy lower church of Assisi, access to which was rediscovered only in the nineteenth century. In 1236 the upper church was finished, the airy and luminous church that crowns the shrine where the apostle sleeps in the peace of eternity.

## VIII

Francis of Assisi bequeathed a lasting and very great work to Italy. The Franciscan Order, carried forward by the soaring imagination called forth by the founder, was destined to pass through many vicissitudes in the peninsula; at one time it defended the See of Rome with ardour and the integrity of the old *Credo*; at another, in the character of a bold innovator, troubled by its own mysticism, it fearlessly embraced the thought of schism. But whatever the dominant inspiration it followed, whether it allowed itself to be carried away by John of Parma, who was the minister-general of the Franciscans from 1247 to 1257, or governed by Bonaventura, who held the same office from 1257 to 1274, or took, in the fourteenth century, the part of the poor Christ against His pontifical vicar, it was always to be faithful to the vocation of its early years ; it was to continue to be the active leaven of men's consciences, and to keep alive in their souls the lofty and tender religious emotions that Francis had aroused. The distinctive features of the Franciscan religion, liberty of mind, love, pity, joyous serenity and familiarity, were long to form the originality of Italian Christianity, so different from the Pharisaical faith of the Byzantines, the fanaticism of the Spaniards, and the scholastic dogmatism of Germany and France. Nothing of all that everywhere else darkened or straitened the conscience, neither subtle metaphysic, nor refined theology, nor the uneasiness of casuistry, nor the excess of discipline and penance, nor the extreme scruples of devotion, was to weigh henceforth upon the Italians. Compare Francis with Dominic, compare the spirit of these two great founders of the mendicants, compare Catherine of Siena with Ignatius Loyola, or Dante with Calderon, or Savonarola with Calvin. The former have no more anguish at the thought of God because they count upon His goodness ; they have no more terror of the Church because they make a church of their own within themselves. Machiavelli, who was no mystic, but who had the profound intelligence of the genius of his race, writes, in his *Discourses upon Titus Livius*, after passing severe judgments upon the social and political work of the Roman Church in Italy, the following lines : "Religions must seek fresh youth by returning to their first principle ; Christianity would have become quite extinct had not Francis and Dominic renewed it and restored it to its place in the heart of men through poverty and the example of Jesus Christ ; they thus saved religion, which the Church was destroying." (42)

But a religious renaissance, by the very fact that it renews the inner life and affects the social life, necessarily takes possession of the whole civilization of a people. The Italian genius which, at the beginning of the thirteenth century, was still seeking its path, thus found itself carried along by the evolution of Italian Christianity. Nevertheless it was enabled to pursue an independent orbit in the bosom of this vast movement. It was never lost in the transcendant mysticism that, after Francis, continued ever more and more to grow in the Franciscan world. A powerful attraction, that of the entirely rationalistic civilization of the Ghibeline south, was to moderate the impetus of men's souls, temper their minds and permeate Christianity itself with its influence (I mean secular Christianity), and, without turning Italy away from the Kingdom of God, to give her back her love for this earthly life.

## CHAPTER IV

# THE EMPEROR FREDERIC II AND THE RATIONALISTIC SPIRIT IN SOUTHERN ITALY

AN original civilization had been founded in the south of Italy and in Sicily at the very time of the first Franciscan apostolate, and was to grow there until the final fall of the house of Suabia. The Norman, and afterwards imperial, provinces of the peninsula, which the abbot Joachim had fascinated towards the end of the twelfth century with his prophecies, suddenly appeared with a culture entirely new for the Christian Middle Ages and a political system remarkable in the eyes of the feudal west. An astonishing man, still in some degree an enigma to us, the emperor Frederic II (1212–1250), seemed to the Church alone responsible for the dangerous inventions that troubled the faith at that time. For history he continues to be the actual creator of a religious and social system of government, of which nothing in the past of Christendom had given an inkling. With him began an intellectual initiation, the effect of which was lasting in the religious conscience of Italy.

## I

If we view the life and work of Frederic II as a whole, we quickly recognize in what respect he changed the traditions upon which the world had been living since the close of the Carolingian age. Between him and his grandfather, Barbarossa, there is undoubtedly a great gulf. Frederic I (1152–1190) was the mediæval emperor *par excellence*, a king of the Romans analogous to all his predecessors: he incarnated the European feudal order, and reigned in virtue of a theological theory; his power emanated from God as well as that of the pope; if he came into collision, as his predecessors had done, with the pontifical authority, it was because, like them, he had formed too great an idea of his divine mission. His right and power were two immovable bases: the right derived from God, Whose vicar he was, and Who had entrusted to him the temporal government of the west; the power of the feudal hierarchy, of which he was the head, and which made him an œcumenical king. The political community over which he presided was also based upon a religious notion, and animated by it: a mystic bond connects all men and all races whom baptism has given to Jesus Christ; it was Christianity which, if it depended upon the emperor for the things of the world, belonged to the Roman pope as far as heavenly things were concerned. God, in this conception of the world, was the universal suzerain. But the pope had received a higher consecration than that of the emperor; he went back to Jesus, whereas the emperor descended only from Cæsar. The emperor could not strike the pope without sacrilege, and every time that he opposed an antipope to him he was violating the integrity of the Holy Church herself; the pope could strike the emperor by means of excommunication, and cut off the master of the world from the communion of the faithful. For nearly three hundred years Christendom had been vainly waiting for some agreement that should restore peace between God's two vicars, each of whom claimed an infinite power, and each of whom, thanks to the feudal system, being placed into too close contact with the other, were constantly under the necessity of limiting and abasing themselves to one another. Such was the age-long problem that Barbarossa's grandson wished to solve in the thirteenth century.

Frederic II had the title, the prestige and the claims of the traditional emperor. Upon several occasions, in the time of his struggle with Rome, he wrote as emperor, and with all the authority of his office, to the kings, counts, and republics of Christian Europe. Nevertheless he abandoned to his sons, Henry, and afterwards Conrad, the exercise of the imperial power north of the Alps, with the title of king of the Romans; he himself, born in Italy, Italian and Greek by education, a Mohammedan even by a sort of secret instinct, took Sicily, the old Magna Græcia, Campania, and Apulia, as his domain. An entire district of northern Italy was handed over to his legate Ezzelino. The attempt he made upon Lombardy, the doctrine he disseminated through the familiars of his court upon the excellence of a Christian pontificate freed from all temporal patrimony, permit us to suppose that one of the first aims of his ambition was the restoration of the Italian kingdom. It was in itself a singular novelty that he effected this geographical revolution in the empire, whose pivot was no longer at Aix-la-Chapelle, Nuremberg, or Spires, but at Naples, Foggia, or Palermo. From the Mediterranean, that opened to him the route to all the political regions of the old world, Frederic looked towards the Greek Empire, Jerusalem, and Egypt. The Italian royalty was for him the starting point for a universal royalty into which the soldan of Cairo and the emperor of Nicæa would enter as allies or vassals, and that would extend from the shores of the Baltic to the steppes of Mongolia. "His heart had no other ambition," wrote Brunetto Latini, "than to be lord and sovereign of the entire world."

But now we come to an innovation of far greater gravity. The fundamental notion of the State, of the relations between the sovereign and those he governs, was radically transformed by Frederic II. The feudal Empire disappeared from the kingdom of the Two Sicilies. The Norman princes had modified the feudal system in these provinces in favour of the nobility, whose baronies had become in some sort independent. Frederic imposed absolute monarchy upon these very barons. The Church, the cities, the corporations, every form of common life, were to be reduced to a common level; here the Middle Ages seem to have ended two and a half centuries before they did so anywhere else in Europe; the modern state, despotically organized, the prototype of the tyranny of the Sforzas or the royalty of Louis XI, was invented. All the functions of the government hitherto exercised by the aristocracy and the bishops and the communal magistrates, were handed over to a hierarchy of imperial officials and functionaries, appointed by the imperial chancellery. Courts of justice, political councils, the regulation of public administration and the imposition of taxes, all depended upon the prince and his delegates. That which was still left of local and feudal jurisdiction was subject to the tribunals of the empire through the right of appeal; the jurisconsulte restored to Frederic, as a terrible weapon against feudality, the essential principle of the Roman law that knows no right of primogeniture or privileged heritage, but which divides patrimonies into equal parts. As to the towns that ventured to renew their old communal elections, they were threatened with devastation, and their inhabitants with servitude. By an edict passed in his youth, dated from the basilica of St. Peter, in 1220, Frederic inflicted infamy, exile and confiscation, upon all heretics, men and women alike, whether Cathari, Patarins, or Arnoldists, and upon all those who claimed the right to think freely about God and the way of salvation, upon the mere suspicion, *sola suspicione notabiles*, of revolt against "the eternal majesty." (43) One only will, one only autonomy, one only reason, therefore, existed, the emperor, who entitled himself "the living law upon earth." Although a story in the *Novellino* credits Frederic with the words of a king devoted to ideal justice and stronger than the seductions of pride, history compels us to suppose that in his eyes the law was merely his own good pleasure. (44) And as he had absorbed in himself all the political rights of his subjects, he attracted to himself all the sources of wealth existing in his kingdom. He filled his treasury by means of the land tax and the duty upon food-stuffs, the monopoly of salt and metals ; he was the privileged shipowner in the ports of the Mediterranean ; he retarded the departure of ships that did not carry his merchandize. The youth of the Two Sicilies were compelled to study in the schools of Naples and Salerno. The emperor felt himself so isolated in the heart of his domains and in his relations with Christendom, and he had so resolutely broken the bonds of feudal fidelity, that he no longer formed the main body of his armies with the help of the feudal chivalry ; his Saracens and Janissaries, who out of their fanatical devotion, were capable of every kind of horror, were at once his knights, his imperial guard, his police officers and his executioners. Such, in its main outlines, was the system of government built up by Frederic II. The men of that age had no difficulty in recognizing in it a disquieting imitation of the political administration of the califs, a wholly Mohammedan conception of government. That Frederic was a despot, crushing without pity all individual liberty, the Middle Ages could well have understood ; but what seemed an unbearable impiety was the imperial attempt against the collective liberties in the bosom of which the Middle Ages, guided by their religious instinct, had sheltered the weakness and curbed the pride of the individual. Mediæval Christendom was disintegrated by the destruction of the framework wherein it had been so long enclosed. The mystic primacy of the Holy See vanished when, in the name of statemanship as well as by the constitution of the state, the emperor placed himself between the bishops and the pope, between the bishop of Rome and the consciences of men. Owing to the mere fact that he completely secularized the state, he appeared to his contemporaries to be the implacable enemy of Christianity.

## II

Frederic, in the eyes of all good orthodox Christians, in the opinion of the Church and the Guelfs, was a type of antichrist. The struggle that he carried on against two inflexible popes, Gregory IX and Innocent IV, had, in the minds of the friends of the Holy See, the grandeur of an apocalyptic drama. Satan alone could have stirred up such malice in the soul of a prince whom the Roman Church, in the time of Innocent III, had held in its arms as a child. "He was an atheist," affirms Frà Salimbene (1221–1288?), who enumerates all the emperor's vices, roguery, avarice, lust, cruelty, and anger, and the strange stories that were whispered concerning him in the secrecy of convents. At the moment when Frederic had denounced Gregory IX to all kings and to the episcopate as a false pope and a false prophet, the latter launched the encyclical *Ascendit de mari*. "See the beast who ascends from the depths of the sea, his mouth full of blasphemies, with the claws of a bear and the fury of a lion, his body like that of a leopard. He opens his mouth to belch forth insults against God; he incessantly hurls his javelins against the tabernacle of the Lord and the saints of heaven." In the following year Gregory wrote: "The emperor, raising himself above all that is called God and making use of unworthy apostates as the agents of his perversity, stands aloft as an angel of light on the mountain of pride. . . . He threatens to overthrow the seat of St. Peter, to substitute for the faith of Christendom the ancient rites of the pagan peoples, and, seated in the temple, he usurps the functions of the priesthood." And the unknown author of the *Life of Gregory IX* asserts that "By dint of associating with the Greeks and Arabs he imagines, reprobate that he is, that he is a god in human form." (45) The pontifical advocate Albert of Beham, familiar friend of Innocent IV, wrote in 1245 that "like another Lucifer, he has attempted to scale heaven, to raise his throne above the stars, in order to become superior to the vicar of the Most High; he has laboured to create a pope; he has set up and pulled down bishops; seated in the temple of the Lord, as if he himself were God, he has had his feet kissed by prelates and clergy, and he gives orders that he is to be called a saint." (46) And further on: "He has desired to sit on God's throne as if he were God; not only has he attempted to create a pope and to subject the apostolic see to his dominion, but he has tried to usurp the divine right, to change the eternal alliance established by the Gospel, and to change the laws and conditions of the life of men." In 1245 and 1248 Innocent IV released the clergy and subjects of the kingdom of the Two Sicilies from their oath of loyalty, removed the Sicilian Church from the imperial jurisdiction, cut off from political society and religious communion the counts and citizens who remained faithful to the emperor's cause, authorized the ecclesiastical lords to fortify their castles against the emperor, and solemnly swore to crush to its last offspring "that race of vipers." (47)

Pietro della Vigna and the courtiers of the Suabian prince replied in as sonorous a tone as that of the champions of the Church. Peter was Frederic's confidant. "I held the two keys to his heart," says his soul to Dante, "which I opened and shut with a very gentle hand." It may be believed that every time he wrote he merely echoed the emperor's thoughts. But the manner in which he exalted the religious mission of his master, in the exaggeration of its ideas and images, is too closely analogous to the invectives launched by the defenders of the Holy See. In the eyes of the chancellor, and even in those of Beraldo, the archbishop of Palermo, in those of Nicholas of Rocca, the imperial notary, and the Ghibeline prelates who paid their court to Cæsar with the help of texts from the Gospel, Frederic was a kind of Messiah, an apostle charged by God to reveal the Holy Spirit, the pontiff of the final Church, "the great eagle with great wings" that Ezekiel prophesied. As to Pietro della Vigna, he was to be Frederic's vicar, as the first Peter was that of Jesus; he was the corner-stone, the fruitful vine whose branches shaded and rejoiced the world. The Galilean thrice denied his Lord, the Capuan will never deny his. The mystical function of the Roman Church was upon the point of coming to an end. "The lofty cedar of Libanus will be cut down," cried the popular prophets. "There will be henceforth but one only God, that is to say one monarch. Woe to the clergy! If they fall a new order is ready to take their place." Innocent IV (1243–1254) found on his table verses announcing the approaching fall of papal Rome. (48) And the Provençal troubadours, the exiles of the Albigensian crusade, who had seen their towns handed over to the inquisitors, sang in the palaces of Palermo and Lucera the furious strophes of William Figueira against Rome: "Treacherous Rome, avarice is ruining you. You shear the sheep's wool too close. Rome, you devour the flesh and bones of the simple; you lead the blind into the ditch. You take money for the pardoning of sins. With too heavy a burden, Rome, do you load yourself. I am glad to think, Rome, that if the emperor, who loves justice, knows how to make use of his fortune and does what he ought to do, soon you will come to a bad end. Rome, I tell you of a truth, your violence will be seen to fall to the ground. Rome, may our true Saviour grant me soon to see your downfall!"

But these war cries and formulas of malediction are very vague evidence for an inquiry into historical reality. We must let the dust settle on this field of battle if we would see clearly what was the action of the emperor against the Holy See and against the Catholic Church. Some considerable documents and one of the most important episodes of his life, the crusade of 1229, permit us, we believe, to discover the main features of the plan of campaign he had conceived.

It is certain, above all things, that Frederic never tried to provoke a schism in the Church. He contemptuously spoke of Milan as "the dregs of the Patarins." He never opposed an antipope to his implacable enemies, Gregory IX and Innocent IV. He did not support the false pope of 1227 who, with the help of the Roman barons, besieged St. Peter's for six weeks. In the deeds of his chancellery he called the Church of Rome "my mother." He called God to witness his fidelity upon the approved symbol of the Roman Church. (49) On his death bed, wrote his son Manfred to king Conrad, "with a penitent heart, humbly, as an orthodox Christian should, he recognized the sacrosanct Roman Church, his mother." Thus till the last he maintained his external adhesion to Roman Christianity. In 1242, in the long interregnum that followed the death of Celestine IV, and at the very time when he was returning again and again to the walls of Rome, which the Guelfic barons defended against him, he wrote to the cardinals in as pressing a manner as Louis IX himself, upon the necessity of restoring to the Church without delay its chief pastor. When Innocent IV was elected, he congratulated him with words of a wholly filial character ; but six months later he threatened the senate and Roman people with his wrath if Rome did not submit "to the absolute master of land and sea, whose every wish ought to be fulfilled." In April 1244 he announced to Conrad his reconciliation with the pope, and rejoiced at having been admitted by the pontiff, in his character of "devout son of the Church, and as a Catholic prince, into the unity of the Church" ; but he added : "as eldest and only son, and patron of the Church, *sicut primus et unicus Ecclesie filius et patronus,* our duty is to uphold its greatness. . . . We are attempting with all our strength and we desire with a sincere heart that reformation of the Church that will give us peace, as well as our friends, and faithful subjects, for ever." (50)

These are words that throw a singular light upon the religious history of Frederic II. The patron and protector of the Church means for him nothing less than the absolute master of the Church. He intended that it should bow as docilely as the feudal nobility and the towns under the rigid law of the state. He claimed the right to dispose of things ecclesiastical as freely as of the secular interests of the empire. Already in 1236 he wrote to Gregory IX upon the question of the collation of benefices : "You are annoyed because we have chosen young and unworthy persons. . . . But is it not, in virtue of the divine right, sacrilege to dispute the merits of our munificence, that is to say, the question of knowing whether those whom the emperor appoints are worthy or not?" In 1246 he was to write to all the princes of Christendom : "The pontiff has not the right to exercise any force against us, even for legitimate causes." (51) In 1248, in a letter to the emperor of Nicæa, his son-in-law, he complained bitterly of the unbearable relations the princes of the west have with the chiefs of the Latin Church ; in all troubles of the state, in all revolts and all wars, he detected the ever-present hand of the Church, that made use of a pestilential liberty. For him the east only, the schismatic east of Byzantium and the Mohammedan califates, have solved the problem of the relations between church and state ; they are not troubled with pontiff-kings ; with them clerical society is not a body politic. That is the plague of Europe and the west. Asia is indeed happy ; she enjoys religious peace ; the power of the prince there knows no limits, because in that part of the world the Church does not exist outside the sanctuary. (52)

But this imperial protectorate, this Cæsarian government of the church by the master of the empire, has for its necessary condition the reformation of the Roman Church. It is not enough that the pope and bishops shall have no more political influence, and that the temporal sovereignty of the pope at Rome shall disappear, as well as the feudal sovereignty of the bishops in their dioceses. The ecclesiastical hierarchy must, in addition, renounce its social power ; the field of its influence must be confined to the direct apostolate of consciences, and Christians must no longer be members of a political society in their relations to the Church, but simply individual souls. In his encyclical of 1246 Frederic wrote : "The clergy have waxed fat upon the alms of the great, and they oppress our sons and subjects, forgetting our paternal rights and no longer respecting in us either the emperor or the king. . . . Our conscience is clear, and therefore God is with us ; we call Him to witness as to the intention we have always had of reducing the clergy of all ranks, and especially the highest placed among them, to such a state that they may return to the condition they occupied in the primitive Church, leading a wholly apostolic life and imitating the humility of

Jesus. The clergy of those days conversed with the angels, performed marvellous miracles, tended the sick, raised the dead, and reigned over kings by the sanctity of their lives and not by force of arms. The clergy of to-day, given up to wholly worldly pursuits, drunk with delights, forget God ; they are too rich and their riches stifle religion in them. It is an act of charity to relieve them of those riches that crush and damn them. And so do all of you join with us in putting hand to this work, that the clergy may lay aside their superfluity and resign themselves to ordinary circumstances in order the better to obey God." (53) In 1249 he accused Innocent IV to the whole of Christendom of having seduced the physician who tried to poison the emperor at Parma ; he invoked the help of all the princes for the salvation of "the Holy Church, my mother", which, he said, he had the right and the will "to reform for the honour of God."

Thus Frederic II returned to the theory of Arnold of Brescia, a theory that his grandfather, Frederic Barbarossa, had thought to destroy in the person of Arnold. But the legendary emperor, who suddenly disappeared in a valley of distant Asia on his way to the deliverance of the Holy Sepulchre, could hardly have foreseen the strange way in which a Hohenstaufen would one day understand the meaning of a crusade and would treat one of the most august historical traditions of the Empire, of Rome, and of Christendom.

This crusade of 1229 is closely connected with the political work of Frederic II. It disconcerted the Middle Ages. The Holy See saw in it merely an act of apostasy ; Gregory IX declared that the emperor started for the Holy Land not as a knight and pilgrim, but as a Mohammedan pirate. He had condemned him for his delay in carrying out the vow made in 1215 to Innocent III ; he excommunicated him for the entirely novel manner in which he proceeded to fulfil that vow. Frederic embarked only after having negotiated with the soldan of Egypt, the master of Palestine, by usurpation from his nephew, the soldan of Damascus. At Jaffa the two princes signed peace and divided the kingdom of Jerusalem between them. The holy city was given back to the Christians, with the exception of the mosque of Omar and the temple of Solomon, into which only the Mohammedans were to enter. The evangelical towns, Nazareth and Bethlehem, and all the chain of posts between Jerusalem and Jaffa, and those between Jaffa and St. John of Acre, were given to the emperor. Frederic and the soldan entered into an alliance against all enemies, even Christian, of their Asiatic domains. This clause was aimed at the Templars and Hospitallers. The treaty was to last ten years, five months, and fourteen days.

On March 17, 1229, Frederic entered Jerusalem. When evening came the Christians illuminated their houses and made the streets resound with festal songs. On the next day the emperor penetrated with a few of the faithful into the Holy Sepulchre, where neither priest nor monk awaited him. There, on the Saviour's tomb, with his own hands, he crowned himself king of Jerusalem. On the day after, in his turn, there came the archbishop of Cæsarea who laid the church and the city under an interdict. The emperor hastily provided for the fortification of Jerusalem. Then, almost alone, he traversed the sacred city, now silent and deserted, and, pursued by the pontifical anathema, made his way towards Jaffa. He was well aware that this conquest, that had not cost Christendom a single drop of blood, was regarded by the Church as a sacrilege, and that, being the result of a diplomacy indifferent to the faith of the age, it could not last.

Nevertheless, this crusade of the excommunicated Cæsar had one very important consequence that Frederic had certainly foreseen and sought. The peaceful alliance between Europe and Asia, between Islam and Christianity, modified the ideas upon which the Middle Ages had been nurtured since the time of Peter the Hermit. The prejudice of the crusades was dissipated on the day when it was made evident that it was by no means necessary to wear the cross, and win a sterile martyrdom, in order to obtain from the infidels permission for the cradle and tomb of Jesus to be made an enclosure reserved to the Christians in the midst of the Saracen country. The enterprise of 1229 marked the limit of the œcumenical crusades. Never again was Christendom to be seen quivering and leaping to arms at the thought of the woes of Jerusalem. From this time forth the Germanic and Italian principalities, and consequently the Empire, renounced Palestine. It was no longer at Jerusalem but in Egypt, and afterwards in Tunis, that the last of the crusading kings tried to recover the key of the Holy Sepulchre. And what Christendom lost thenceforth in enthusiasm, the Holy See was to lose in prestige; that age-long duel, that judgment of God, had been a cause of greatness to the Papacy; every time the Holy See had summoned a crusade it had made an impressive display of its spiritual strength and had evoked a recognition of the claim of the bishop of Rome to include in his diocese no less than the entire Christian world. Henceforth, until the sixteenth century, each time it appealed to princes and peoples to undertake a crusade it was to make manifest its powerlessness, to reveal itself to be a *vox clamantis in deserto*. An ideal patrimony had just been taken from the Church; a very noble period in its apostolate was closed for ever.

## III

The system of government set up by Frederic II, so little favourable to the liberties of public life, encouraged the liberties of the mind by the very attack it delivered upon the traditions of the Middle Ages. Southern Italy, that had been kept awake by the sight of new things, lent itself with a kind of joy to this revival of human thought. Upon the other hand, the emperor's religious policy called forth against the Church and the faith the spirit of criticism and all the boldness of unbelief. It was dangerous, doubtless, to profess in the Two Sicilies the old heresies of the Catharians or to appeal to Arnold of Brescia ; in such a case a man was looked upon as a revolutionary, or at least as an old-fashioned thinker. There the state of men's consciences, in which doubt and indifference and irony were already interacting with a wholly modern grace, was really philosophic. Reflection was applied to matters of faith quite calmly, as though they were objects of disinterested research ; the value of religion was pondered by souls no longer tormented by concern for their religious destiny, that were accustomed to compare one with another the known religions of the age and to judge them with serenity.

A book that is invaluable for the understanding of this singular epoch in the history of southern civilization, the *Novellino*, has preserved for us some of the popular recollections of Italy about the crisis that Christianity passed through at that time. The *Novellino*, which is, in its earliest texts, the work of a single compiler, probably a Florentine of the last thirty years of the thirteenth century, contains a distinct group of stories proceeding from the Suabian court and the friends of Frederic II. The emperor is celebrated in them as "the veritable mirror of the universe for wisdom", the spirit of moderation, justice and liberality ; his son Conrad, still a child, out of a delicate feeling of pity, watches over his own faults in order to save his pages from being punished for them. In that court, in which men's souls soared so high, the narrow practice and pharisaical customs of the conventional Christian worship are disdained; they disappeared before the upright intention of the conscience. A smith, "who worked continuously at his art, who respected neither Sunday nor Easter, nor, indeed, any other festival great or small," was denounced to Frederic. (54) The emperor, as "lord and master of the law", had the artizan summoned into his presence and questioned him. "I must earn four sous a day; I give twelve deniers to God, twelve to my father for his living, for he is now so old that he can no longer earn anything; I throw twelve out of the window, the ones I give my wife; the last twelve are for my own expenses." The emperor resolved without difficulty to sacrifice the letter of religious observance, upon condition that the workman could prove his words and avoid a snare. The artizan successfully achieved an ingenious test, and obtained at the same time a hundred golden bezants from the lords of the court. The emperor, hearing his story, began to laugh and said to him: "Go, my worthy fellow, thou hast been stronger than all my wise men. God give thee good luck!" The smith returned home, therefore, safe and sound, with permission to do as he pleased.

As a foil to Frederic, we find in the *Novellino*, Saladin (1138–1193), the soldan of the third crusade, "a very noble lord, chivalrous and liberal." Through him Islam occupied a splendid position by the side of the Christian religion; upon one occasion he even gave a lesson in piety to the Christian knights. One day, in the midst of a truce, Saladin paid a visit to the camp of the crusaders. He saw the lords eating at tables "covered with very white table-cloths"; he saw the repast of the king of France, and highly praised its order and seemliness. "But he saw the poor folk seated miserably on the ground, and loudly blamed their leaders, saying that the friends of the Christian God ate in a viler fashion than other men." Then it was the turn of the crusaders to go to Saladin's camp.

The soldan received them in his tent, where they trod a bright carpet whose design consisted of crosses; "they spat on it as if on the bare earth." Then he spoke, severely rebuking them: "You preach the cross, yet you come and insult it under my very eyes; you love your God in word and seeming only, not in deed." (55)

There remained one religion to be uplifted, the old Jewish faith, the mother of the two others which, in the west and the east alike, treated it with great harshness. It was in Saladin's presence that the *Old Testament,* according to the story-teller, revenged itself upon the *New Testament* and the *Koran*. The soldan had need of money; he had a rich Jew brought to him in order to despoil him. He asked him which of the three faiths was the best. If the Jew answered the Jewish, it was an insult to his master's faith; if he said the Saracen, it was apostasy; in either case an excuse for confiscation. But the Jew had an edifying story in reserve, one that goes back, perhaps, as far as the Babylonian captivity. "My lord, there was a father who had three sons and a ring, the best in the world, adorned with a precious stone. Each of the sons begged the father to leave him the ring at his death. And the father, to content each of them, called a good goldsmith and said to him: 'Master, make me two rings like this one and put in each a stone similar to this.' The goldsmith made the rings so alike that no one but the father could distinguish the true one. He called each of his sons to him separately, and each believed he had received the true ring, which only the father really knew. That, my lord, is the story of the three religions. The father who gave them knows which is the best, and each of his sons, that is to say we men, believe that we have the good one." The soldan was amazed, and let the Jew go without doing him any harm. (56)

That is an apologue that was bound to be very

popular in that southern land which was so little prone to fanaticism, whether religious or political. After the Byzantines, the Italian south had accepted the Arabs in Sicily, then the Normans in the Two Sicilies ; it had seen, without surprise, the Suabian princes take the place of the Norman adventurers, and when at the semi-oriental court of Frederic II it contemplated the good understanding between Latin and Greek bishops, Arab imams and Jewish rabbins, this harmony of all religions and all clergy seemed to it a touching symbol of its varied history. But this religious peace, viewed from afar by Guelfic Italy and the world of monks, looked like an abominable compact with Satan, a new and more odious treason against the Christian faith upon the part of the emperor. The very peculiar manner in which Rome has at all times regarded opinions contrary to Roman orthodoxy was bound to display the reality to the partisans of the Holy See in a strange light. To tolerate and conciliate as equally good all revelations had soon the effect of an insult inflicted equally upon them all. Moses, Jesus, and Mohammed thus received the same buffet from the imperial hand. The *De Tribus Impostoribus*, that caused the Middle Ages a terror all the more profound because no one ever saw a single line of it, that legendary book, was accordingly attributed, without hesitation, to Frederic. At first the title, *The Three Imposters*, had been only a blasphemy gratuitously attributed by the scholastics to the Arabic philosopher Averroes. Pope Gregory IX made a doctrine of it, and deliberately named the inventor of it : " That pestilential king asserts that the universe has been deceived by three imposters, *tribus baratoribus* ; that two of them died in glory, while Jesus was hanged on the cross." (57) And of this devilish doctrine the popular imagination, inflamed mercilessly by the preaching of the mendicant orders, made in the emperor's lifetime a book that was searched for and whose authorship was disputed for five centuries.

After Frederic II, Pietro della Vigna, Machiavelli, and Giordano Bruno ; one of the last philosophers accused of having written it was Spinoza.

## IV.

And Gregory IX said of Frederic II, in the same document from which I have just quoted : " He lies to the extent of affirming that all those are fools who believe that God, creator of the universe and omnipotent, was born of a virgin. . . . He adds that it is impossible to believe anything absolutely except that which is proved by the laws of things and by natural reason." We have at last reached the emperor's real heresy. It is now no longer a matter of reducing the political power of the Church, of taking from the popes the supreme control of Christendom ; it is the very prestige of the conventional Christian faith that he wishes to assail ; and, just as he has secularized the state, by subjecting all the forces of society, the Church included, to the will of a single master, so he is bent upon secularizing knowledge, philosophy, and faith, by giving to them reason as their sole and sovereign mistress.

To carry out this great revolution Frederic has allies drawn from many sides, who have no difficulty in agreeing with each other and with him, the Arabs, the Jews, and the Epicureans, that is to say, the infidels scattered throughout all Italy. Add to this army that is recruited throughout the entire world, in Syria and in Spain alike, learned Greeks, Asiatics or Sicilians, such as Master Theodoros, who was a kind of philosophical chancellor to the emperor, who drew up his master's correspondence with the sultans of Cairo, Tunis, and Morocco ; mathematicians, such as Leonardo Fibonacci of Pisa, the first Christian algebraist ; refugees from the Albigensian lands of southern France, troubadours or rabbins, who brought memories of a country where the chivalric civilization had accommodated itself both to heresy and to religious indifference. With the aid of all these free-thinkers or malcontents, Frederic showed the Middle Ages, at the very moment when scholasticism was about to begin its most brilliant period in France, that human thought, emancipated from all theological discipline and texts of *Scripture*, could investigate the secrets of God, search into the mysteries of the soul, and discover the laws of nature.

What chiefly characterizes the intellectual revival directed by the Hohenstaufen is the predominance of the Arabic culture. But, we must remark, it was not Islam that the emperor opposed to the conventional Christianity of his day ; the Mohammedan tradition to which he attached himself was that of the dissidents from Islam. The movement in favour of free investigation, inaugurated at Bagdad as early as the eighth century, and directed against the divinity of the *Koran* and the dogma of predestination, had passed into Spain with the Ommiades. There, in spite of the popular fanaticism and violent conduct of the Almoravides, it had spread in Andalusia, in the school of Cordova, and in the twelfth century had been incarnated in the person of Averroes. Averroes (1126–1198) was for the Middle Ages the philosopher *par excellence,* and the sum total of negations, accumulated by four centuries of dialectic and gathered together by him, seemed so monstrous an impiety that the Church designated him in his turn as " patriarch of atheism " and antichrist. Ibn Tofail, who passed as one of his masters, had already professed absolute indifference in matters of religion and the right of the conscience freely to distinguish the good and the true. Averroes was filled with utter aristocratic disdain for the mediocre devotee, condemned to the faith of the simple, and to theological superstitions ; he proved from the *Koran* itself that God orders inquiry into the truth by the reason and by science, and that philosophy alone truly understands religion. "The proper religion for philosophers", he says, "is the study of what is". (58) The current beliefs about God, the angels, prophets, sacred ceremonies, prayer and penitence, are excellent for the ignorant, for the common man. As to the sage, he governs his conscience as he pleases, he can choose the noblest among several religions, or content himself with an idealistic interpretation of the creeds and dogmas of the established religion. His reason contains in itself a complete revelation; in it he finds his doctrine, morality and worship, according to the measure in which they reside in a choice soul.

Averroism, therefore, was welcome to the Suabian court, where, for some time, according to an uncertain tradition, the two sons of Averroes represented their father's wisdom. Sicilian civilization gladly allowed itself to be penetrated by that elegant scepticism of the Arabs that became its ally against the enemies of the emperor, the intolerance of the popes, the gloomy zeal of the Guelfs, and the outcry of monks and petty clergy. Frederic II showed, by the entire conduct of his life, to what an extent the disdainful eclecticism of the Mohammedan doctors suited his temperament; he succeeded in maintaining with the dominant religion of the west those relations that were indispensable for the policy of the empire, while at the same time waging an incessant war against the Holy See and reserving for himself, in his secret harems at Lucera and Capua, among his eunuchs and astrologers, opportunities of perpetual recourse to Islam.

But the Arabs, and side by side with them the Spanish or Provençal Jews, their immediate disciples, were destined to initiate the Two Sicilies into a rational work loftier than scepticism or religious indifference. The natural function of the reason, as soon as it is disengaged from theology or faith, is to propound to itself the problems that religion solves, and to explain the sum total of things without having recourse to divine action. This very free inquiry, of which science is the fruit, had been inaugurated by the Greek philosophers, and now for some centuries the Arabs, guided by the unerring sentiment of intellectual traditions, had been advancing along the road once trodden for humanity by Greece. On this highway of thought the Arabs had at once come across Aristotle ; they had read him, commented upon and translated the prodigious encyclopædia. Under their guidance the Christian west and the University of Paris had formed for themselves an idea, often a very confused one, of the peripatetic philosophy and ancient wisdom. The Church, surprised that solutions so contradictory could be derived from Aristotle, at one time condemned and at another embraced with veneration the old master. It put forth all its energies to bend him beneath the scholastic system, to put Greek rationalism at the service of theology, to find in the treatises of the Stagirite a continuous interpretation for its religious metaphysics, physics, and cosmology. At the very period at which we have arrived, towards the middle of the thirteenth century, Aristotle was about to reign over the school through his great interpreters, Alexander of Hales ( ? –1245), whose *Summa Theologia,* of slight intrinsic value, is the first work of the mediæval centuries based upon a knowledge of all the writings of Aristotle and those of the Arabian commentators, Albertus Magnus (1206–1280), and Thomas Aquinas (1225?–1274). But that Aristotle, whom the Church regarded at that time as a sort of pagan forerunner of Christ, and who, in the fourteenth century, in the paintings of Orcagna, Gozzoli, Gaddi, and Traini, stands, sometimes after the manner of a deacon, beside Aquinas trampling under foot Averroes and Mohammed, was no longer a very disturbing teacher ; he was the master of the syllogism, who allowed the scholastics to reason in a very innocuous way upon matter and form, the principle of individuation, the last incorruptible heaven, and the first immovable source of motion.

The Aristotle of the scholastics was by no means the heresiarch Aristotle of Averroes and the Arabs with whom the Emperor Frederic had associated himself in his philosophical enterprise. At Bagdad, Cairo, Toledo, and Cordova, the Mohammedan peripateticism had extracted from the *Metaphysics* or the *Treatise upon the Soul* two dangerous questions, the solution of which singularly confirmed the revolt of unbelieving consciences in the very bosom of Islam. Now the books of Averroes clearly presented the last phase of these questions, the one, the eternity of matter, which implies the negation of a creating God, the other, the active and universal intellect, which leads to the negation of personal immortality. (59) Upon the first of these problems, the gravest problems that every theology has to solve, the Arabic interpretation very closely followed the ideas of the Stagirite. If original matter is only the simple possibility of being, every substance is thus eternal by its matter, that is to say, by its power to be. Matter was not engendered, it is incorruptible. The series of generations proceeding from this eternal source is infinite ; movement, which is the condition of coming into being, is also eternal and continuous, since every movement has its cause in that which precedes it. The world therefore is uncreated and eternal ; God knows only general laws ; He is occupied with the species and not with the individual, for if He knew the particular there would be perpetual innovation in His being. The doctrine of the one and only intellect is parallel to this metaphysical system ; but, as it proceeds with less precision from Aristotle's work, the philosophical imagination of the Arabs, who never had, says Ernest Renan, a very clear sense of the personality of the conscience, left a less definite impress upon it. With Averroes the active intellect, common to all the human race, is nothing else than the universality of the principles of reason, the unity of psychological nature in the entire species. The reason, independent of the individual, is an absolute and impassible thing ; humanity, which is the very act of this reason, is necessary and eternally springing to birth. The universal intellect, separable from the body, is incorruptible. It alone is immortal, like the laws that it conceives ; the individual intellect, sensibility, memory, passion, suffering, love, all that makes of a man a person distinct from other men, is corruptible and perishable, and it is dissipated with the mortal elements of the body. But the immortal intellect is absolutely devoid of conscience. Therefore let not man expect resurrection or the joys of Paradise and let him laugh at eternal woe. The Arabic peripateticism drove away as the dreams of a child the two great hopes, as well as the supreme anguish of humanity, the creating and paternal God and the future life.

Frederic II (1212–1250) was sincerely interested in these lofty problems, not as a Christian who asks for the confirmation of his faith from profane wisdom, but as a free spirit that aspires to the truth, however distressing it may be for the common beliefs of his age. He presided over a regular philosophical academy at his court. A disciple of the schools of Oxford, Paris, and Toledo, Michael Scot (1175 ?–1234 ?), an orthodox Christian, patronized by Gregory IX, had brought him in 1227 the chief Aristotelian treatises of Averroes translated into Latin, and among them that of the *Treatise upon the Soul*. In 1229 the emperor, while negotiating with the soldan, charged the Mohammedan ambassadors with learned questions addressed to the doctors of Arabia, Egypt, and Syria. Later on he again questioned upon the same metaphysical points Juda ben Salomo Cahen, a Spanish Jew, author of an encyclopædia, the *Inquisitio Sapientiæ* ; finally, towards 1240, he renewed this rational inquiry throughout the whole of Islam, and then to Ibn Sabin of Murcia, the most celebrated dialectician in Spain. The latter replied, "for the love of God and the triumph of Islam", and the Arabic text of his answers has been preserved, under the title of "Sicilian Questions", together with the inquiries of the emperor, in a manuscript at Oxford. "Did Aristotle", Frederic asked, "prove the eternity of the world? If he did not, of what use are his arguments? What is the aim of theological science, and what are the preliminary principles, if it depends upon pure reason? What is the nature of the soul? Is it immortal? What is the proof of its immortality? What is the meaning of these words of Mohammed: The heart of the believer is in the hands of the merciful?" (60)

These bold ideas, towards which thus far the Middle Ages had turned only to exorcize them, passed through the civilization of imperial Italy, following, in a kind of parallel course, the same direction as the emperor's politics. The Ghibeline party felt itself all the freer in dealing with the Church of Rome in that, to a still greater extent, the philosophy patronized by its prince resolutely enfranchised the human reason from the obsession of the supernatural. And as all metaphysics conceals at its basis a moral doctrine, the partisans of the emperor, those who loved temporal power and earthly riches and happiness, while troubling very little about the eternity of the world and the one and only intellect, eagerly welcomed a wisdom that reassured them about what comes after death, rendered the present life more agreeable, disconcerted the priest and inquisitor, and extinguished the pope's thunderbolts. The "Epicureans" of Florence, in whom the twelfth century had seen the worst enemies of the social peace, since they brought down the anger of heaven upon the city, were upon two occasions, towards the end of the reign of Frederic and under Manfred, the masters of their republic. The Uberti at that time were at the head of the imperial party in upper Italy; they ruled with harshness and grandeur of soul, and, by their side, "more than a hundred thousand nobles", says Benvenuto of Imola, "men of high condition, who believed, with their captain Farinata and Epicurus, that Paradise should be sought only in the present world." (61) Until the end of the thirteenth century, through all the vicissitudes of their political fortune, these indomitable Ghibelines carried their religious unbelief to a very high degree, perhaps even to a radical materialism. "When the good folk saw Guido Calvalcanti passing in deep meditation through the streets of Florence," says Boccaccio, "they used to say, 'He is seeking reasons to prove that there is no God'". (62) The same had been said of Manfred, who did not believe, says Villani, "either in God, or in the saints, but solely in the pleasures of the flesh." To the Tuscan cardinal Ubaldini, who valiantly upheld the accursed part of the Hohenstaufen at Rome, were attributed these words, which are quite Voltairean in their flavour: "If the soul exists, I have lost mine in the cause of the Ghibelines." We can see that in these freethinkers all the characteristic features of unbelief are the same; they have rejected, as superstitious, the essential beliefs of all the conventional theologies; whether they know it or not, they are pupils of Averroes. Dante has grouped some of them, Farinata, Frederic II, Ubaldini, and Cavalcante Calvalcanti, in the same pit in hell; but the most "magnanimous" of them all, Farinata, will not believe in hell, whose flames are devouring him; he holds himself erect, from the waist upwards, from out his fiery sarcophagus, and casts a haughty eye over the horrible region which he will despise through all eternity:

> *Ed ei s'ergea col petto e colla fronte,*
> *Come avesse l'inferno in gran dispitto.* (63)

To this metaphysic of unbelief and this effacement of the supernatural in the life of the conscience there corresponds a new view of nature. Here miracle has vanished ; the omnipresence of God, that joy of pure souls, and the perpetual ambush of the devil, that terror of weak spirits, have both disappeared ; there remains nothing but the unalterable laws that rule the indefinite evolution of living things, the combinations of forces and elements. The revival of the natural sciences had as its first condition a wholly rational theory of nature.

It was once more toward Aristotle, the natural and physical philosopher, that the Arabs, as alchemists and physicians, brought southern Italy back. About 1230 Michael Scot translated for Frederic the abridgment made by Avicenna (980–1037) of the *History of Animals.* Master Theodore was the chemist of the court and prepared syrups and sundry kinds of sugar for the imperial table. The great school at Salerno renewed medical study for the west, following the methods of Arabic science, the direct observation of the organs and functions of the human body, the quest of salutary plants, the analysis of poisons and experiments with thermal waters. Frederic revived the regulation of the Roman emperors that forbade the practice of medicine to any one who had not undergone an examination and obtained a degree. He fixed the medical and surgical course at five years. He had the properties of the warm springs at Pozzuoli studied. He himself gave prescriptions to his friends and invented receipts. There were brought him from Asia and Africa the rarest animals, and he observed their habits ; the book *De arte venandi cum avibus,* that is attributed to him, is a treatise upon the anatomy and training of birds of chase. Simple people told tales about his experiments. He disembowelled men, it was said, in order to study the process of digestion ; he brought up children in isolation to see what tongue they would invent, whether Hebrew, Greek, Latin, Arabic, or the language of their parents, says Frà Salimbene, whose mind was much perturbed by all these strange things ;

he had the whirlpools in the Strait of Messina sounded by his divers ; he was interested in the distance that separates the earth from the stars. The monks were scandalized by this universal curiosity ; they saw in it the signs of pride and impiety ; Salimbene, with ineffable disdain, characterizes it as superstition, accursed perversity, criminal presumption and madness. (64) The Middle Ages did not like the secrets of the divine operations to be too closely scrutinized, or the play of human life or the celestial machine to be investigated. The natural sciences seemed to them to be suspect of witchcraft and sorcery. Italy, led by the Hohenstaufen in the path of experimental observation, was long to be the only province in Christendom where men could contemplate the phenomena and laws of the visible world without uneasiness.

## V

Finally, wherever the Suabian culture spread, we find centres of poetry in the vulgar tongue, in which the religious indifference and natural philosophy I have just described are once more manifest. Love is its only theme, but it is no longer a love purified by a kind of mysticism, love stronger than death itself, such as northern France knew in the romances of the Round Table ; nor was it ardent and sensual love, yet tortured by shame and the fear of sin, such as the woeful letters of Abelard and Héloïse had revealed to the Middle Ages. It was instead an elegant passion, curious of pleasure, a stranger to all acute suffering, very resigned to change and with a keen enjoyment of the little storms it delighted to raise, the refined love of which the Provençals had been singing for the last two centuries. Here obviously the models, too closely imitated by the Sicilian troubadours, have somewhat impaired the originality of the sentiment ; one can hardly suspect the violent voluptuousness of the seraglios of the Two Sicilies in the caressing sighs, the petty quarrels in subtle language, the charming, thoughtless and childish music of the Provençal lyre. (66) All, the emperor, king Frederic, king Enzo, Pietro della Vigna, as well as poets of less illustrious name, sing in the same tone the smiles and treachery of their mistress, "flower among flowers".

*La fiore d'ogne fiore ;*

so delicate, of so pure a countenance,

*Tant è fine e pura ;*

fair, with face white as silver,

*Bionda, viso d'argiento.*

Believe only half what they say when they tell you, as does Pietro della Vigna, that they "are dying of love", or, like Tommaso di Sasso di Messina, that they "are going mad because of their love".

*Son divenuto paccio, troppo amando.*

This chivalrous devotion is only a *jeu d'esprit* ; these rationalistic souls have too frankly renounced idealism to bear with the great anguish of unhappy love ; they are too ingenuously on the lookout for the actual pleasures of passion, willingly to taste its disenchantments and bitterness. If they bewail the death of their mistress, they give us to understand that all is over and hopeless ; they have not a glimpse of that "other world" of the true love poets, the region where the immortal phantom of earthly love survives. The past and its joys, now destroyed, occupy all their heart. A lover cries : "Cruel, pitiless death . . . thou hast taken from me my pleasures and delights",

*Tolto m'dì 'l sollazo e'l gioco.*

A mistress who is weeping for her lover says to death: "Thou hast taken away from me my delights and gladness, thou hast changed my joys into great sorrow", (67)

*del mio disporto*
*Messa m'dì in gran tristeza.*

This emotion is sincere. It owes nothing to literary artifice. It is the cry of Boccaccio's Fiammetta, deserted by her lover. The Epicurean, to use the name given by the Italian Middle Ages to the representatives of the Suabian world, cannot find consolation for the lost joy in the melancholy charm of memory, still less can he live for a love without voluptuousness, and, as it were, enfranchised from its natural law. It is not easy to imagine Dante or Petrarch singing of Beatrice or Laura at the Saracenic festivals of Frederic II.

## VI

We can now determine with precision what was the importance of the Ghibeline civilization for the Italian conscience. In the emperor's historical work, the enterprises that most struck the imagination of the age, namely, the struggle against the Holy See, the endeavour he made to despoil the pope of his social primacy, the wholly diplomatic crusade of 1229, the constitution of a despotic empire freed from the feudal compact and the old mystical tradition about the balance of the two powers, were, we believe, the least serious innovations; they merely confirmed the Italian Middle Ages in some of their most ancient ideas, those, for example, that the state of political society, as well as that of the Church itself, was by no means unalterable as a dogma ; that the relations between men and their temporal or spiritual masters might be changed to meet the needs of the time ; that the ascendency of the Church over humanity was the result of transitory conditions, and consequently as mobile as those very conditions. We shall see almost immediately, in the course of the thirteenth century, that the most dangerous enemies, not only of the Holy See, but of Roman orthodoxy, were the most fanatical in their Christianity, that they believed themselves to be the followers of Joachim of Flora and Francis of Assisi, and cursed in the most vehement manner the name and memory of Frederic II. No. It was not by means of such external events as these that Frederic most deeply and permanently influenced Italian thought and life. It was through the philosophical spirit of the civilization that he encouraged that something new brought into the religious life of Italy. This spirit showed that it is possible, by the natural development of the reason, for a man to detach himself absolutely from Christianity. But as the Hohenstaufen, with their really free minds, never sought to substitute a different religion for the Roman communion, or a hostile heresy, they never gave men to understand that it was rigorously necessary to abandon orthodox Christianity. They gave the peninsula a lesson in intellectual independence. Therein they responded to the profound instincts of the Italian soul. They permitted men convinced of the excellence of the rational life, as well as those who most openly resisted the influence of the priest over the individual and the influence of the Church over society, to reserve in their hearts that measure of the Christian faith which they thought good for them. The Sicilian culture gave birth to many unbelievers or persons who were indifferent, but it strengthened in the Italians the taste for personal religion and the free investigation of divine things. In the age of Francis, and as Francis himself did, it removed them for a long time from the scholastic Christianity that Abelard had withstood in the twelfth century, and which the University of Paris was about to set up with so toilsome an effort. Only, by the mere efforts of its dominant philosophy, it placed in the heart of Italian Christendom a very useful ballast that kept the most reasonable of its Christians far from the extremes of individual mysticism.

## CHAPTER V

# EXALTATION OF THE FRANCISCAN MYSTICISM. THE ETERNAL GOSPEL. JOHN OF PARMA. FRÀ SALIMBENE

FRANCIS of Assisi, like all religious founders, had formed a very high opinion of human nature. He believed that the ideal of purity, asceticism and charity, embraced by his first followers would always continue to be the light of his Order and the consolation of Italy. His excellent soul was only half mistaken. For more than a century the mystical impulse survived in the institution of Assisi, at times it even went so high and so far that the Franciscans, who sincerely wished to remain faithful to the master's revelation, lost sight of earth, civil society, and even of the Church. Francis had not foreseen that the virtues that formed the nobility of the rising Order would become a danger when that Order, permeating all Christendom, would manifest an apostolic Christianity contradicting the discipline, the historical traditions, and the temporal needs of the Roman Church. The apprehension of a conflict between the "religions" perhaps crossed the mind of Innocent III for a moment. Francis was incapable of suspecting it. At the most he had an inkling, in the last days of his life, that many of his brothers would soon grow weary of too rigid a rule, and, through weakness or discouragement, would seek to compromise with the world. He may have thought of apostasies, but he had too simple a confidence in God for the sad thought of schism ever to enter his mind.

## I

The increasing exaltation of Franciscan Christianity is explained by two very cogent reasons. The first lies in the very prestige of Francis. He had left an almost divine image in the memory of his disciples. The people used to say even in his lifetime: "He listens to those whom God will no longer hear." He was regarded as a sort of Messiah, charged by God to fulfil the promises of Jesus. It needed but a step to pass from that view to regard the good tidings of Assisi as the definite canon of religious belief, and the chapel of Portiuncula as the tabernacle of the universal Church. The second reason is the extraordinary liberty given by Francis to individual consciences that were fired by zeal for an ever-higher perfection. It was a ferment ever at work that uplifted the thirteenth century in Italy and brought forth a whole crop of religious creations. Moreover, men believed they were imitating the founder by seeking to draw nearer to God, as he had formerly done, through a purely personal movement. Thus the adoration of this great figure and the high esteem in which individual findings of the way of salvation were held were bound to cause the Franciscan body to look upon themselves as a chosen family, more jealous of the independence of its faith than of common obedience to the ecclesiastical hierarchy and of respect for the narrow letter of doctrine.

It was the characteristic virtue of the Order, perfect poverty, the one most easy for each affiliated member to practise, since it was at the cost of the entire community, that was the occasion of a long crisis, of which only the first period comes within the scope of this book. Down to 1312, at the time of the Council of Vienne, the debate apparently turned only upon a question of Franciscan discipline. The truly faithful followers of Francis, the Observants or Spirituals, defended the precept of absolute renunciation against those known as the Conventuals, who built great convents, and who returned to monastic property, to humane letters, and to the profane sciences. From 1312 onwards the question assumed larger proportions; the very poverty of Jesus and the apostles came into debate. It was held by the Spirituals that Jesus and the chosen twelve, having possessed nothing of their own, had made the virtue of perfect poverty a strict article of faith for Christians. The secular Church and the Papacy of Avignon were profoundly moved by this new view sustained by the most ardent of the Spirituals, of the Little Brothers or the *Fraticelli*. The matter was complicated, moreover, by the intrusion of politics into theology, and by the interest shown by the emperor and the princes in a doctrine well calculated to diminish the temporal power of the Church. The Franciscan Order at that time had heretics and martyrs in its ranks, especially in the south of France. (68)

We are dealing here only with the long preparation for that acute crisis, with the period marked by the singular book of Frà Angelo Clareno (1247 ?–1337), the *Historia Septem Tribulationum ordinis Minorum*, with which Wadding was only imperfectly acquainted. (69) Angelo in this book, in conformity with the chronological method of the Joachimites, summed up in six epochs of tribulation the struggles and woes of the community of the Spirituals from the middle of the thirteenth century onwards; the seventh epoch, that began at the time when the author was writing, was to carry the true brothers to the day of the final triumph of their form of Christianity. Frà Angelo struggled against persecution for seventy years; he was accused of heresy, condemned to perpetual imprisonment, delivered in 1289 by the general of the Order, Raymond Gaufridi; and then, after a short period of repose under the pontificate of Celestine V

(1294), he was obliged to hide in an island of the Adriatic, or in the hermitages of the Roman Campagna and the kingdom of Naples, in order to escape from Boniface VIII. He died in 1337, well stricken in years, after having collected in his chronicle the recollections of the last companions of Francis of Assisi and the evidence of the great fight he himself had carried on for more than half a century, between the age of John of Parma, who was the general of the Franciscans from 1247 and 1257, and that of Dante, on behalf of the doctrine.

In 1317 Angelo had written to pope John XXII (1316–1334) a long apologetic letter defending the orthodoxy of his brothers ; at the same time, from his residence at Avignon, and later on from the neighbourhood of Rome or the recesses of the Basilicate, he wrote letters to the Spirituals, scattered throughout all Italy, in order to confirm them in their faith, according to the tradition of the first apostles. These documents are most precious ; they expound, with greater clearness and serenity than the *History of the Tribulations* the foundations of the doctrine of the strict Franciscans, in the manner in which they were fixed immediately after the death of Francis and were perpetuated as a creed adopted by all kinds of sects, accepted by the Joachimites of the thirteenth century, down to the crisis of the *Fraticelli*. The *Epistola excusatoria* bears witness to a firm attachment to the faith of the Roman Church, " the only true Church ". It refutes the calumnies with which the mystics had been overwhelmed under Boniface VIII, those, among others, that in their view the Church of Rome had lost the Holy Spirit, that the true priesthood resided in the communion of the Spirituals, and that the Eastern Church is better than the Western. " We are merely poor men or hermit brothers, who observe in the desert the poverty to which we have pledged our lives." But to his brothers Angelo wrote in less humble a tone.

"Christ has spoken to us by the fathers, the apostles, the prophets, the martyrs, the doctors, and the saints. He has spoken to us in the last place by His seraphic son Francis, heir of all His other witnesses. . . . The blessed Francis was in the world under the form of Jesus crucified. He humbled himself and that is why Christ has exalted him. Jesus called Francis to the practise of perfect poverty; He chose him for that mission and bade him adopt the evangelic rule. And pope Innocent proclaimed to the world, in a general council, that, by obedience to the Holy See, Francis had chosen the evangelical life and had promised to keep it to please Christ." "To seek heavenly things, desire the spiritual and despise the earthly, reach out to those things that are before, forget those that are behind, that is our vow, the imitation of Christ, the pledge of our immortality, the perfect observance against which neither law nor decree can avail anything, to which all authority and all power must yield. . . . If king or even a pope bade us do anything contrary to this faith, to the confession of this faith, to this charity and its works, we will obey God rather than men. . . . Christ, the only Saviour, teaches all men, by the example of His life and His divine preaching, the way of salvation and justice, to husbands who have wives and goods, to the clergy and canons who possess in common, to those who, imitating His life and that of the apostles, possess nothing, make a vow that they will possess nothing and wish to have nought of their own. . . . Fly from those who live evil lives and obey their belly and their greediness; speak not to them, but weep over them and pray for them. Honour the lord archbishop and the other clergy, and consider not their sins, for you have promised to live as if you were dead to them and strangers to the things they do. . . . The Rule is superior to all other authority; obedience to the Rule goes before obedience to the ministers, the general, the cardinal-patron. . . . There is no authority in the Rule against the Rule, as there is none in the Church against the Church. . . . The Rule is the remedy against the tyranny of false prelates, for nothing can prevail against it. . . . Francis put nothing therein of himself, he wrote under the dictation of Jesus Christ." The bold Franciscan ended this letter with a very curious consultation upon the case of a man "of good and holy will," to whom the ecclesiastical authority has forbidden the holy mysteries, and who craves the pontiff's absolution. Angelo quoted the apostle: "All that proceedeth not from faith is sin"; faith, he added, is the very judgment of the conscience. Doubtless it would be good for the pope to give absolution to this man, but Angelo did not wish the conscience to be straightened by casuistry and this sinner to be frightened by the difficulties of the sacrament. "We are all confined, by reason of our sins, in the shadow of death; let us therefore pray with a penitent heart, in order that grace may wash out the stains of our faults; thus we shall have, through this anticipated confession, *confessione previa,* a remission and internal absolution wider than those who would absolve us could comprehend. All fear will be driven from our hearts, we shall enjoy peace through faith and the testimony of our heart and the spirit of Christ. For, when the spirit of contrition touches the soul, it removes the stain of sin, and it then teaches us the obedience and respect that are seemly to accord to the ministers of the Church and the divine sacraments".

## II

This theory, written only at the beginning of the fourteenth century, corresponds, from the middle of the thirteenth century, to the inevitable evolution of the Christianity of Assisi. Through poverty and the inner life this world of the Spirituals was escaping from the hand of the Church. He who is devoid of all things, but who will never suffer from lack of alms, is unassailable ; he is as free as the birds. And the man who undertakes to purify himself and his own conscience by his tears need no longer trouble about the priest, the works he enjoins and the penance he imposes ; salvation results from a direct understanding between the Christian and God. It is clear that a religious society in which so free a theology is manifested forms a church within the Church, a Christendom independent of all conventional Christianity. The mystics detached themselves from Rome, returned to the solitude of the old hermits, and gradually removed themselves from the orthodox Christian family. They went back to the asceticism of Joachim of Flora, thus compromising the very foundation of Francis in its work of charity.

Scarcely was the apostle dead when the conflict broke out between the brothers who wished to remain united to the Holy See and those for whom the evangelical inspiration was superior to the hierarchical discipline. The Spirituals of the early days came into collision with the vicar of Francis, Elias of Cortona, who from 1232 to 1239 governed the Franciscan society with remarkable energy and cleverness.

Elias was a politician and a capable man, not averse from cunning, and perhaps a man of letters. He thought of substituting a despotic form of government for the parliamentary constitution of the Order. He told the brothers that the strict Rule was very harsh, intended only for men like the founder and " neighbours of God " ; at the same time he obtained from the Holy See mitigations in the law of poverty and permission to receive money *per interpositas personas*. That was a way of evading the Rule and bringing the Order nearer the Church by community of earthly interests. All those " who maintained the inspiration of Francis " secretly combined, for fear " of the power of this man and the number of his adherents ". Elias, it was said, lived like a prince, thanks to the money received for the basilica of Assisi ; he had valets, horses, a sumptuous table, the train of a feudal bishop ; the worthy Bernard of Quintavalle, the first disciple of Francis, used sometimes to enter the general's house at the dinner-hour and sit down without being invited, saying : " I also wish to eat with you the good things that God lavishes upon His poor ". But Antony of Padua (1195–1231) took things tragically : he reproached Elias for ruining the Order by these privileges and with destroying " the evangelical state that they had promised to observe." This Portuguese theologian, a man of action, irascible and obstinate, who ventured to attack the vicar of Frederic II, Ezzelino, gathered together the timid flock of mystics and took them to the feet of Gregory IX (1227–1241). The pope, troubled by Antony's outcry, sighed and consented to depose Elias. The latter took his fall with admirable good feeling ; he quietly passed over to the emperor Frederic, with whom he stayed at first as pacific intermediary between the pope and Cæsar. Later on, under Innocent IV, defeated at each chapter at Portiuncula for the generalship which he sought anew, he openly revolted and embraced the imperial cause ; he was even for a time Frederic's ambassador at the court of Constantinople. When the emperor died, Elias returned to his home at Cortona. There he built a great Franciscan church with his riches ; excommunicated, he was free, very happy, obeying neither bishop nor pope, with no uneasiness about his salvation until his last hour. When upon the point of death he made his peace with the Holy See and God " in the name of the merits of Francis ".

Elias had outlived his adversary Antony more than twenty years. If these two heirs of the work of Francis of Assisi, instead of making war upon each other and driving the Order to a dogmatic crisis of which the consequences were so grave, had combined their good will, passion and genius, the Franciscan history and the religious history of Italy, and even that of Christendom, would have been very different from what they were. The apostasy of Elias caused scandal in the Church ; Antony of Padua was canonized. Nevertheless it was with the party of Elias that the Church of Rome was soon to find it most easy to agree. The Conventuals, rendered prudent by the care of their secular interests, soon made common cause with the Holy See, which, in exchange for their services, lavished bulls upon them tempering the severity of the primitive Rule. Antony, who died in 1231, had time to train his brothers in the most characteristic attitudes of mind of the Spirituals. He inspired in them their superstitious respect for the very letter of the Rule. We can see, from the sermons of the fiery Franciscan, what value he attributed to the words of every sacred text. They are nothing but quotations from the *Scripture,* rapidly commented upon. Even the symbolical figures of the *Old Testament* are rigorously applied to his demonstration ; it was at Coimbra, beneath the learned pulpits of the Augustinians, that he had acquired this very scholastic method of preaching. Now the precept of poverty having been once embraced, for the sole reason that it was found in the canonical words of the Rule, it was no longer possible to mitigate it by the spirit of moderation and charity that had been the soul of the Franciscan constitution and one of the apostolic gifts of its founder. Antony moreover bequeathed to his followers an original tradition of the Observants, distrust of the secular clergy, prelates and bishops, carried at times to the length of contempt. He preached against the Church in as passionate a tone as Savonarola, reproaching it for its riches, its power, its sensuality and the decline of morality, with as much passion as the Florentine friar, and sought in the biblical texts the lively images with which, in the famous Lent of 1493, Savonarola was to make so powerful an appeal.

*Circumdederunt me vituli multi; tauri pingues obsederunt me.* He aggravated this first text by the biting insult that Savonarola was to borrow in his turn from the prophet Amos: *Audite verbum, vaccæ pingues.* From this inspiration he drew a picture of a wholly popular triviality that Savonarola did not dare to present to the Florentines of Lorenzo de' Medici's day: "The flesh of heifers is hung in the smoke, where it waits to be eaten. Thus the demons will hang the flesh of the wicked prelates in the smoke of hell, where it will await a burning yet more cruel, the fiery heat whereof the *Scripture* speaks, that is to say, hell, the place of anathema, mourning and ineffable pain". Brother Antony, to whom Francis had given neither his tenderness nor his pity, again and again returned to this vehement satire upon the clergy; the friars were long to repeat the same invectives; but this Portuguese cried aloud to Italy the conclusion for which he had prepared his hearers, namely, that the worship celebrated by the covetous and libertine clergy was illusory and sterile, unworthy of God, who rejected it, and useless for the salvation of souls. "Our fat canons think they are quit in the sight of God if they sing in a clear voice in the choir an alleluia or a response; then they return home to amuse themselves and sup well with their mummers and jugglers". Antony was too good a logician not to carry his ideas to their conclusion, extraordinary as it might be; true religion had departed from the Church of the secular clergy, prelates and doctors, to take refuge with the laity. "Carmel is invaded by the brambles of the desert, for the clergy bear no more fruit, the laity alone have a fruitful faith, *clerici sunt infructuosi et laici fructuosi*."

Thus on the one hand the split was final between the moderate and the rigid; on the other it was beginning to be foreseen between the mystics and the secular Church. The contradictions of the chroniclers of the Order as to the names and succession of the early generals prevent us from seeing clearly the formation of two irreconcilable communities, distinguished from each other by theology and discipline and even by dress. Brother Crescentius, canonist and physician, who was general from 1244 to 1248, according to the *History of the Tribulations,* followed in the same path as his predecessor Elias of Cortona, showed the same eagerness for riches and knowledge, the same aversion for the poor convents scattered in the solitudes, that he changed into sumptuous monasteries ; under his guidance the brothers became legacy-hunters, summoned their debtors before the courts, attached themselves to schools of dialectic, and neglected prayer and the *Scriptures* for the "useless curiosities of Aristotle ". Crescentius surrounded himself with arch-scoundrels, such as Bonadies, his jurisconsult, "who drank fraud and lying like water " ; he looked with a malevolent eye upon the growing sect of the Spirituals, "who did not walk," he thought, "according to the truth of the Gospel, who despised the rules of the Order, who believed themselves better than the others, who lived according to their own pleasure, who referred everything to the spirit, *omnia spiritui tribuebant,* and who even wore their mantles too short, *mantellos curtes usque ad nates*." (72) Soon Crescentius openly accused before the pope those brothers who "in appearance and in the opinion of the laity are saints, but who in reality are superstitious, proud, turbulent, indocile, and champions of dangerous innovations ". Innocent IV, who was then engaged in his great war against Frederic II, expected the Church as a whole to marshal itself under his crosier ; so he granted Crescentius permission to pursue and correct the dissidents, and to tear up by the roots "these occasions of schism in the Order ". The general, "with the agility and treachery of the leopard ", laid an ambush for the "pious and simple brothers, who were steadfast in truth and charity ", and they, in their turn, journeyed to Rome; he had them arrested, overwhelmed them with ill-usage, and then sent them, two by two, preceded by calumnious letters, as arrant heretics, to the guardians of the most remote provinces. "But God wished that their virtue should spread abroad as a light and a perfume among the brothers charged with their punishment, who were rejoiced by their angelic conversation", says Angelo Clareno. The hand of God was stretched forth over the Spirituals. The election of 1247 or 1248 raised Brother John of Parma to the government of the Minorites, a man "illustrious for learning and saintliness". The first act of John was to recall the proscribed. The house of Assisi thrilled with joy; the old friends of Francis, the last apostles of the first Franciscan community, "Egidio, Masseo, Angelo, Leo, burst into transports of gladness, because they believed they saw in John of Parma the very soul of Francis come to life again"; Egidio, enlightened by the prophetic spirit, said to him: "It is well, thy coming is welcome, yet thou comest but late". (73)

## III

The ten years, ending with 1257, that John of Parma spent at the head of the Order of Assisi are of vital importance for the religious history of the Middle Ages. Round the new general were grouped the whims of opposition, the bitter rancour and still vague aspirations of the Spirituals. The Joachimite ideas that, for nearly half a century, had been floating in Italian Christendom, suddenly showed an extraordinary recrudescence and became fixed in certain very precise views to which the mystics eagerly rallied. Already in 1240 Brother Aymon, an Englishman by birth, the predecessor of Crescentius, had returned to the prophetic method of the Calabrian monk by a commentary upon Isaiah. Immediately upon his election John of Parma appeared to his brethren as the representative of the purest Franciscan ideal. Against the Conventuals and the lukewarm he played the part of a reformer, going incessantly from house to house to restore the Rule of 1209. (74) The enthusiasm for Francis, brought back to its first impetus, had no difficulty in carrying this body of exalted men back to Joachim of Flora. Had not Joachim, moreover, been the forerunner of the Messiah in Umbria? Had not the "man clothed in linen" announced the approach of the "angel bearing the sign of the living God?" Were not those perfect Christians of the last religious epoch, who were to live by contemplation and love, the children of Assisi, who, delivered by their evangelical poverty from all earthly care, would enter into ineffable communion with the Holy Ghost? Doubtless it was forgotten that Francis had provoked a reaction against that monastic egotism proclaimed by Joachim as the condition of sanctity, and that he had commanded his Minorites to work with their hands and to watch unceasingly over human pain. They were about to forget that the founder had always proclaimed himself the most submissive and the humblest of the sons of the Church; in the effervescence of religious invention, towards the middle of the thirteenth century, the Spirituals were to look upon themselves as the final Church, better than the former one, and, driving the abbot Joachim himself into heresy, were eagerly to seek in his works, interpreted by the aid of a feverish exegesis, the date of the great day when the religion of the Holy Ghost was to take the place of the law and the Word. Now Joachim, who had passed the last years of his life in calculating the moment when the *spirituales viri*, the perfect cenobites, would uplift the Church and Christendom, had fixed the year 1260 as the final term of expectation. One of the most curious witnesses of this singular age, Frà Salimbene, sincerely expected the fatal year, that seemed to be confirmed by the death of the emperor Frederic. The emperor had been regarded as the apocalyptic beast whose appearance, conformably with the old theory of the millennium, was to precede the radiant Church of the perfect. But Salimbene, who feared the crisis although he gloried in being a Joachimite, breathed again on the last day of 1260. "I abandoned that doctrine for ever, and determined to believe only those things I saw."

This mighty religious movement and this fermentation in the Franciscan society resulted partly from the action of John of Parma. Salimbene's interlocutor says, on that same page of the *Chronicle:* Brother John of Parma troubled himself and his Order; his life was so saintly, he was so learned, that he might at that time have amended the Roman curia; but, having followed the prophecies of men who were half mad, he greatly injured himself and did much evil to his friends. . . . If Brother John had imitated your prudence, he would have pacified the minds of his brethren." I believe, nevertheless, that it would be a mistake to look upon John of Parma as a sectary who played with heresy, a visionary haunted by the thought of an approaching overthrow of the Church. The portrait of him drawn by Salimbene, in conformity with that of the *History of the Tribulations,* is that of a very gentle mystic, "with an angelic countenance, gracious and ever smiling", of a singular patience, humility and charity. *Consolabatur mæstos, corripiebat inquietos, suscipiebat infirmos, fovebat debiles, simplices familiariter et læte erudiebat.* Very eloquent when he preached the divine word, of a melting piety when he celebrated the holy mysteries, he spoke but rarely. In church he never sat or leant against the wall, but always stood upright with bare head. He was of middle height, very brisk in his gait, and charming. The old brothers could trace in him the dear form of their founder. His Joachimism probably did not go beyond the moderate provisions of the abbot Joachim.

But that was enough to encourage the fancy of the Spirituals, whose hazardous hypotheses were already no longer contented with the authentic works of Joachim. They needed more precise prophecies, and they found them incessantly, commentaries upon Jeremiah, Ezekiel, Merlin, the *Sibyl Erythræa*, and fearful books against the emperor Frederic or the Holy See. This pseudo-Joachimite literature occupied the ample leisure of the brothers ; in case of need they tried to decipher sure tidings of the antichrist between the verses of the Bible, for "he is already born and come to man's estate ", and revelations concerning the kings of Europe. Salimbene and Gerard of San-Donnino, *Bible* in hand, conversed upon these formidable themes, one summer afternoon, beneath the shade of a vine arbour, in the garden of the convent of Modena.

These dreams did not disturb the noble conscience of John of Parma. He wished nothing more than the greatest progress of men's souls in spirituality, the perfection of his brothers by poverty, contemplation and love. He attached himself to the memory of the Seraphic Father with the tenderness that John had for that of Jesus. He wrote a book, *De sacro commercio sancti Francisci cum Domina Paupertate*. Around him the legends about Francis continued to grow, becoming ever more marvellous ; the *Tres Socii* embellished the primitive biography of Thomas Celano ; the Messianic theory of the thaumaturge of Assisi, that was to end in the *Liber Conformitatum* of Bartolomeo of Pisa, had already begun. But the current that carried the Franciscan family far beyond Francis was stronger than the wisdom of John of Parma. The Joachimites, escaping from the discipline of the Order, multiplied in Italy and France, far from the general's eye. In the convents of Provins and Hyères were elaborated the most audacious prophecies of the sect. Hughues de Digne (?–1285?), "one of the greatest clerics of the world ", says Salimbene, a friend of John of Parma, seems to have been the recognized chief of French Joachimism ; a popular preacher, ardent in dispute, *paratus ad omnia*, admirable when he pictured paradise or hell, a strange mystic, *spiritualis homo ultra modum*, like Paul or Elisha ; when he spoke men trembled "like reeds in the water." Hughues preached before Louis IX. He possessed all the books written by the Calabrian abbot ; he delivered oracles in his cell at Hyères. At his table nothing was spoken of but Joachimite hopes. But, side by side with his open-air Joachimism, upon which the neighbourhood of the episcopal inquisition, the malevolent curiosity of the Dominicans, and the distrust of the secular authorities, imposed a certain amount of reserve, a glimpse could be caught, in the recesses of the small convents, of the mystery of an occult doctrine, the turbid effervescence of the secret society. Salimbene saw, about 1240, an old abbot of the Order of Flora, *vetulus et sanctus homo*, furtively bringing the books of the sect into the Franciscan house at Pisa, in order, he supposed, to remove them from the violent hands of Frederic II. Was it not rather from the pope and his theologians that the Joachimites were hiding at that time? The prophetic, but apocryphal treatises of the Calabrian hermit were slipped from hand to hand ; they were concealed in the least suspected cells, *in angulis et nostris*, say the acts of the Council of Arles. Conferences were carried on in whispers at Provins and Hyères ; the affiliated laymen of the Third Order took part in them ; in Hughues de Digne's room, on the great festival days, we find notaries, judges, physicians, men of letters, scrutinizing the dark sayings of the *Scriptures* under the direction of the Provençal prophet. They were evidently somewhat troubled in conscience ; they felt they were impairing the integrity of the old *Credo*, that they were deserting the Church and creating a new religion that appealed to them with the attraction of forbidden fruit. On the other hand the good folk who remained faithful to the age-long faith looked upon Joachimism with extreme terror. About 1250, in Sicily, men crossed themselves in the name of the Father, the Son, and Matthew, in order not to compromise either with the Holy Ghost or with the *Gospel of John*. *Signumi in Patre, e in Filio, et in Santo Matteo,* we read in the *Contrasto* of Ciullo of Alcamo.

The mystic exaltation rapidly passed through all ranks of society. It was not until 1260 that the epidemic of flagellants was seen. But as early as 1248 Provence and the region of Genoa were full of penitents, male and female, who crucified their flesh in the privacy of their own houses. A singular woman, Douceline, sister of Hughues de Digne, stirred up the south of France. "She never entered a religious order", says Salimbene, "but always lived chastely and holily in the world." She wore the girdle of Francis of Assisi and traversed Provence, followed by eighty ladies of Marseilles ; the gift of healing and even of raising little children from the dead was attributed to her. She entered into all the churches of the Franciscans that she passed on her way ; she stopped in them in ecstasy, with her arms raised aloft, from the first mass until compline ; "she was entirely absorbed in God." And her biographer adds that "She made a vow, with her hands in those of the holy father Brother Hugues de Digne, that she would preserve with the greatest ardour the holy poverty of Jesus, as Francis observed it and gave it to his followers." (75) She founded an institution of Beguines ; "women, virgins, and widows, and even those who were married, left their husbands and children and came to her." She could not hear God or our Lady or Francis spoken of without being carried into an ecstacy, "and, experiencing in that state superhuman emotions, she knew nothing of what was going on around her. . . . Sometimes she was suspended in the air, without any support, without touching the earth with her feet, or only with her big toes. . . . She was one day enraptured in a church of the Minorites, someone approached her, and, as doubting the truth of the ecstasy, drew out a bodkin and cruelly plunged it into her. The holy mother did not move or feel it. But afterwards the cruel pricks were found that had been given her, so that the saint, upon returning to her ordinary state, felt great pain from them. . . . The first time that king Charles saw her in a trance, he wished to try whether it were genuine. . . . He had a quantity of lead melted and thrown boiling over her bare feet in his presence. The saint did not feel it. In consequence the king conceived such an affection for her that he made her his intimate friend." "She could not hear any sound, or almost any song, even that of the birds, without becoming beside herself. One day she heard a solitary sparrow singing, and she said to her companions, 'What a lonely song that bird has!' Immediately she fell into a trance, drawn to God by the song of that bird."

Charles of Anjou, who was somewhat afraid of Douceline, did not fail to consult her upon all important matters. When she was plunged into her mystic slumber, her words were observed as a divine revelation. One Good Friday, at the moment when the cross was raised, she began to cry with sobs: "O false and deceitful world, what a terrible chastisement awaits thee! Come, come, enter the boat, for all who are left out of it will perish." Then, raising her voice: "Do you not hear the pilot cry? Do you not hear he cries: 'Enter the boat, for all who are left out of it will perish'? Alas! they are souls covered with the blood of Jesus!" And to the anxious question of a sister she replied cheerfully: "Yes, verily, under the wings of Francis you will all be saved." But one night, in the convent dormitory, she was seen walking "as if she had followed a procession." She was singing in a melting manner and repeating at times: "A new Jesus! a new Jesus!" At other times she sang: "A new Jerusalem! a new holy city!" The poor Beguines comprehended nothing of what she said. The great dream of Joachim of Flora, the vision of an ideal faith and a purer Paradise, had just crossed the soul of the prophetess.

## IV

The Middle Ages were too fond of dogmatic show and the authority of written texts to leave Joachimism long in the state of a floating and secret doctrine. The new religion needed a Gospel; Joachim had predicted "the Eternal Gospel", but none of his books bore that title. It was at Paris, in 1254, in the bosom of the University, that the manifesto of the final Church of the Holy Ghost burst forth. This strange book, that we know only by the denunciations of its enemies and the condemnation of Rome, was the *Introductorius ad Evangelium æternum*, by Gerard de Borgo-San-Donnino, a colleague of Frà Salimbene and a disciple of John of Parma. According to Jean de Meung, who is wrong by a year, the book appeared,

> By evil intention,
> In the year of the Incarnation
> One thousand two hundred and fifty-five;

and it was publicly exposed

> In the parvis before Notre-Dame. (76)

This book, *The Eternal Gospel*, contained the most radical revolution that the Church, and, indeed, all conventional Christianity, had ever had to face. The three great works of Joachim, the *Concordia*, the *Expositio in Apocalypsim*, and the *Psalterium*, formed its three chapters. Gerard himself had perhaps time to publish only the first, the *Concordia*. The only original parts of the book were the introduction and the comments ; these explained the mystery contained in the hermit's writings. (77) According to the Protocol of the inquisitors of Anagni, Gerard said, at the beginning of the Introduction, that about the year 1200, that is to say at the period when Joachim had finished writing his revelation, the spirit of life had departed from both the *Old Testament* and the *New Testament*, to pass into *The Eternal Gospel*. In this very first proposition Gerard impaired the primitive Joachimism by a truly schismatic view. While Joachim had regarded the Gospel of the future only as a wholly mystic intelligence of the two *Testaments*, reserved, according to him, to the spiritual Christians of the final Church, the author of the Introduction announces that the hermit's three works constitute the very text of the *Eternal Gospel* and are the last to appear of the *tria sacra volumina*, that they are the completion of the *triplex littera* that began with the *Old Testament* and was continued with the *New Testament*. What was for Joachim only an interpretation of the *Scriptures*, contained within the limits of the traditional dogmas of Christianity, became for Gerard a new Scripture, a revelation of a third Law, the Law of the Holy Ghost, that was to replace and extinguish the Law of Christ, as the latter had replaced the Law of the Father. For the Church of the monks, living on the quintessence of Christianity that Joachim had imagined in his desert at Flora, Gerard substituted the communion of souls that henceforth, indifferent to the sacramental symbols, will at last enjoy the fulness of divine things.

Did the man who thus derived a heresy from the prophecies of his master represent, in the middle of the thirteenth century, the actual belief of all the Joachimite family, or was he only an isolated innovator? Father Heinrich Denifle (1844–1905), a great palæographer and historian, is of the opinion that he spoke only for a very restricted group of persons. I believe rather that he expressed with a compromising precision the vague faith that was troubling many souls, in Italy still more than in France. He it was who first dared to show towards what goal men's consciences agitated by the Franciscan apostolate were journeying. For he proceeded no less from Francis than from Joachim. The latter is in his view "the man clothed in linen, angel and teacher, who came down from heaven, holding an open book in his hands"; but Francis is the angel who appeared, about the year 1200 after the Lord's Incarnation, bearing the sign of the living God, and the Order that he founded "came equally from the laity and the clergy." It is the immense militia of brothers "who walk bare foot", Franciscans of the strict letter, already separated from the Church of Rome, who lend to the Messiah of Assisi, as to his forerunner of Flora, a formidable revelation, the new faith, destined to put an end to the prevailing Christianity of the time in five years, and to reign "from one sea to the other." The scandal caused by the Introduction, the outcry of orthodox Christians and the sentence of the Holy See were soon to open the eyes of these enthusiasts; they were to perceive the abyss into which they were upon the point of falling. Many disowned Gerard. Salimbene cannot find words severe enough to condemn the "follies" of this madman who has seduced "the ignorant brothers" by his book, and who was "so well punished", *valde bene fuit punitus;* in other respects, the most amiable man in the world, courteous, modest, temperate, gentle and humble, but one who spoilt all these gifts by a criminal belief.

Assuredly Gerard had chosen the most suitable place

and time to give his heresy a singular celebrity. The University of Paris did not allow any theological novelty to pass without discussing it to death. The age-long practice of the syllogism, the incessant interpretation of the *Scriptures* and the passion for long disputes, put into the hands of the doctors of the institution terrible weapons against all suspected doctrines. By means of its scholastic function the University really held, in the words of the *Romaunt of the Rose*, the "key of Christendom." It was then asleep, says Jean de Meung, but

> At the sound of the book it awoke,
> And could hardly go to sleep again;
> So it armed itself for the encounter
> When it saw this horrible monster,
> All ready to give battle.

Whatever the troubadour, Jean, may say, the University of Paris was wide awake at the time when the first part of the *Everlasting Gospel* was published. The quarrel of the masters with the begging friars, Dominicans and Franciscans, who claimed the right to teach publicly, had for some time been agitating the Latin quarter of Paris. The most fiery defender of the privileges of the University, Guillaume de Saint-Amour ( ? –1273 ?), without waiting till the *Commentary upon the Apocalypse* and the *Psaltery* were published in their turn, preached against the accursed book that, represented by the Introduction and the *Concordia*, seemed to him more voluminous than the *Bible* itself. Matthew of Paris ( ? –1259) tells us that the doctors appointed a commission instructed to convey the grievances of the University to the pope. Then the preaching friars hastened to choose a counter embassy, *ut magistris in faciem contradicerent.* (78)

According to Richer de Senones, Guillaume himself sent to Alexander IV (1254–1261) a copy of the Introduction. In 1256 Guillaume, at the synod of

Paris, once more demanded an inquiry into the conduct of the false preachers "who are creeping into the house of God". His book *De Periculis novissimorum temporum* is full of vehement accusations, mainly directed against the Dominicans, "who claim to give a new discipline to life and to reform the Church." The University displayed such passion in seeking heresy between the lines of Gerard's book and in those of Joachim, and so feverishly drew up a list of the doctrinal errors in the new Gospel, that it did violence to the text and falsified its propositions in a very serious manner. This singular proceeding at first astonished the theologians of the Holy See. "Charges of heresy have been brought before us", says the brief of Alexander IV to the bishop of Paris, "that cannot be found in this book, and that have been treacherously inserted in it". The famous *Excerpta*, to the number of thirty-one propositions, that have been transmitted to us by several manuscripts, by the *Chronicle* of Matthew Paris, the *Liber de Rebus memorabilioribus* of Henry of Hertford ( ? –1370), and the *Directorium* of Nicholas Eymeric (1320?–1399), a Spanish theologian and inquisitor, are thus a most suspicious source for the religious history of the thirteenth century. For instance, not Gerard but Joachim himself is made to say in them that God will grant peace and salvation to certain Jews, however obstinate they may be in their blindness, whereas Joachim had asserted upon several occasions that at the beginning of the third religious state of the world new apostles would evangelize the Jewish people and bring back to "Our Saviour Jesus Christ" the last remnant of the Synagogue. The *Excerpta* declare that, according to the *Concordia*, upon the approach of the third revelation, many chiefs of orders will detach themselves from the secular Church, that is to say, from Rome, and will prepare to return to the ancient faith of the Jews; the *Concordia* says on the contrary that at that time the Jews will allow themselves to be touched, and will see the pure light of the faith, that the Church will find again the joy of the apostolic times, and will embrace, as formerly, with the same closeness the Jewish family and the crowd of the Gentiles. Joachim had said: "One day the preachers will go to the infidels to bear them the good tidings, and these new converts will serve as a defence to the apostles against the wicked Christians of the old community." The *Excerpta* translated: "The preachers, persuaded by the clergy, will pass over to the infidels, and it must be feared that they will unite them to lead them to the assault of the Roman Church." But perhaps the most audacious alteration of the original text is the following. In the second book of the *Concordia*, Joachim, recalling the separation of the Greek and Latin churches and the schismatic pontificate of the bishop of Constantinople, he added: *ambulantes usque in finem in erroribus suis*. In the fifth book he had reproached the Greeks with having, in their forgetfulness of God, embraced the things of the flesh and persecuted, even to that present day, those who live according to the Holy Spirit: *persequuntur eos qui ambulant secundum spiritum usque in presentem diem*. Now the *Excerpta* deliberately translated the passage thus: "Sixth error—the Greek pope, or the Greek people are more in the ways of the Spirit than the Latin pope or the Latin people; that is why they are more in a condition to attain salvation, and we ought rather to attach ourselves to them than to the Roman pope or to the Roman Church."

The theological tribunal of Anagni, formed by the cardinals Odo, Ugo, and Stefano, accordingly heard, in July 1255, the accusation brought by the clergy of the University of Paris, and perhaps aggravated by the opening speech of the prosecutor, Florentius, bishop of Acres. But the inquisitors carefully read the impeached passages not only in the *Concordia* but also in the *Apocalypsis* and the *Psalterion*. Guillaume de Saint-Amour had not been mistaken when he announced in the preceding year that these books had their defenders in the councils of the Holy See. The orthodoxy of the old abbot of Flora came out unscathed from the long "Protocol" of Anagni, which is really the most complete explanation of the Joachimite system. The heresies peculiar to Gerard of San-Donnino were alone retained. The *Introductorius* was therefore condemned by three bulls of Alexander IV, but with a real moderation, without anger and, so to speak, without criticism ; (79) while, a little later, the provincial synod of Arles, presided over by that same Florentine, fulminated against Joachim and all the Joachimites as guilty of sacrilege. Alexander IV, with the greatest urgency, recommended the bishop of Paris not to disturb the Franciscan Order by investigations in the monastic libraries. He ordered that the copies of the "new book" should be burnt, says Matthew Paris, *secrete, sine fratrum scandalo*. But it does not appear that Rome itself was very severe towards Gerard's person ; he was merely, in the first instance, deprived of the priestly functions, preaching and the hearing of confessions ; the harsher penalties inflicted upon him subsequently, the dungeon, the bread and water of affliction, and the deprivation of ecclesiastical burial, were, according to Salimbene and Angelo Clareno, the doing of the Minorite brothers who were irritated at the obstinacy that Gerard showed in not abjuring the Joachimite belief. Guillaume de Saint-Amour paid very dearly for the scandal that he had trumpeted abroad ; he found himself dispossessed of his pulpit in consequence of his book *De Periculis*, exiled from France and deprived for ever of the right of preaching and teaching. (80) John of Parma was in his turn implicated in the effects of this serious affair. "He had received", says the *History of the Tribulations*, "from Francis himself the chalice full of the spirit of life, and having devoutly drunk it, he became as luminous as the sun". (81) But he was to drink it to the dregs. The Franciscans who were loyal to the Holy See summoned him before a chapter of the Order, the first one limited in its membership, at Castello della Pieve; he had to defend himself against a suspicion of heresy, says Frà Angelo, "though filled with the Holy Spirit", against the calumnies "of the least fervent Christians." To the furious brothers who obeyed the directions of Bonaventura he replied in a lofty tone: *Credo in unum Deum, Patrem omnipotentem.* Cardinal Ottoboni, the future Adrian V, contrived that the general of the Minorites should not be cast into prison. In 1257, at the general chapter of Ara Cœli, he resigned his office, and then he retired to the little convent of the Greccia, near Rieti, in the alpine valley, where Francis of Assisi had celebrated the mysteries on Christmas night. There he passed thirty-two years, "in an angelic life", writes Angelo, honoured and flattered by the popes, who upon several occasions offered him the cardinal's hat. In 1288, at the age of eighty, he obtained from Nicholas IV (1288–1292) permission to go to Greece in order to convert the schismatics and restore the unity of Christendom. In the neighbourhood of Camerino he felt his end approaching and said to his companions: "Here is my eternal rest, here I shall dwell for ever." Some days later he died, at peace with the Church.

## V

It is easy for us to appreciate the part, sometimes an unexpected one, taken by the University of Paris and the Holy See in this singular crisis. The former was certainly disconcerted by the hesitating attitude of the Church; Rome must have been astonished by the noisy zeal of the Parisian doctors who seemed to take upon their own shoulders the exclusive task of saving Christendom and preserving the integrity of dogma. I believe, however, that Paris and Rome dealt with the *Eternal Gospel* in the manner most conformable with their respective interests and traditions.

For the University the enterprise of Brother Gerard was an excellent opportunity for compromising the begging orders and getting rid of its rivals for a long time to come. By accusing them of heresy it was undoubtedly *pro domo sua* that it was working. But let us not see in all this the action of a mediocre egotism. It was a question with the University of a nobler privilege than the possession of pulpits, coveted by the Franciscans and the Dominicans. Joachimism, whether taken from the authentic writings of Joachim or the pseudo-prophecies attributed to him after his death, was the contradiction of scholasticism. To the deductive reasoning, based at times upon a sophism, the new sect opposed the direct intuition of eternal things, the intimate conversation with God. All the work of the human mind, of which the University had been the centre since the time of Abelard, was thus nothing but vanity and falsehood ; the whole of science, deprived of its age-long method, was to be started afresh ; or rather it became useless. Mysticism has no need either of syllogisms or of experience. It reads, without any effort of demonstration, the secrets of God and disdains real things as pure illusions of the senses. The mystics live on dreams and ecstasy, at an infinite distance from nature, society and history ; like Francis of Assisi, they are content, for all nourishment, with the chirping of a grasshopper.

Now the University of Paris represented in a certain way the practical and sober spirit of France, I will even say the lay spirit, that was to grow without ceasing until the period of Philip the Fair. It distrusted the mystics and had no love for idealism. More and more it was assimilating the rational genius of the philosophy of Aristotle. It used its influence to clear from its path the metaphysical chimeras of Scotus Eriugena and Guillaume de Champeaux, that doctrine of the universals that always came back to it, like the stone of Sisyphus. It saw in Gerard's *Introductorius* a more dangerous innovation even than the heresy of Amaury of Chartres had been fifty years before. The Joachimite prophecy seemed in fact to have been already half realized ; and was not the swarm of friars, who were impatiently awaiting a religious revival, beginning the final era of the *spirituales viri?* The preaching of the new Gospel was about to close with a triple seal of the two *Testaments*, the revelation of Moses as well as that of Jesus. The *Holy Scripture*, the light of the old science, whose texts were perpetually illuminating the reason of the doctors, for physical researches no less than for political theories—was that *Scripture* about to fail and deprive the human mind of an august collaboration? If, then, this group of *illuminati* succeeded in imposing itself upon the world, what would become of the *Trivium* and the *Quadrivium*, the methodical labour of the reason, the culture of the school, aye, of the school itself?

Quite other was the interest of the Church and the Holy See in this affair. Rome felt no uneasiness about the orthodoxy of the father of the sect, Joachim ; and it held the huge family of the Mendicants too firmly in its hand to feel much anxiety about the credit enjoyed by John of Parma in the Order. The reign of the Spirituals and the ascendency of monasticism constituted no new historical phenomenon. Had not the Church of Gregory VII been the Church of the monks? Had it not even in former days favoured the Lombard *Pataria*, that is to say, the insurrection of the regulars against the secular clergy of Milan? The Holy See, since the days of Innocent III, had been passing through a period of increasing greatness. The boldness of the *Eternal Gospel* seemed to it without doubt to be weakened by its very excess. What could be feared from the prophecies of a few visionaries fixing the downfall of traditional Christianity for so near a date? The terror of the year 1260 would soon pass. And so Italy measured with a tranquil eye the value of this strange heresy. Rome was by no means ignorant that, among the Franciscans of the peninsula, many, without waiting for the issue of the fateful year, treated the dream of the Joachimites with irony. As early as 1248 Peter of Apulia said to Hugues de Digne, in the presence of the principal members affiliated to the sect: "I have certainly read the books of Joachim, and I do not believe them". He said also to John of Naples: "I regard Joachim as the fifth wheel of a carriage, *quantum de quinta rota plaustri*". (82) In reality the theory of absolute poverty, that from the second half of the thirteenth century onwards was directly aimed at the temporal power of the Church, caused the Holy See far more affliction than the preaching of the *Eternal Gospel*.

Rome, finally, at this period of the Middle Ages, had much to ask of the friars. In the crisis it had been passing through since the revolt of Frederic II it found itself closely bound up with monasticism. The emperor was dead, but the "nest of vipers", the family of the Hohenstaufen, was not yet crushed. What subsisted of the work of Frederic, the entirely rational civilization, religious indifference and the spirit of irony as well as that of tolerance, compelled the Holy See to gather about itself the militia of the regulars, and consequently to close its eyes to the errors of their interpretation and the exaggeration of their mysticism. Exact theologians would have been of less service to the Church at that time. Unbelievers or mockers are not to be answered with scholastic discussion, but with enthusiasm and the glorification of the ideal. The mendicant friars, that is to say the active and democratic monasticism of the time, counted at that time for far too much in the moral life of the Italian communes for Rome, whose buckler they were, not to pardon them a little theological licence. The Ghibeline and imperial party, Frederic II, Pietro della Vigna, and king Manfred, who claimed to be restoring civil society outside the Church or in opposition to the Church, had no more constant adversaries than these pious vagabonds who preached to the crowds at the cross-roads of towns, under the trees in the fields, and talked to them of public liberties as much as of the kingdom of God. As to the direct descendants of the abbot Joachim, the reformed Cistercians of Flora, whose convents filled southern Italy, the policy of Rome had again good reasons for treating them with forbearance. At all times the Holy See had coveted the suzerainty, at any rate in name, of the Neapolitan provinces. It had solicited it from the Normans ; it was about to impose it upon the Angevins ; could it therefore embroil itself with monks whose founder was famed as a prophet and a saint, who were its certain political allies, and who, from the point of view of the primacy of the Latin Church, alone seemed capable of balancing in that region, isolated from the rest of Italy and attached by a thousand bonds to the east, the still very powerful influence of the Greek communion?

## VI

The University of Paris had thought it recognized in the excessive Joachimism of Gerard of San-Donnino an invention all the more disturbing, in that it manifested itself on the northern side of the Alps as an isolated and unexpected phenomenon. But for the Holy See this sect was only an evidence of the spirit of religious liberty that the Church granted to Italy, and of which it hindered only the most glaring errors. Never, since the Alexandrine period and the time of the Council of Nicæa, had such a ferment of the faith been seen, so rich a harvest of mysticism. The precious *Chronicle* of Frà Salimbene of Parma gives a glimpse of the degree to which Italy was at that time alive and what fertile germs Francis had sown in the consciences of all men.

Undoubtedly the Parisian scholastics would have been disconcerted by so strange a spectacle ; they would have failed utterly to have understood the very particular notion of orthodoxy that animated Italian Christendom in the middle of the thirteenth century. There, under the motherly eye of the Church, it was agreed that the faithful, individually or combined in free communities, might seek the way of salvation at their will. And each went his own way according to his own humour. One, a layman of Parma, shut himself up in a Cistercian convent to write prophecies. Another, a friend of the Minorites, founded a religion "for himself alone, *sibi ipsi vivebat*". He recalled the person of John the Baptist, with his long beard, his Armenian cloak, his skin tunic, his leathern girdle and "a terrible copper trumpet". He preached in churches and on the squares, surrounded by a band of children bearing branches of trees and lighted tapers. The text of his sermons was always the same and in the vulgar tongue : "*Laudato e benedetto e glorificato sia lo Patre*." The children would repeat these words. And then the preacher would glorify the Son and the Holy Ghost, and all the listeners would cry Alleluia!

Hermits multiplied—hermits of Augustine, hermits of William of Monte Vergine, and hermits of John the Good. The fraternities were of the most diverse sorts. In 1260, the great Joachimite year, the flagellants appeared in the north of Italy. "All, great and small, nobles, soldiers, common folk, bare to the waist, went in procession through the towns and lashed themselves, preceded by bishops and monks". The mystic panic spread like wild fire; all men lost their heads, confessed, restored what they had stolen, embraced their enemies and composed canticles. The end of all things seemed to be at hand. He who did not lash himself was reputed "worse than the devil", he was pointed at and ill-treated. On All Saints' Day they came from Modena to Reggio, and then marched to Parma and Cremona. The *podestà* of the latter town refused them entry and raised a gibbet on the banks of the Po for the use of flagellants who forced the passage; no one presented himself. At Perugia and Rome the inhabitants lashed themselves on their naked bodies in the streets. (83) With the *gaudentes* the scene changes. These latter did not lash themselves, but lived merrily in chivalrous fraternity; they were instituted by Bartolomeo of Vicenza, who was a bishop. They devoured their substance *cum hystrionibus,* writes Salimbene. They never gave alms or contributed to any pious work. They derived as much as they could from rapine. Once ruined, they had the audacity to ask the pope to assign them the richest convents in Italy. Dante met them in the procession of the hypocrites in copes of gilded lead, and he conversed with Loderingo, one of the founders named by Salimbene.

Undoubtedly tares were abundantly mixed with the good seed. The *ribaldi,* the *trutani,* and the *trufatores,* the ribalds, the vagabonds, and the rogues, are denounced by Salimbene. In his *Chronicle* we have the *saccati* or *boscarioli,* men clothed in sacks or men of the woods. They were a sect of false Minorites, proceeding from the Joachimite group of Hughues de Digne, who had usurped the Franciscan costume. Hughues had said to them: "Go into the forests, live upon roots, for the tribulations are at hand". They swarmed in the woods, on the highways, in the towns, preaching, confessing, and begging, for they were furious foragers, more alert than the real mendicants and leaving them nothing but the crumbs. One of them became archbiship of Arles. Among them were *apostoli*, false apostles, vagabonds, *tota die otiosi, qui volunt vivere de labore et sudore aliorum*. They lived in a state of anarchy, did not work or pray, preach or confess; they sought only to "see the women". These wanderers attracted children to their ranks, making them preach; and women, *mulierculas*, clad in long mantles, attached themselves to the *apostoli*, calling themselves their sisters. With these women complete communism was practised. Their chief, Gerard Sagarelli, whom the Minorites had expelled from their Order, passed himself off as the son of God. Around him his followers chanted *Pater! Pater! Pater!* But he had his gallant adventures, copied from Robert d'Abrissel, that revolted Salimbene's sense of decency. This scandal roused the bishop of Parma, who imprisoned all the apostles upon whom he could lay his hands. Then Gregory X condemned the sect, but they refused to submit. The *saccati*, however, who were more humble, had already done so.

Everything is found in Salimbene's *Chronicle:* the enthusiasm of a whole district that built a church for the preachers at Reggio in Emilia; soldiers, women, peasants and citizens carried the stones and lime on their shoulders; the pious industry of the Franciscans and Dominicans who, at Parma, "came to an understanding as to the miracles that should be wrought that year at the feast of Easter"; the joyous miracles of Nicholas of Montefeltro, who, simply by pulling his nose behind the altar at the close of mass, cured a novice whose noisy sleep had disturbed the whole convent; the false relic of St. Albert of Cremona, that the clergy of Parma had adored in their churches and honoured with edifying pictures, *ut melius oblationes a populo obtinerent;* the testamentary song of an epicurean canon, who vowed he would end, glass in hand, a life enlivened by all the deadly sins. In this astonishing Christendom boon companions elbowed ascetics, charlatans honoured saints with their friendship, and the Church let all these people play at their ease in the house of God. Had it not words that could stop, whenever it pleased, the want of religious discipline, and had it not a strong hold upon the most intractable of its children through the mystery of death? (84)

## VII

But the most curious personage in this Christendom is its own historian, Brother Salimbene. This good friar was born in 1221 at Parma. At seventeen years of age, in spite of his parents and the emperor Frederic II, to whom his father had recourse, he took the Franciscan habit. He drew up his *Chronicle* between 1283 and 1288. He died without doubt in 1289. As a child he might have looked upon Francis of Assisi; he saw the first flowers of the seraphic legend in bloom in all their spring-time sweetness. For the space of forty years he journeyed in Italy and France, from convent to convent. He conversed with the greatest men of his century. He saw Frederic II, the antichrist, face to face, *vidi eum et aliquando dilexi;* he was upon familiar terms with John of Parma and Hughues de Digne. At Sens he heard John de Plano Carpini, the predecessor of Marco Polo, explain his book on "the Tartars". At Lyons he accosted Innocent IV, the haughty pope, who had sworn to exterminate the race of the Hohenstaufen. Lastly, in 1248, he saw Louis IX at Sens at Whitsuntide. The king was setting out for the crusade, travelling on foot, apart from the escort of his chivalry, praying and visiting the poor, "a monk rather than a soldier", he says. The portrait that Salimbene drew of Louis is an exquisite one, and cannot be translated: "*Erat autem rex subtilis et gracilis, macilentus convenienter et longus, habens vultum angelicum et faciem gratiosam*". Our little friar accompanied the king as far as the Rhone. One morning he entered a country church with him that was not paved. Louis, out of humility, wished to sit in the dust, and said to the brothers: *Venite ad me, fratres mei dulcissimi, et audite verba mea;* and so the band of cowled friars sat round the king of France.

Surely, for an obscure friar, that was a life with experiences of no common sort. Add thereto Salimbene's great mystical adventure, his vocation to Joachimism, that he embraced with simplicity, because all around him were becoming Joachimites. In the refreshing silence of the Italian cloisters he questioned the prophet Gerard of San-Donnino, and knew all the charm of the apocalyptic terror. And yet, in spite of the moral shocks that fortune had in store for him, Salimbene continued to be an innocent friar, of very moderate intelligence, a little timid soul, who would not give, if one judged too quickly, a very high idea of the Franciscan society thirty years after the death of its founder. He had all the harmless vices of those members of the clergy who wished to be neither saints, nor doctors, nor apostles. His egotism is wonderful. When quite a child he was in his cradle at the time a hurricane was passing over Parma; his mother, fearing the baptistery would fall on the house, took her two little girls in her arms, leaving the future chronicler to the grace of God. "So I never loved her very much", he says, "for she ought to have carried me away, the boy". When his father begged him to renounce the convent, he replied: *Qui amat patrem aut matrem plus quam me, non est me dignus.* Yet he was a very moderate friar, discreet in his zeal.

He speaks of liturgical matters with an astonishing offhandedness. "It is very tedious to read the psalms at the office on Sunday night before chanting the *Te Deum*. And it is very annoying, as much in summer as in winter. For in summer, with the short nights and great heat, one is really too much tormented by the fleas". And he adds "moreover, there are in the ecclesiastical office many things that might be changed for the better". He was fond of the large monasteries, "where the brothers have delights and consolations greater than are found in the small ones". He makes no mystery about these "consolations", fish, game, capons, and tarts, temporal graces that God lavishes upon those who make a vow to be His. You will find in the *Chronicle* four or five Franciscan dinners, all very succulent. The most curious is the "fish" dinner offered by king Louis to the brothers on Whitsun Eve. First the noble wine, the king's, then cherries, fresh beans cooked in milk, fish, lobsters, eel pies seasoned with "an excellent sauce", tarts and fruit. This was very different from the dry bread and spring water of Francis and Frà Masseo. But the founder had said in his Rule: "Eat all dishes that are put before you, *necessitas non habet legem*. And Salimbene on that day humbly submitted to the Rule.

At bottom this by no means ascetic soul was really good and Christian. He was a sheep belonging to the great monastic flock, somewhat wandering by nature, but always ready to come back to the shepherd's side. He resigned himself to discipline, but did not trouble himself with too minute a devotion; incapable of the slightest tendency to revolt, he had made for himself a quiet retreat within himself. As he believed himself to be assured of a good place in Paradise, he willingly tarried to enjoy the pleasures of his earthly pilgrimage, and by no means aspired, with the melancholy impatience of the monks of old, to the splendours of the heavenly Jerusalem. He amused himself at times in a somewhat trivial manner; he tells us convent stories of a very Gallic flavour; he quotes drinking couplets, received from wandering students, that he must have sung many a time to the melody of some hymn on the afternoons of holy days. But I am not sure that in the very circle of Francis of Assisi there was not formerly more than one Salimbene, and that the Seraphic Father did not smile, with the indulgence of the truly great at heart, at the sallies of their good humour. Had he not prescribed gladness as a virtue of the Order: *ostendant se gaudentes in Domino*. And all the promises of the Eternal Gospel were not worth the joy that Francis had awakened in the soul of the old Church, and that new beatitude he seemed to have added to the Sermon on the Mount: *Beati qui rident!*

## CHAPTER VI

# THE HOLY SEE AND THE SPIRITUAL FRANCISCANS. POPULAR ART AND POETRY

THE condemnation of the *Eternal Gospel* by no means relaxed the zeal of the Spiritual Franciscans, who, according to the words of John of Parma, "cared only for eternal things, desired nothing carnal or earthly, looked only to Jesus, and, attaching themselves to the evangelical life, naked and dead to the world, carried the bare cross of the Saviour". The deposition of John of Parma, brought about in 1257 by their opponents, the Conventual Franciscans, seemed to them the accomplishment of the words of Francis of Assisi announcing the religious falling away of certain brethren, the tribulations that his better disciples would suffer, and even the persecution that several popes would visit upon them. The mystics, therefore, were expecting the dark days of war and schism. Hughues de Digne had said at Lyons: "The Christians are about to lose the Holy Land. The Templars will be destroyed. The Franciscans will be divided. The Dominicans will aspire to riches". John of Parma said in his turn: "Those who wish to observe the testament of the founder must sever themselves from those who claim privileges contrary to the Rule." (85) Italy, for half a century and down to the Avignonese captivity, was to be occupied with this gross question of heresy: Is the true Christian life, based upon a pure imitation of the *Gospel*, always in agreement with the spirit of the secular Church?

## I

The problem would have been easy of solution if monastic society had remained faithful to the tradition of wisdom and liberty belonging to the first Franciscan epoch. The Holy See wished only for religious peace. It had always left great independence to the ascetics and hermits. It had just given evidence, in the case of Joachimism, of its indulgence of the mystics. Between Innocent IV and Boniface VIII the Church elected several popes of a very gentle disposition and of true political genius, who asked for nothing better than to welcome under their mantle the more adventurous of the Franciscans. These genial pontiffs were Alexander IV (1254–1261), *vir placidus, sanguineus, jucundus, risibilis*, says the chronicler of St. Bertin; Gregory X (1271–1276), who was elected under the inspiration of Bonaventura, general of the Minorites, and who endeavoured to reconcile all the hostile brothers in Christendom, Ghibeline and Guelf, Greek and Latin, the Papacy and the Empire; then, after the Portuguese John XXI (1276–1277), who hated the regular clergy, who occupied himself with medicine and scholasticism, and who was accused by the regulars of magic, the Church chose a cardinal-patron of the Order of Assisi, John Gaetani Orsini, Nicholas III (1277–1280), the author of the constitution of 1278, who restored civil liberty to the Sacred College and to the pontiff by casting out of the senate and the magistracies of Rome every prince or captain who did not belong to the Roman families. After Honorius IV (1285–1287), a valetudinarian pope, who pacified his states to the advantage of his family, the first Franciscan pope appeared in the person of Nicholas IV (1288–1292), who organized the Tertiaries into a society independent of the parochial clergy and the bishops, a society that left them subject only to the supervision of the regular Minorites. Finally, towards the close of the century, a hermit, a *Fraticello*, Celestine V (1294), sat for a few days in the chair of St. Peter. (86)

But the causes of dissension between the two great factions of the Franciscan Order, and those between the Holy See and the mystics, were too deep to be easily eradicated. The Spirituals no longer accepted any but the heroic aspects of Christianity, and the more they detached themselves from the earthly life, the more they isolated themselves by the harshness of their discipline from the common life, the more they supposed they were carrying out the intention of their founder and the *Gospel*. They were no longer capable of understanding moderation in faith and virtue. As soon as a brother interested himself in the government of religious affairs or of temporal society, as soon as he entered into the councils of the Church or devoted himself to the study of profane science, he became suspect and lost all authority. The powerlessness of Bonaventura to pacify these restless souls is well worth attention. Bonaventura (1221–1274), known as the Seraphic Doctor, was himself a mystic; but he had been a deep student of scholasticism and had taught with distinction in the School of Paris; dialectic and exegesis had developed in him a respect for the reason, and, as he was rational, his actions were for a long time very influential in the Order as well as with the Holy See. There was not in the thirteenth century, and after John of Parma, any Franciscan leader who more poetically retained the memory of Francis and who was more suited to put the first tradition of Assisi in agreement with the real conditions of Latin Christianity. But he was a cardinal and a doctor, a theologian who had the ear of Rome, the enemy of pious chimeras, convinced that the doctrine of absolute poverty would weaken the social value of the

Order; finally, he succeeded John of Parma, and although the latter had nominated him to the chapter for election, he seemed to the exalted to be in possession of an illegitimate power. "He was created general", says Angelo Clareno, "and under him began the fourth persecution". Angelo is not afraid of accusing Bonaventura of duplicity and lying; in the course of the inquiry set on foot to deal with the faith of John of Parma, "when he shut himself up with John in his cell, he thought as he did; but in the presence of the brothers he spoke against John". Bonaventura, having read in a sermon by a Spiritual a vehement criticism of prevaricating prelates, recognized his own portrait and wept, and that was one of the four cases of the new persecution. When it was necessary to pronounce sentence against John, the wisdom and saintliness of Brother Bonaventura suffered eclipse, his gentleness changed into furious anger, and he cried: "If I had not regard for the honour of the Order I would chastise him as a heretic". The Spirituals saw, in their ecstasies, John of Parma clothed in light, and Bonaventura, with his fingers equipped with iron talons, rushing upon the saint to tear him into pieces. Jesus and Francis then appeared and disarmed the hands of the sacrilegious man. (87)

But in dealing with the Holy See the Spirituals closed their ranks and put themselves on the defensive, after the manner of a sect decided to resist to the point of schism. The Seraphic Father, in communicating to his sons the free inner life, had formerly relaxed the bonds that united the faithful to the hierarchy; but he maintained for the Church a tender veneration, and for the dogma of which the Church is the tabernacle the simple faith of a child. Here religious liberty was troubled by a breath of revolt. The excessive contempt for things of the earth threw the mystics into a very peculiar form of Christianity, one that was no longer that of the Church of Rome. The secular progress of the Church, begun by Innocent III (1198–1216) under the eyes of Francis, grew so rapidly that the strict Christians, who hated riches and power, looked upon Rome with no feelings but those of anguish; they asked of themselves whether this bishop, so keen in his search for the good things of the world, was still the vicar of God contemplated by the Bible. The thought never occurred to them that perhaps the very history of the age imposed upon the pontiffs that extraordinary passion for temporal greatness. In the desperate struggle they sustained against Frederic II (1212–1250) and Manfred, a natural son of Frederic, who was crowned king in 1258, the popes had judged that the basis given by the masterful Innocent III to the apostolic authority was too narrow. It was no longer sufficient for them to be masters of Rome now that the Empire claimed to be mistress of all Italy. In order to preserve the hegemony of the Guelfic party they had to assure themselves of the alliance of Guelfic Tuscany, and, consequently, they had to guarantee this political compact by their territorial and military power. So too with the Angevin alliance. When the house of Suabia had fallen for ever at Benevento and Tagliacozzo, the Holy See understood that, if it were not as strong as possible, it ran the risk of becoming the client of its French vassal; later still it seemed to it that Florence would be a dangerous ally if not pacified by the very heavy arm of Charles of Valois. Between Clement IV (1265–1268) and Boniface VIII (1294–1303) the Papacy undertook finally to free itself from the constraint imposed upon it by the old theory of the imperial law. At the council of Lyons, in 1274, Gregory X (1271–1276) had no difficulty in obtaining the greatest results. Rudolf of Hapsburg (1218–1291) recognized the ecclesiastical state and renounced the exercise of the traditional powers of his predecessors at Rome and in the patrimony; he accepted Charles of Anjou as king of Sicily (1266–1285); he bowed himself, and so did all the princes of Germany with him, before the religious primacy of the pontiff, "the greatest luminary"; he avowed himself ready to draw his sword for the defence of the Church at the first sign made by the Holy See. The emperor in 1278 confirmed these engagements and in addition recognized, at the request of Nicholas III (1277–1280), the old donations granted to the Holy See as far back as the Carolingian era, the Pentapolis and Romagna, "the garden of the empire". The tyrants of the Romagna saw the pontifical suzerainty imposed upon them. Then the pope took from Charles of Anjou the function of senator of Rome. But these conquests of the Holy See, every day compromised by the permanent revolution of the Roman commune, were quite illusory. The Roman families, upon which the hand of the foreigner no longer weighed, became very formidable to the pontiffs. Nepotism, that is to say, dynastic security, seemed then to be a constitutional necessity of the papal monarchy.

Nicholas III made the Orsini, of which family he was himself a member, the greatest lords in his domain. He dreamt of creating military tyrannies for them in Lombardy and Tuscany. "He was too fond of his family," writes Ptolemy of Lucca. "He built up Sion for the benefit of his relatives, as several Roman popes had done," writes Salimbene. He was also fond of gold, the first instrument of all political power. Dante met him in hell, in the region of the simoniacs. "I was so greedy to enrich my bear cubs up there that I filled my purse, and here I am cast to the very bottom of the infernal pit". (88)

This pope, whom Dante damned, was certainly considered by the Spirituals as unworthy to preside over the Church of God. From that time forward the thought of schism, that was to break out quite frankly only after Boniface VIII, silently grew in the conscience of the mystics. The idea that they formed of true Christianity is clearly characterized by these words of a bull of John XXII in 1318: "They imagine two churches, one carnal, overwhelmed with riches, lost in luxury, soiled with crime, over which, they say, the Roman pope reigns; the other spiritual and free in its poverty" This separated Church of the Spirituals had to wait until the election of the antipope Nicholas V (1328), the Franciscan Peter of Corbara, before it got a government distinct from the Holy See. But for half a century past it had been nurtured on the sentiments expressed by Angelo Clareno. Francis of Assisi, writes Angelo, predicted that "there would be seen on the papal throne a man who had not been catholically elected, who would think ill of the way of Christ and the Rule that Christ has given by Francis to his sons and that the Church has confirmed. If the sovereign pontiff, by his decrees, renders sure truths doubtful, and defines as heresies what the Church, the doctors and the rules of the saints, teach as articles of the Catholic faith and the consummation of all perfection, no one will judge him, but he judges himself and condemns himself by the decrees that he precipitately promulgates, urged by his own will and in virtue of his authority, against the doctrine of the saints and the rules approved by the Church". (89)

## II

Between the Franciscans of the strict rule and the Conventuals reconciliation was as difficult as between the mystics and the Holy See. Those Minorites who were attached to the monastic tradition of Elias of Cortona thought that Rome interpreted the Gospel more sanely and that the rigid penance, the bed of cinders and the black bread, were by no means the best conditions of the apostolic life. Then they replied to the intolerant austerity of their brethren by the hatred that the rich are fond of showing to the wretched and revolutionary. Each time the Conventuals felt themselves the stronger, they treated the Spirituals with an implacable harshness, hunted out suspected doctrines, burnt books and, not yet daring to burn them, subjected the theologians to the most odious tortures. From the deposition of John of Parma onwards the *History of the Tribulations,* by Frà Angelo, becomes a veritable martyrology.

Pierre Jean d'Olive, a Franciscan friar of the diocese of Béziers, a pupil of the University of Paris, (90) was, under Nicholas IV and Boniface VIII, the most interesting victim of the religious rancour of his brethren. He wrote much, saw all his books condemned, and was even obliged to burn some of them with his own hand. He was moderately chastised by several generals of the Order, by Jerome of Ascoli, the future Nicholas IV, by Bonagratia, at Strasburg and afterwards at Avignon, and by Arlotto of Prato at Paris ; a second time, in 1292, at Paris, he had to explain himself before the general chapter presided over by Raymond Gaufridi. He died quietly in the convent of Narbonne in 1298, after an edifying profession of the Catholic faith and an act of submission to pope Boniface. For the space of some years the festival of his death was celebrated with great devotion by the clergy and humble folk of Provence. Later on, under John XXII, those friars who, in spite of numerous censures, persisted in reading his writings, were ill-treated. Finally he was formally accused of heresy, and his body was disinterred and burnt.

Pierre Jean d'Olive had written two treatises, the *De paupere usu* and the *De Perfectione evangelica,* that have disappeared, and commentaries upon *Genesis,* the *Psalms,* the *Proverbs,* the *Song of Songs*, the *Gospels*, and the *Apocalypse,* a treatise *On the Authority of the*

*Pope and the Council,* and an *Explanation of the Rule of Francis,* of which we possess the manuscripts. His views upon poverty, that are summed up by the historian of the *Tribulations,* are very clear; he grants his brothers merely the use of the daily necessaries of life and the objects, breviaries or sacred vestments, that are used in the divine office. He forbids them to exact payment for burials permitted in the churches of the Minorites or to receive legacies. The basis of his doctrine was, according to his censors and his apologists, a Joachimite idea. He proclaimed a future state of the Church more perfect than the preceding, of which Francis was the forerunner and the coming of which was to be hastened by the reform of monasticism. He came back to the Joachimite vision of the angel who carries the Eternal Gospel. Nicholas Eymeric did not fail to transcribe in his *Directorium Inquisitorum* the list of the heresies exumed from books of Pierre Jean d'Olive. The articles that follow recall the pure tradition of the *Eternal Gospel,* but with a singular accent of violence: "The Rule of Francis is truly the evangelical law. The law of the Franciscans is reproved by the carnal Church, as the law of the Christians was by the Synagogue. It is inevitable that the carnal Church, in order to merit its destruction completely, should condemn the Rule of Francis. The evangelical law of Francis is called to prosper among the Greeks, the Jews, the Saracens and the Tartars, more than in the carnal Church of the Latins. That Church, which is called universal, catholic and militant, is merely the impure Babylon, the great prostitute, *meretrix magna,* precipitated into hell by simony, pride, and all other vices. It appertains to the doctors of the perfect state, much more than it ever appertained to the apostles, to open the spiritual gates of the Christian wisdom". Later on, when the storm called up by the revolt of the *Fraticelli* had long been dissipated, the Church itself proved more indulgent to the memory of Pierre Jean d'Olive. Antoninus, a Dominican, praised him for his orthodoxy and docility; Sixtus IV (1471–1484), a Franciscan pope, permitted the reading of his books. But we know, through the chronicler of the *Seven Tribulations,* to what excesses the Italian Conventuals were carried against the immediate disciples of Pierre Jean. One of them, Ponce of Buontugato, who had refused to surrender the master's books, was chained at the bottom of a dark well and fastened in some manner to the wall; his food, consisting of *panem artum et aquam brevem,* was lowered to him; greatly cramped, and sickened by the filth of his dungeon, he awaited death "with a joyous soul and burning with love." The same fate was in store for Thomas of Casteldemilio. Some others, such as Peter of Macerata, who had likewise been condemned to perpetual imprisonment, the deprivation of their breviary, of confession and of ecclesiastical burial, were delivered in time by the general Raymond Gaufridi. They asked to be sent as missionaries to the east, convinced that they would find among the Saracens the pity and liberty they no longer expected from their brothers.

Thus, in the last years of the thirteenth century, the rupture between the religious of Italy, who laid claim to absolute perfection, and the rest of the Franciscan family, between the rational and the lukewarm, who, satisfied with a less sublime state, chose, after the manner of the secular Church, a less thorny path to salvation, was completed. This detachment from all things was at that time very noticeable even among a great number of afflicted members of the Third Order, who endeavoured to escape the obligations of their social condition and sought the peace and egotism of the cloister in the midst of the populous towns. The Franciscan pope, Nicholas IV, had in 1289 renewed, by the bull *Supra montem,* the constitution of the Tertiaries, or the Brothers of Penitence, whose first Rule was five or six years subsequent to the death of Francis. In 1290, by the bull *Unigenitus*, he confirmed the visitors of the Order in the privilege of watching over the afflicted members who, withdrawn from the inquisition of their bishops, thus formed a kind of religious institution. A considerable part of the middle class in each commune was, by virtue of this new Rule, dependent upon the chiefs of the Minorites and in consequence upon the Holy See. In 1291, by the bull *Ad audientiam*, addressed to the bishop of Florence, Nicholas IV published information to the world regarding the crisis that had rapidly been produced among the Tertiaries ; those among them who, rebellious to the constitution of the bull *Supra montem*, had rallied round their bishop, and who had received as a reward for their attachment to the old discipline the privileges, breviaries, furniture and goods of the old fraternity. The pope thus took up the cudgels in defence of the others, more docile to the Holy See, who, in the eyes of the bishop and parochial clergy of Florence, are the real apostates. This resistance of the Italian episcopate to the reforms of Nicholas IV is one of the numerous incidents in the struggle of the secular Church against the mendicant orders. But in the very course of this crisis we can perceive a conflict no less serious between civil society and the Brothers of Penitence. The relations between the state and this vast community were extremely difficult. From the very first the Tertiaries had escaped from military service, from their feudal duty, and from the exercise of public offices. The popes were constantly occupied in withdrawing them from the requirements of the communal law. Gregory IX determined the strict cases in which they could take an oath in a court of law, and assist in the solemn engagements of their cities. Nicholas IV confirmed, " by the indulgence of the apostolic see ", these exceptions to the general rule of civil abstention. He moreover renewed the privilege accorded to the

Tertiaries of disposing of their goods in favour of the poor or the Church, to the exclusion of their families or the State, to which these strict Christians refused bread and taxes, in the name of the Gospel poverty. (91)

## III

As soon as the ideal embraced by the exalted members of the Franciscan religion detached them more and more from the real world, the return to solitude and the flight to the desert were bound to appear excellent things to these intemperate mystics. So they went back in great numbers to the distant tradition of Romuald (950 ?–1027), who seems to have wandered up and down Italy for thirty years founding monasteries and hermitages, and Nilus the Younger (910–1005). They buried themselves in the woods, in the wastes of the Roman Campagna, in the desolate gorges of the Apennines, praying and sleeping beneath a roof of rushes, waiting for a raven sent by God to bring them their daily bread, as in the legendary time of the hermits of Syria or Egypt. Under the last pontificates of the century a certain Pietro, a peasant of the Abruzzi, a narrow-minded fanatic, had gathered together a few deserters from the Franciscan Order on Mount Murrone, near Sulmona. Nothing was spoken of in Italy but the sanctity of this solitary. Had not the founder of the new community, in the presence of Gregory X (1271–1276), hung up his cloak on a sunbeam? But this miracle seems even less surprising than the election of Pietro himself to the pontificate. The conclave that gathered after the death of Nicholas IV (1288–1292) divided hopelessly between the Orsini and Colonna, terrified by the anarchy that for two years reigned in Rome, had fled, or a part of it had fled, to Rieti, and then at the end of 1293 had proceeded to Perugia.

The Church, dominated by a revolutionary senate, and threatened by Charles II of Anjou, was upon the eve of a schism. Cardinal Latino Orsini then conceived the extraordinary idea of proposing for the choice of the Sacred College the hermit of Mount Murrone, whose prophetic visions were disturbing the peninsula. On July 5, 1294, Pietro was elected. Three bishops were deputed to take to him, amid the rocks and moors where he hid, the news of his election. In a rude hut, whose window was defended by a grating, they found an old man covered with a ragged shirt, with a wild beard and a face emaciated by fasting, and eyes worn with tears. The bishops uncovered their heads and threw themselves on their knees. Pietro, in his turn, thinking it a miraculous vision, knelt also. The deputies of the Church then told him that he was pope and handed him the parchment bearing the report of the election. Pietro, terrified, wished to escape, but his brothers, who saw old Joachim's Gospel being suddenly fulfilled, constrained him to accept the tiara. Thus the new pope was carried off, and before long he met upon the way, ascending the mountain, king Charles and his son, claimant to the crown of Hungary, with barons, priests, and an immense crowd of people. The procession entered Aquila; the pope, still clad in his miserable robe, rode on an ass, the bridle of which was held by the two kings, followed by the Angevin chivalry and all the regular clergy of the district. The author of the election, cardinal Orsini, died at this moment at Perugia. Pietro ordered the Sacred College to join him at Aquila. The cardinals, and among them the proud Benedict Gaetani, the future Boniface VIII, came therefore to look upon the pontifical mummy they had just placed on the throne of Gregory VII and Innocent III.

On August 29, 1294, Frà Pietro was consecrated and took the name of Celestine V. His very short reign was assuredly one of the most astonishing pages in the history of the Church. If he had possessed political genius, and had had sufficient time, he might perhaps have given an unheard-of shock to Christendom. But from the very first he found himself in the hands of Charles II, who took him to Naples, in spite of the resistance of the cardinals. Altogether bewildered by the noise of the great city, he at first shut himself up for some weeks in a cell of the New Castle, like, says a chronicler, "the pheasant that hides its head under its wing and thinks thus to escape the eyes of the hunter". On that pontifical throne, whereon he had seen himself flung as in a dream, the unhappy man felt himself seized by a terrible giddiness. He regretted the peace of his retreat in the sacred silence of the lofty plateaus of the Apennines, his long colloquies with God, his childish ignorance of the things of the world. For five months he struggled in the anguish of his weakness, then, perhaps induced by the treacherous counsels of cardinal Gaetani, he suddenly decided to abdicate. On December 13, after having read to the consistory a bull sanctioning the act of renunciation, he laid down the supreme power in the Church. Outside a popular rising brought about by the hermits and *Fraticelli* tried in vain to alter Celestine's resolution. Under the eyes of the cardinals he took off the pontifical cope and resumed his patched shirt. The Sacred College and king Charles let him return to his mountain. But Boniface VIII, directly after his election, took measures to suppress this vagabond pope whom a religious or political crisis might bring back to the government of the Church, and in face of whom he himself, for the turbulent mob of the regulars, was but an antipope. Celestine V, pursued as a wild beast in the woods of Apulia by the emissaries of his successor, succeeded in reaching the sea; he went on board a fishing-boat, hoping to gain the shores of Dalmatia, but he was carried by a storm back to Italy. The inhabitants of the coast where he was driven ashore paid homage to him and begged him to declare himself the true pope. Celestine simply went to give himself up to the *podestà* of the district ; the latter handed him over to the king of Naples. In May, 1295, the constable of Charles II conducted him to the frontier of the Papal State. Boniface had no difficulty in persuading the old hermit to submit to perpetual seclusion. He was shut up in a tower, at the top of a mountain, near Alatri. The cell was so narrow that he slept with his head resting on the altar where he celebrated mass. He died in the following year. He had suffered sufficiently to be venerated as a martyr. In 1313 the Church canonized him. But Dante, who could not pardon him for having ceded the tiara to Gaetani, placed him in hell, among the colourless souls that had lived "without infamy or glory", and that were "disdained alike by the divine pity and the divine justice",

> *l'ombra di colui*
> *Che fece per viltate il gran rifiuto.* (92.)

## IV

Celestine V left the Church two instruments to avenge his memory, a new religious order, that took the name of *Pauperes heremitæ domini Celestini,* and a poet, Jacopone of Todi. The Celestines, who were no other than the former anonymous community of Frà Pietro, with which the last devotees of Pierre Jean d'Olive had affiliated themselves, were destined to seek exile in Greece in order to escape the pursuit of Boniface VIII. They lived for some time in peace on the coasts of Morea, on the shore of the Gulf of Lepanto, in Thessaly and in the islands of the archipelago. But the Minorites, hearing from merchants and sailors the manner of life led by these hermits "who ate no meat, drank no wine, lived far from men, heard no mass, and recognized neither pope nor Church", denounced them to the Latin bishops and the barons. The majority of these reports were false, but they came to the ears of Boniface VIII, who ordered the patriarch of Constantinople and the archbishops of Athens and Patras to recall the Celestines to the Catholic faith. Solemnly excommunicated, to the sound of the sacred bells, in the church at Negropont, the hermits, led by their chief Frà Liberato, resolved to return to Italy, in order to plead their own cause before the pope. The general of the Minorites, hearing that they were in hiding in the hermitages of the kingdom of Naples, had them arrested by the police of Charles II and handed over to the judgment of the inquisitor, Thomas of Aversa. The latter, a Dominican, who formerly under Nicholas IV had been deprived of the right of preaching in consequence of a disrespectful sermon upon the stigmata of Francis, hastened to absolve these poor people; he advised them to disperse, travelling by night, by devious ways, promising them his support in the councils of the pope. Frà Liberato went to die near Viterbo in the seclusion of a hermitage. The part played by the Celestines was ephemeral, as had been the pontificate of their founder. But the seed of schism that the anchorites of Murrone had received from the hands of Celestine V was gathered up by the *Fraticelli* of the fourteenth century who made it bear a rich harvest. The chronicler of the *Tribulations* tells us, in fact, that the hermit-pope, immediately after his elevation, had absolved his brothers in solitude from all obedience towards the heads of the Order of Assisi, and delegated to Frà Liberato, for the government of this community of dreamers, the plenitude of apostolic power. This was a most artless way of recognizing the right of religious insurrection. Thus, from the earliest days of the reign of Boniface VIII (1294–1303) we see reappear in Italy, in the little sects that were formed here and there under the inspiration of the

Holy Ghost, the anarchy whereby the Church had been troubled forty years before in the days in the Joachimite ferment. (93)

But this host of turbulent sectaries would have passed almost unnoticed through the tragic pontificate of Boniface VIII if a singular poet, Frà Jacopone of Todi (?–1306?), had not made himself the mouthpiece of all the religious and political hatred that had combined against the Holy See. Ser Jacomo Benedetti had adopted the mystic life somewhat late in his career. Born about 1230 on the confines of Umbria and the Papal State, he had studied law, taken the red robe of the doctorate, and for some time carried on the profession of a lawyer. He was at that time looked upon as a man of a very harsh nature, proud, rapacious and impious. (94) A domestic catastrophe made him change his vocation completely. His wife, who was of a Ghibeline family, perished in 1268, being crushed beneath the ruins of a platform at the time of a festival. Under her rich garments was found a hair shirt. That was enough to convert Ser Jacomo to God. He bade farewell to jurisprudence, distributed his goods to the poor, and, clad in a coarse tunic with a cowl, became a Tertiary of St. Francis and a hermit. At the end of ten years of penitence, he entered the Minorite Order as a lay brother. His devotion was displayed in a somewhat strange manner. He reproduced the excesses of fervour whereby Francis of Assisi had marked his rupture with the world: he was seen walking, half naked, on all fours, saddled and bridled like an ass; or perhaps, with his body smeared with resin, he would roll in a mass of feathers and thus face the ridicule and insults of the mob. He was then surnamed Jacopone out of mockery. At night, far from all prying eyes, he wept, prayed and smote his breast. This painful piety, this "madness for Christ", was by no means a novelty for those who remembered the extraordinary epoch of the flagellants. But

Jacopone also appeared in the character of the troubadour or "*jongleur* of God". He exhorted himself, he glorified his God and his penitence, in vehement language, as unequal and free as the theology that was therein contained. "I am going to a great battle, a great labour. O Christ, help me, in order that I may be victorious. I am going to love the cross with a burning ardour and ask it to penetrate me with its madness. I am going to find peace and joy in the sweetness of agony. . . . I shall see whether I can enter Paradise by the path I have chosen, to enjoy there the songs and the smiles of eternity. Lord, permit me to know and fulfil Thy will here below; what matters it then whether Thou dost damn or save me according to Thy good pleasure?" This disdain of salvation, in a mystic of the Middle Ages, is a novelty that testifies to the revolutionary genius of Jacopone. "I have asked God for hell", he says again, "loving Him and losing myself; all evil that comes from Him is sweetness to me." When Celestine was carried to the Holy See, Jacopone thought he had at last a pope after his own heart. After the *rifiuto* he refused allegiance to Boniface VIII, who denied the hermits the privileges granted them by Celestine, and declaimed against the new master of the Church with a fury that Dante himself did not surpass.

## V

The conflict offered itself to Jacopone of its own accord. In 1297 the pope took part in a family quarrel that divided the Colonna, and became embroiled with the cardinals Giacomo and Pietro, uncle and nephew, the two greatest lords in the Roman Church. They, aided by their cousins, Stefano and Sciarra, rallied the Ghibeline party to their side, entered into an intrigue with James of Aragon against the Angevin dynasty, and, crying aloud that Boniface was not a lawful pope, refused to accept the pontifical garrisons in their fiefs in the district of Palestrina. Boniface launched a bull against them and despoiled the two cardinals of their ecclesiastical dignity. The Colonna took up the challenge hurled at them by the pontiff. On May 10th they held a family and war council at Longhezza on the Anio, at which there were present doctors of jurisprudence, French prelates, and two Minorite brothers, Diodati and Jacopone. The conspirators drew up a manifesto in which they declared Boniface an antipope and the abdication of Celestine invalid because of fraud and violence; they finally demanded the convocation of a general council. This deed was published at Rome and even on the altar at St. Peter's. But Celestine had been dead two years, the cardinals Colonna had voted at the conclave for Gaetani, and the latter, strong in his right, excommunicated by a bull all the rebellious Colonna as traitors and schismatics. He stigmatized them with infamy and cursed any who gave them asylum. The Colonna fortified themselves in their towers and in the citadel of Palestrina. The pope, by a third bull, summoned all Christendom to the crusade against his enemies and sold indulgences to pay for the zeal of the crusaders. A fairly large number of them came from Tuscany and Umbria, while the Colonna saw themselves abandoned by king Frederic of Sicily, by the Ghibelines of the Papal State, and by the aristocracy and people of Rome. It was undoubtedly at the end of this year 1297 that Jacopone composed rimed pamphlets against Boniface and the secular Church. "O pope Boniface, thou hast played deeply the game of the world. I believe that thou wilt not leave it with pleasure. . . . Thou hast shown great diligence in heaping up riches; things permissible are not enough for thy insatiable hunger, and behold thou dost rob like a highwayman. . . . When thou didst celebrate thy first mass, darkness fell upon the city and the sanctuary remained without light. . . . When thou wast consecrated forty men perished on coming out of the church, and by this miracle God showed how far thou wast well pleasing to Him." Then Jacopone pictured the Church in tears, weeping for the apostles, martyrs, and priests, of the ages of faith ; he stigmatized, by the mouth of Jesus Christ, the ingratitude of the Church of Rome that had shown itself unworthy of the Saviour's love. "The false clergy have slain and destroyed Me ; they have caused Me to lose the fruit of My labours, and they have inflicted on Me pain greater than death :

*Lo falso clericato*
*Si m' ha morto e destrutto :*
*D' ogne mio lavereccio*
*Me fon perder lo frutto ;*
*Major dolor de morte*
*Da loro aggio portato."*

The cyclopean fortress of Palestrina, the last refuge of the Colonna, was compelled to capitulate. The cardinals Giacomo and Pietro were taken to Rome, dressed in mourning garments and with ropes round their necks ; they knelt at the feet of Boniface, who was surrounded by the Sacred College, and they were compelled to honour him as pontiff. Palestrina, which Sulla had razed to the ground fourteen hundred years before, was utterly destroyed by the Holy Father's orders, although it was one of the seven episcopal mother cities of the Church of Rome. All the heads of the Colonna family fled into exile, loaded with fresh excommunications ; the cardinals retired to the Ghibelines of Tuscany ; Sciarra, after hiding in the woods and marshes, reached the coast, where he was captured by pirates and compelled to row as a galley-slave ; Stefano, whom Petrarch was to compare with Scipio Africanus, found refuge in Sicily. Frà Jacopone was taken and shut up in a dungeon at Palestrina itself, a living witness, among those ruins, of the implacable wrath of Boniface. Fastened to the wall, in perpetual night, he continued to sing his verses : " I am chained for ever, chained like a lion " ; he disputed his bread with the voracity of the rats ; he paid his tavern-keeper for his pittance with *Paternosters*. During the first months of his imprisonment he retained his schismatic's pride and his cheerfulness, as a *Fraticello* whom God at last permitted to know absolute poverty. " Come, Jacopone, behold thou art put to the test. . . . Thou hast been given a subterranean dwelling as thy prebend, thou must be content therewith. . . . Behold for thirty years I aspired to the suffering that is being inflicted upon me ; the day of consolation has at last come. . . . I lie beneath the earth, chained for ever ; so good a benefice have I gained at the court of Rome ! " But little by little the weariness of the darkness told upon him ; he solicited the pope's pardon in tones more and more humble. At the Jubilee of 1300 he asked for grace in the name of the universal peace that was reigning in men's souls ; he bleats, he says, " to the shepherd who has driven him from the fold "; he would fain see the sun rise again and once more chant on Palm Sunday the hosanna of the little children.

*Messer, chi io riveggio la luce !*
*Ch' io possa cantar a voce*
*Quello osanna puerile.*

Let Boniface resign him into the fatherly hands of Francis and cry to him : " *Vecchio, surge* ! Old man, arise ! " Legend would have it that one day the pope, passing by the prison of Palestrina, said to the " *jongleur* of God " : " When wilt thou come forth from here? " Jacopone replied : " On the day when thou dost enter here ". (95)

As a matter of fact Jacopone did not recover his freedom until the year 1303, in the pontificate of

Benedict XI (1303–1304), the successor of Boniface. He was then nearly seventy-five years old. He went to the door of the convent of Collazzone and knocked thereon as a last haven of refuge. There he lived yet three years longer. When he was upon the point of death, on Christmas night 1306, he declared that he would receive the sacraments only from the hands of Giovanni della Verna, his old friend, and as the brothers were dismayed at this dangerous fancy, the dying man, in a joyous voice, began to sing the laud: "*Anima benedetta,* soul blessed by the Creator, look to thy Saviour, Who awaits thee on His cross." Hardly had he finished when Giovanni della Verna appeared on the threshold of his cell. Jacopone then turned towards God, and afterwards sang the first words of the popular canticle,

*Jesu, nostra fidanza,*
*Del cor somma speranza,*

and gave up the ghost at the very moment when, in the convent church, the priest who was celebrating the midnight mass began to intone the *Gloria in excelsis.*

## VI

Over the tomb of Frà Jacopone there reappeared the religious enthusiasm with which the humble folk had formerly greeted the death of Francis of Assisi. He had suffered persecution and exalted the religion of the poor and humble; that was enough to make him reckoned among the best friends of God. In him was venerated not only the ascetic and the martyr, but also the poet. The satires and war songs by which the hermit of Todi had buffeted Boniface VIII were doubtless soon forgotten; but his lauds, written in the vulgar tongue, and his Latin hymns, had been piously stored up in the heart of the crowd. These compositions with their tender smiles, full of the love of Jesus, corresponded marvellously with the artless mysticism of worthy people. They were sung in the churches, in order to enliven the austerity of the liturgy; they were sung by the processions of pilgrims as they passed through the fields in the sunshine, in order to beguile the weariness of the way.

It is not quite certain that Jacopone, as Ozanam thought, was the author of the *Stabat Mater* of the cross, or even of the charming *Stabat Mater* of the crib. "The gracious mother was standing joyfully near the hay on which the little one was lying:

*Stabat Mater speciosa,*
*Juxta fœnum gaudiosa,*
*Dum jacebat parvulus.*

But the laud *Di'Maria dolce* is of a very similar sentiment to that of this second *Stabat*. "Thou hast laid the Child in the hay of the crib, thou hast wrapped Him in some poor swaddling clothes, then thou didst admire him with extreme joy." M. d'Ancona sees in this hymn the delicate work of some Florentine of the fifteenth century rather than the fresh fancy of Jacopone. The same inspiration, however, appears more than once in the lauds of the Umbrian poet, with a descriptive charm that seems to announce the tradition at once free and pious of the first efforts of Italian painting. "See how the *Bambino* kicked in the straw; the mother was there and covered him and put the little mouth to her breast. And the Child seized the teat with His little lips; He pressed it with His mouth that had as yet no teeth; with her left hand she rocked Him, and with holy songs lulled her dear Love to sleep. . . . And all around danced the angels, singing verses most sweet and speaking of nought but love. . . . A new star appeared to the kings of the east ; they found Him all radiant, between the ox and the ass ; the tender Flower did not rest on a bed of fine linen ; the dazzling Lily was laid on a handful of straw. . . . What didst thou feel, Mary, gracious lady, when God sucked thy milk? Oh ! how is it thou didst not die of joy in embracing Him? " Do we not already see in these verses the saintly pictures of Lorenzo di Credi or those of Sandro Botticelli?

We must perhaps refer to Jacopone the canticle of passionate love, long attributed to Francis of Assisi :

*Amore, Amore, chesi m' hai ferito,*
*Altro che Amore non posso gridare ;*
*Amore, Amore, teco so unito,*
*Altro non posso che te abbracciare.*

But it matters little enough whether the paternity of this poem remains doubtful between the two troubadours of Jesus ; both of them made Umbria hear the same cry of loving suffering. There was less serenity, nevertheless, in the soul of Jacopone than in that of the founder of the Franciscans. The thought of death extends its shadow at times over the poetry of the lauds. And it is no longer the angel of peace descending towards the faithful that was summoned up by Jacopone, but the funereal figure that Orcagna was at a later time to fix on the walls of the Campo-Santo :

*Ecco la pallida morte,*
*Laida, scura e sfigurata.*

He displays, with a mournful emphasis, all the miseries of the tomb. "Their flesh, that was so brilliant, is all eaten by worms. Behold this is death, that slays knights, ladies and pages, that gives back to the earth nuns and monks, priests and laymen, the ugly as well as the beautiful. . . . Human filth, be no longer so proud ; ashes, glorify not yourselves ; earthworm, thou must die ; grass of a day, thou must be withered.

To-day a man all brilliant with glory walks with head erect, proud and haughty ; to-morrow he lies as a vile thing, hideous and dead, and his corrupt flesh is full of worms."

## VII

Jacopone's laud is a plebian song, and owes nothing to the imitation of ecclesiastical hymns. The first bands of flagellants, who in 1258 arose at the voice of an old hermit of Umbria, Raineri Fasani, and afterwards the *disciplinati di Gesù Cristo,* who multiplied in central Italy, used to sing, according to Salimbene, lauds in honour of God and the Blessed Virgin, while they marched and lashed their shoulders". (96) When these pious vagabonds were organized into lay brotherhoods, attached to the parishes, the laud, towards the end of the thirteenth century, gradually took the dramatic form. The dialogue seemed more touching than the earlier form of the monologue. On certain church festivals the devout members of the laity, aided at times by a few of the clergy, dressed themselves in the costumes of Gospel characters and sang a scene from the sacred legends. The oldest of these popular dramas had been the midnight mass, celebrated in a barn, where Francis preached beside the crib between the ox and the ass. Soon the imagination of the faithful added to the liturgical text "what might have happened", for, said Bonaventura, "the evangelists did not write everything". (97) The same doctor, in his *Meditations,* imagines all sorts of incidents of a pathetic kind and pictures that fitted into the framework of the historians of Jesus. There was no need of a practised art thus to detach from the *Gospel* a few scenes in dialogue, in which the Brothers of Penitence sometimes spoilt the great simplicity of Mark or Matthew by somewhat poor developments. At times even the monologue was sufficient to the Umbrian poet in order to edify the audience ; thus Jesus would relate simply to his disciples, who remained silent, the parable of the Prodigal Son, from which the authors of the mystery plays were afterwards to deduce a whole drama.

Two subjects, however, the greatest to be found in the *New Testament*, gave the primitive theatre of Umbria material for the amplest invention, the Last Judgment and the Passion. The laud for the Sunday of Advent was recited by numerous personages : antichrist and the kings of his court, the people of Jerusalem, the archangel Gabriel, Satan and his demons, the elect and the damned, Mary beseeching her Son, Christ the sovereign judge. Jesus reminds the accursed of all the trials of His earthly life, of which He accuses them as the authors : " You who saw Me suffering hunger and thirst and gave Me nought to eat or drink. . . . I was wandering as a pilgrim and you refused me a lodging ; I was walking naked on the road and you turned aside your heads as if I were unknown to you ; I was sick and in prison and you visited me not ". The damned answer : " Lord, when we saw Thee overwhelmed with such evils we knew not Thy distress ; why, O Lord, hast Thou condemned us? " " When a poor man asked alms of you ", replies the judge, " it was I who was in him. At every sin you have crucified Me, and yet I have waited with gentleness, hoping always that I need not smite you. . . . Depart, accursed race ! " The sinners turn to Mary and beseech her to intercede, and the Virgin tries in vain, in the name of her miraculous motherhood, to alter the terrible decree of the Church. " By the milk wherewith I nourished Thee, hearken to me a while, my Son, pardon those for whom I plead. . . . Nine months I bore Thee in my virgin womb, and Thou didst drink of these breasts when Thou wast a little child ; I pray Thee, if it may be, repeal Thy sentence ".

The *Lamentation of the Madonna of the Passion of her Son Jesus Christ* makes the voice of the people, the voice of the martyrs, or even that of the poet, alternative with the desperate words of the mother, showing the Virgin the successive scenes of the drama. " O Pilate, torture not my Son, I can prove to thee that He is wrongfully accused ". " Crucify Him, crucify Him, the man Who says He is our King : according to our law He has sinned against the senate. Let them bring the thieves to be His companions ! Let them crown Him with thorns, Him who is called our King." " Woman, behold, they have taken His arm, they have stretched Him on the cross, and have nailed His hand ". " Mother, wherefore art thou come? Thou dost pierce My heart with thy tears ". " My Son, they called me ; my Child, my Father, my Husband, my Child, who has smitten Thee, my Child, who has stripped Thee of Thy garments? . . . My Son, Thou hast given up the ghost, my Son so white and red, Thou hast abandoned me ; my Son so white and fair, my Son with Thy charming face, why has the world so cruelly outraged Thee? John, son that has just been given me, thy Brother is dead, and I have felt the sword concerning which it was prophesied me and which with the same stroke has slain both the mother and her Son ".

These poems, still more lyrical than dramatic, that have been attributed to Jacopone of Todi, sufficed for the edification of the faithful of the thirteenth century. They were devotions in popular language, celebrated, at the close of the parochical mass, by the Brotherhood of Penitence, either in the nave or in some chapel of the church. The *Dramatic Offices of the Penitents of Umbria,* of which several are remarkable for the presence of the strophe in *ottava rima,* derived from Sicily, already testify to a precise distribution of the parts, of a commencing evolution of the drama and even of the decoration of the stage. (98) The *Laud of Good Friday* opens with these words from a group of devout persons: "Raise your eyes and behold. Jesus Christ died for us to-day, His hands and feet nailed to the cross, His side pierced". And the Virgin, Mary Magdalene, the apostle John, and the holy women, relate at the foot of the cross the different pictures of the Passion, down to the Lord's pardon of the good thief, and the last cry of Jesus, that rent the veil of the Temple.

It was thus that, little by little, the dramatic movement and the picture of holiness, added to the edifying words and the procession of the characters in the sacred tradition, made the primitive laud assume the scenic form of the mystery-play. The Italian mystery-play of the fourteenth century is, in a general way, very like the pious representations of the rest of Christendom. An original element, nevertheless, shows itself there more than elsewhere, irony. I mean the Florentine irony of Boccaccio and Sacchetti directed towards both the regular and the secular clergy, as bitter at times as that of Dante, that reveals, in the simple theatre of this people, the influence of the lay spirit, curious of criticism and easily moved to mockery, that grew so rapidly in Italy. There were doubtless scenes of a comic kind in that famous pantomine of Hell celebrated in 1303 at Florence, that ended with so lamentable an accident. And in the drama *A Holy Father and a Monk,* the date of which is undecided, but which is certainly very old, the following words contain even at that early period a very lively satire upon the monastic life: "Nowadays they are nothing but merchants, and under the device of their order they wish to be venerated, holding all others as damned . . . a proud, ungrateful and foolish race, who show to others the narrow path to salvation, and, if they thought they could win a great gain, would not hesitate to kill Christ a second time . . . greedy people, full of all impiety, who think they have the right to enter Paradise when they have separated a son from his father". (99)

## VIII

At the very time when the Italian imagination began to return to the evangelical past of the Church, in order to seek there subjects for a religious drama, a mystic writer had set out to collect, with charming simplicity, the most venerable memories of the apostolic history and the traditions scattered as well in the memory of the faithful as in the tales of the hagiographers about the saints inscribed in the breviary, disciples of Jesus, martyrs, doctors, bishops, fathers of the desert, virgins, and thaumaturges. From John and Paul to Francis, Dominic and Bonaventura, the old bishop of Genoa, Jacobus de Voragine, gives us a procession in his *Golden Legend* of the noblest figures in the Church triumphant, without any historical order, without criticism, and without theological theory. He believed with a childlike faith in the Seven Sleepers of Ephesus who, flying from the persecution of Decius, slept in the recesses of a cavern for two centuries and whose countenances, when they awoke, "had the freshness of roses", no less than in the existence of Thomas Aquinas, with whom he had certainly conversed at some time or other. "They say they had slept three hundred and seventy-two years, but that is not certain, for they revived in the year of the Lord 448, and Decius reigned one year and three months, in the year 252; so that they slept only one hundred and ninety-six years." He believed in the most surprising miracles, even in magic spells and enchanted formulas that summon up or drive away the demons; he had no doubt whatever that the devil is incessantly coming to tempt, in the guise of a young girl or a young man of ravishing beauty, the modesty of virgins and the chastity of ascetics. Simple as a Christian lulled to sleep by the legend of Assisi, Jacobus believed in the familiar intercourse of wild beasts with the confessors, in the wolf who led

Antony to the cell of Paul the Hermit, in the raven which, on that day, brought the two solitaries a double ration of bread and fruit, in the two lions who, on the very evening of that day, piously presented themselves in order to dig Paul's grave, "and, when they had buried him, they retired into the woods".

Although the *Golden Legend* is dedicated mainly to the history of martyrs and the stern penance of the most faithful friends of God, it contains only consoling lessons for simple souls, and seems to endeavour to fill up the abyss that separates the very pure and glorious saints from the humble crowd of Christians engaged in the seductions of the world. It does not exhibit evil and sin as enemies of too formidable a kind; it takes pleasure in pointing out the shameful and sometimes ridiculous defeats of the demon. Here the devil, in spite of his malice, carries off only a very meagre booty—here and there, the soul of some pagan proconsul who insisted upon commanding the worship of his gods of bronze and clay. With a little good will, Christians, surrounded by a strengthening atmosphere of miracles, succeeded in assuring their salvation. God holds out a helping hand to them and complaisantly lifts them up to His throne. The virtues that are within the reach of the humble, goodness of heart, charity, uprightness, tenderness, and faith, are, equally with the bitter sacrifice of life or the renunciation of all earthly joy, certain pledges of bliss. The priest is little found in the *Legend*; he does not trouble the faithful about his heavenly Father. Here faith is of more account than works; an emotion of penitence is sufficient to purify one's conscience. A young man whom John the Evangelist had converted made himself the chief of a band of robbers. The apostle went in search of him and pursued him to the mountain crying: "My dear son, why dost thou fly from thy father? Fear nought, for I will offer up prayers for thee to Jesus Christ, and I will willingly die for thee, as Jesus

Christ died for us. Return then, my son, for Jesus Christ has sent me to thee". And, when the young man heard that, he repented and returned and shed very bitter tears, and the apostle fell at his feet and kissed his hand, as if he had been made white by penitence." A woman who had committed a horrible sin did not dare to confess it to John the Almoner, patriarch of Alexander. "At least write it down", said the indulgent confessor, "and seal the writing, and bring it to me, and I will pray for you". The woman brought her sin written down and sealed; some days later John died; the woman, uneasy for her honour, went to weep at the tomb of John in order that he might restore her secret to her. He came forth from the tomb, dressed as a bishop, and handed the woman the confession, the seal of which was unbroken. She opened it, found her sin obliterated, and in its place these words: "Thy sin is done away by the merits of My servant John". One day when the same bishop was praying alone, he saw by his side a very beautiful virgin, who wore a crown of olives on her head, and when he saw her he was seized with astonishment and asked her who she was. And she said: "I am Mercy, who caused the Son of God to come from heaven; take me for thy wife, and it shall be well with thee". And John, understanding that the olive signified mercy, began from that day to be so merciful that he was surnamed the Almoner and always called the poor his lords. But is not the spirit of this Christianity that smiles at the weakness of men already to be found in those words of John the Evangelist, that are recalled by Jacobus de Voragine as having been told by St. Jerome: "John was at Ephesus, having arrived at an extreme old age, and, when he was brought to the church, he could no longer say anything but these words, which he repeated to his disciples: 'My children, love one another'. And at last the brethren who were with him were astonished that he always repeated the same words, and they asked him : 'Master, why dost thou always say these words?' And he answered : 'Because that is the commandment of our Lord, and if that alone is fulfilled, it is enough' ".

## IX

Italian art, in its early youth, painting and sculpture, drew upon the same sources as the popular poetry, the sacred drama and the edifying history of the distant ages of Christianity. The school of the Pisan masters and that of Giotto present two original features that are always to be met with down to the end of the sixteenth century : the sense of living nature and the taste for the pathetic and for religious tenderness. The education that a few remains of Greek sculpture gave the Pisans, the delicate instinct of the antique nobility that can be recognized in Giotto, maintained Tuscan art, whose naturalism was for ever preserved from the middle-class vulgarity of the French artists of the fourteenth century. And this naturalism, in its turn, at the time when Dante wrote the *Paradise*, protected Italian painting from the seduction of mystic candour that, in the middle of the fifteenth century, reappeared under the brush of the friar Angelico of Fiesole.

Religious art possesses its full historical value only if it is very sincere and corresponds by its very artlessness to the conscience of the faithful. The hieratic art of the Italians, the mosaics that lasted without interruption from the Byzantine epoch to the Roman school of the Cosmati in the thirteenth century, the painting in fresco or distemper of the image masters, anterior to Cimabue, well expressed, in spite of the awkwardness of the compositions or the inexperience of the processes, the sentiment of sadness, often of terror, with which men's souls were filled in the Middle Ages. The idea that these old artists form of the divine majesty is painful. He is a judge, an emperor, seated on an inaccessible throne high up in the apse ; still in his sacerdotal purple, He looks far off into vague space, and never lowers His black eyes towards the crowd prostrated on the stones of the church. The first painters of Italy, down to Cimabue, dare not imagine anything beyond the inert Madonna and the Crucifix, that is to say, personages of the Passion grouped round the cross, with their emaciated bodies, grimacing faces, stiff hair, looking at the Saviour Whose suffering is exhibited in a manner that is grim rather than touching.

The religious revival of Assisi gave new life to Italian art at the same time that it raised man's consciences. The airy and luminous church that Jacopo, faithful to the tradition of the cathedral of Pisa, built above the sombre Romanic church where the remains of Francis lie, is truly the symbol of the renewed youth of all the arts. The thirteenth century had by that time rejected the age-long anguish of the Middle Ages ; it sought the brightness of day, nature, the human heart, it threw itself open to pity and to love. On all sides, at Pistoia, Orveito, Siena, Arezzo, and Lucca, the house of God, by its external decoration, the delicate tracery of its porches adorned with foliage, flowers and fruit, by its covering of marble courses in various colours and the marquetry of the framing that occupies the level surfaces, called Christians from afar as to a place of festival ; inside, it grouped and harmonized, for the delight of the eye, the original elements of the diverse architectural periods of the peninsula ; it made the Norman arch rest lightly on the solid pillars with capitals at once Norman and Corinthian ; it resumed the oriental arabesque and the paving of many-coloured mosaics. All glittering in the sun, with its chiselled garlands like an ivory jewel, the Italian church of this time seemed to be singing the *Canticle of all Creatures* of Francis ; every living form was welcomed by it ; on the galleries of Santa Maria Maggiore, the mosaist of Nicholas IV, Jacopo della Turrita, represented, on a background of azure, the crowning of the Virgin by the Saviour's hands ; above pray the angels ; on the two sides Peter and Paul stand in adoration, with the two Johns, Francis of Assisi and Antony of Padua ; lower down the two donors, Nicholas IV and cardinal Jacopo Colonna lie prostrate ; but on the golden mosaic that represents the ground are green vine stocks round which fly all sorts of birds, that remind us of the winged hearers of the sermon of the *Fioretti*. The disquieting beasts, shapeless as the dreams of a sick man, which the Romanic sculptors lavished on the front of churches, disappeared from the Italian church ; the *Gospel* beasts, symbols of gentleness and fidelity, took their place. Guglielmo d'Agnello, the greatest of the pupils of Nicholas of Pisa, in the pulpit of San-Giovanni-Fuor-Civitas, at Pistoia, showed, in life-like attitudes and appearance, the ox and ass looking at the crib, the three browsing sheep, forgotten for the moment by their shepherd, and the crouching greyhound, attentive to the adoration of the three Magi. At Assisi, a pupil of Giotto, Puccio Capanna, in the Christ at the Column, put a monkey, going on all fours, on the roof of a house ; in the Last Supper there is a dog licking a platter, and beside it a curled-up cat. And, at Padua, Giotto painted in profile, with a striking correctness of movement, the colt of the ass ridden by Jesus when he entered Jerusalem. (100)

The austere and sacerdotal art of the early Middle Ages would certainly never have admitted into religious scenes this amiable familiarity that the schools of Italy preserved down to Titian and Veronese. It would perhaps have accepted the grave architectural sculpture of Nicholas of Pisa (1207?–1280), while at the same time making reserves for the antique reminiscences that the master put into the sarcophagus of Dominic, and the classical attitudes of his Nativity. But the tendency to realism that appears in the Last Judgment of the

Baptistery of Pisa, in the twisting and writhing bodies of the damned, permits us to see what progress Nicholas owed to a sincere observation of nature. His son Giovanni (1240–1320) rushed into complete naturalism by his violent work in the pulpit of the cathedral at Pisa and that of Sant-Andrea at Pistoia. But the blows of his rude chisel were always ennobled by some generous emotion derived from the most striking pages of the Gospel. In the Massacre of the Innocents at Pisa the distracted mothers tear their little ones from the hands of the assassins, clasp them wildly in their arms, turn them over and feel them to assure themselves they are dead, and then, cowering down, weep over their beloved ones *quia non sunt*. At the top of the picture Herod, sitting with his crown on his head, turns to the right towards the executioners, and with his outstretched arm makes them a gesture both imperious and impatient, while on the other side the mothers beseech his mercy. In the Massacre at Pistoia the Jewish king looks down with a grim pleasure on the lamentable crowd of executioners and victims at his feet. But the school of the Pisan sculptors could also express the religious serenity of the century that had just ended ; it showed a singular sweetness in honouring "our sister bodily death", so joyfully greeted by Francis. At the tomb of Benedict XI in the church of St. Dominic, at Perugia, two angels, despoiled of their hieratic wings, bend over the head and feet of the pope who sleeps on his marble couch ; with a familiar gesture, as if they were watching the pontiff as he sleeps, they lift the curtains of the mortuary canopy. At the feet of St. Margaret at Cortona there lies the dog that led the young woman to the blood-stained corpse of her lover. Giovanni's fellow student, in the studio of Nicholas, Arnolfo del Lapo, attaches as a pledge of hope to the tomb of the cardinal De Braye, at Orvieto, the purest vision that Italian art ever saw, even down to its latest days. While the dead man is supported by two angels whose faces breathe a great sadness, higher up, in the arch of a gothic tabernacle raised on two wreathed columns, the Madonna is seated on a throne, grave and benignant, crowned with a diadem whose veil falls down on her shoulders ; she holds on her knees the *Bambino* and quietly rests her right hand on the arm of the chair. This Florentine with his delicate genius communicated to the school of Pisa, in the person of Andrew of Pisa (1270–1348?), the author of the first bronze door of the Baptistery of San-Giovanni, in Florence, the touching candour, sustained by the simple harmony of the attitudes, that was in all the arts the character peculiar to the genius of Florence.

Through Giotto (1276–1336) this originality seems to have become fixed in its principal features for Florentine painting. Dante's words about his friend, *ed ora ha Giotto il grido,* were true as long as the school of Florence lasted, of which he was the perpetual master. It is well known that he practised miniature. In Italy that delicate art, celebrated by Dante in the person of Oderisi, the *onor d' Agobbio,* rivalled French illumination towards the end of the thirteenth century. Giotto retained from his essays in miniature not only the bright and smiling colouring and the piety of composition, but also the liberty of invention so dear to the painters of missals, who, narrowly confined to the margin of the liturgical parchment and compelled to interpret the scenes of the sacred text by minute details, enlivened the grave tradition of the Scriptures by the intimacy of the ornamentation and the familiarity of the sentiment. But the constant study of nature prevented, in Giotto and his pupils, that familiarity of religious painting from becoming fixed in a school of convention. The spectacle of life gave the master an abundant store of picturesque variety ; in his first frescoes in the upper church at Assisi we see a man running along devoured by thirst, who, coming across a spring, rushes feverishly towards it as if he wished to plunge therein. While the brothers bend over the bed on which Francis has just expired and weep, one of them, looking upward has seen the soul borne off by angels, and the astonishment that enraptures him is so powerful that he seems to be rising himself and ready to follow the miraculous ascension of the apostle. And this unrestrained art, that rejects no feature of reality, will never be vulgarized by the faces or gestures of the characters, the disposition of the groups or the decoration of the scene ; the painter evokes only noble scenes, while in France the gothic painting and sculpture, stricken by a premature malady, are about to fall into triviality in the representation of Madonnas with the Child, who, playing with an apple or a toy, " is merely a burgher's son amusing himself ".

Giotto had the generous faith of the Italians of his age. In the two churches at Assisi as well as in the chapel of the Bardi in the Franciscan church of Santa-Croce, in Florence, he wished to glorify Francis, his miracles inspired by a great charity for the humble, and the lofty virtues of his Order, obedience and poverty, that render man purer and more gentle. In the chapel of the Scrovegni at Padua, under the eyes of Dante, he painted the great scenes of the Gospel : the Resurrection of Lazarus, the Kiss of Judas, the Watch in the Garden on the Mount of Olives, the Crucifixion, and the Descent from the Cross. His Christianity confines itself by preference to the evangelical cycle that proceeds from the legend of Joachim, grandfather of John, to the Ascension and of which the drama of the Passion forms the chief poem. At Padua he painted a Hell more calculated to excite the curiosity of little children than anguish in the breasts of sinners. The Hells of the Campo-Santo at Pisa and of Santa-Maria Novella at Florence were not to be much more awe-inspiring to gaze upon ; fear of everlasting torture was to be manifested for the first time in Italian art in the frescoes of Luca Signorelli at Orvieto, and then in the Last Judgment of Michelangelo. The story of the Redemption, from the stable of Bethlehem to Calvary, the miracles of mercy lavished by the Saviour upon all who came to him with a cry of suffering or a word of love, became the *Credo* of the Italian schools, following the example of Giotto. Giotto's Christ has laid aside the formidable majesty of the Byzantines; He is rather the Son of man, superior to His disciples in the solemn grace of His demeanour and the melancholy purity of His features; such He appears at the grave of Lazarus, and above all in the Garden of Gethsemane, half enveloped by the red mantle of Judas, as though by the wings of a bird of prey, and receiving with a sad disdain the traitor's kiss. This Christ, incessantly ennobled by the progress of art, was to appear later on in the frescoes of Masaccio (1402–1429?), then in the *Cenacolo* of Leonardo and that of Andrea del Sarto, blessing the last supper of the apostolic family.

But the most tragic work of the old master is the Descent from the Cross at Padua. The holy women, John and the friends who were present at the last hour, standing or prostrate, adore and weep for Jesus Whose head rests on His mother's heart. Mary seeks in the discoloured face of her Son the traces of the life extinguished; the Magdalene holds the Saviour's feet; a tree covered with spring buds stands on the slope of the hill, and, from the mourning sky, angels, their faces covered with their hands or their arms wide open, hasten with outstretched wings to greet the dead God with their lamentations.

This religious idealism, that Giotto received from the thirteenth century, deservedly attracts the attention. It continued in Italy down to the schools of the Renaissance at its height. It succeeded in holding its own with the painters and sculptors outside of all positive belief or convinced adherence to the supernatural and the very rules of the Christian life. It is to be found again in Frà Filippo Lippi (1406–1469), despite the disorders of an adventurous youth more worthy of a corsair than a friar of old. It sometimes visited even Benvenuto Cellini (1500–1570), who, when sick in a dungeon in the castle of St. Angelo, sang psalms and conversed with Christ and His angels. Raphael maintained it intact in the midst of the elegant corruption of the court of Leo X ; it re-appears again in Sodoma's Christ at the Column, as well as in Perugino's Descent from the Cross. Here, beyond the persons kneeling in the foreground and gathered as it were at the foot of an altar, nature seems to be keeping holiday, and celebrating by the serenity of the landscape, the smile of the sky, the peace of the azure hills, the transparent waters and the flowering meadows, the hope of the approaching resurrection. And yet the Umbrian master, who was penetrated by the incredulous spirit of Florence, "had no religion", writes Vasari, "and could never be persuaded of the immortality of the soul ; but with words well worthy of his granite brain he ever refused with obstinacy the good way. He believed only in earthly goods".

Thus Giotto was the initiator, for all the succeeding Italian art, of a mysticism without which truly Christian painting could not live, and which, combining the veneration for holy traditions with the sentiment of their ineffable poetry, continues even in our day deep down in many souls long since alienated from the ancient Church. But in Giotto's heart there also reposed emotions and hopes that the world will never know again, the last religious visions of the age whose conscience I have just been studying. For the chapel of the Peruzzi at Santa-Croce he painted the apostle John, lonely and asleep on the rock of Patmos, while above his head the great mysteries of the future, that the Middle Ages had endeavoured to decipher among the verses of the *Apocalypse* or the *Fourth Gospel*, march on the clouds like gods. Then in the neighbouring fresco we have the evangelist's resurrection, when he came forth from his tomb before his astonished, terrified, and dazzled disciples. It was the farewell that Italian art sent from its cradle to the Johannine tradition, its farewell to Joachim of Flora, to John of Parma, and to Jacopone of Todi.

## CHAPTER VII

# THE MYSTICISM, THE MORAL PHILOSOPHY, AND THE FAITH OF DANTE

AMID the vicissitudes of Italian Christianity in the Middle Ages we have marked three replies to the problem of the relations of the soul to God and the relations of the Christian to the Church : (1) the communion of Arnold of Brescia ; (2) that of the abbot Joachim, Francis of Assisi, and John of Parma ; and finally (3) that of the emperor Frederic and his suite of philosophers. At the bottom of each of these three theories is a doctrine of liberty, the absolute liberty of political society in relation to the temporal Church, the liberty of individual religion, in which faith and love are superior to obedience and penance, the liberty of the individual reason in its relation to dogma and its ministers. The Arnoldists, the Joachimites, the intemperate Franciscans, the *Fraticelli,* and the unbelievers of Ghibeline Italy, caused some bitter hours to the Church of Rome. Against these refractory persons who disobeyed the old discipline the popes launched resounding bulls. Yet nevertheless these very free bodies of Christians never brought about a rupture with the creed of the Church, never fell into formal heresy or schism. Dante, who was the greatest witness of his race and century, received all these influences of religious liberty. In him were reconciled all the original manifestations of Italian religion. This austere Christian, whose orthodoxy many suspected, has been placed by Raphael, in the Dispute of the Holy Sacrament, by the side of the fathers and doctors of the universal Church. He is, with Francis, the loftiest figure of the story I have just sketched.

## I

But the features of this figure are very complex, for Dante's soul was as troubled as his life. While Francis of Assisi, in the earthly paradise of Umbria, sings, in company with the birds, a perpetual *Lætare*, Dante writes about himself: "I am a ship without sails or rudder, driven by the tempest from port to port and from shore to shore". He lost one after the other the objects of his first tender affection; Beatrice, whom he had loved while quite a child, his mother city and his baptistery, his "beautiful San Giovanni", his political faith, and his Florentine devotion to the Church of Rome. From a moderate Guelf, partisan of the Holy See, and still more of the communal liberties of Florence, he had become a Ghibeline when Boniface VIII had with his own hands destroyed the Guelfic party. But after the descent of Henry VII he despaired of the empire as he had despaired of the Church; he was then seen travelling with his sadness and dreams throughout Italy, the "hostelry of sorrow". One evening he laid down and died in the shadow of one of the beautiful Byzantine basilicas of Ravenna.

Among so many ruins one thing, in which consisted all his genius, was left to Dante,—his faith. God, redeemer and spirit of life, the justice of God the supreme mistress of the unjust history that men make, consoler of those to whom the world refuses earthly happiness; and then the noble certainties whose beam God has planted in the human reason, and the immortal love wherewith He enchants the human heart; Dante embraces all these truths with the adoring emotion of the priest who bends over the Host and the quiet conviction of the geometer who proves a theorem. He not only believes but sees; he moves in the region of the supernatural without more astonishment than the thaumaturges of the *Golden Legend*, and the children who fled at the sight of his cowl were not mistaken when they cried: "There is the man who has come back from hell!"

It is in the first awakening of his heart, at the dawn of his "new life", that we must first study him. He was nine years old when, on the first of May, the festival of the *Primavera*, he met little Beatrice Portinari. She was clad in a blood-coloured dress. At the sight of the young girl he trembled and heard a voice within him that said: *Ecce Deus, fortior me.* Nine years later he saw her again for a second time; she was clad in a white dress and returned his salutation so courteously that he thought he was carried away into bliss. One day when Beatrice had not returned his salutation he saw a young man all in white who wept and said: "My son". The *Vita Nuova* contains eight visions. In it Dante is always hearing airy voices, and meeting phantoms of light. Someone speaks within his heart. The last of these visions, on the day when Beatrice died, was so astonishing that he had not the strength to tell it. He closes his story by praying God to give him in Paradise the sight of Beatrice, "who gloriously beholds the face of Him Who is blessed for ever and ever".

Here we discover in the child and the youth the extraordinary gift that has visited the souls of the greatest saints and also those of philosophers possessed by the perpetual thought of the divine, namely, the faculty of mysticism. But these others had suffered in their manhood some profound shock to their conscience, some incurable weariness of things here below; they had experienced either the emptiness of sensuous happiness, or the weakness of the reason, or the terror of the unseen, and the shock that detached them from passion or knowledge threw them into the bosom of God, whence they never again wished or were able to escape. The visionary who wrote the *Apocalypse* has passed through the fatal days of Nero's reign; Plotinus (204–270) and Proclus (410–485) the most systematic of all the Neo-Platonists, had lived amid the strangest ferment of religious dreams that history has ever known and had had recourse to the dangerous seductions of theurgy. Joachim of Flora had known the pomp of the Norman court, and before hearing the Holy Ghost speaking into his ear he had traversed oriental Europe, Constantinople, and Asia Minor. Francis of Assisi had stirred his imagination by reading romances of chivalry and, as a young man, had devoted himself to all kinds of pleasures; a long sickness and disgust for all voluptuousness and then his desire for superhuman charity had brought him back to the *Gospel*. All these mystics, by contemplation and asceticism, had destroyed in themselves all earthly affection and put off, like a garment soiled with mud, their carnal covering. Their union with God was so intimate that they abandoned themselves distractedly and felt themselves fall into His arms as into an abyss. "I am about to rest in the peaceful sea, God Eternal", Catherine of Siena was to say on her death bed. Plotinus had said at his last hour: "I feel that God is departing from me". Almost all, even those who, like Francis and Catherine, took part in the affairs of the world, reached without effort the last term of the ecstatic life, the familiar vision of God and the mysteries of the other world. For them sensible objects seemed to be as nothing but shadows of beings; the conscience of each of them was dissipated and mingled with the conscience of God, and the last personal and living sentiment that remained in it was the ineffable joy given them by this daily communion with things eternal.

But here we have a young boy, the son of middle-class parents, belonging to a family of legists, brought up in the study of the Latin poets and early trained in military exercises ; he grew up in that commune of Italy that was most tormented by political violence ; his grandparents and his father, engulfed by the eternal conflict at Florence between Ghibeline and Guelf, had known the sorrows of exile. In that city of merchants and bankers, where only earthly passions had strength and where religion was of so moderate a temperament that, down to Antoninus (1389–1459) in the fifteenth century, none of her sons obtained an illustrious place in the Italian Paradise, in that Florence that loved joy, that invented the ironical *conte* and had, as far back as the eleventh century, rediscovered the incredulity of Epicurus, the child, still too young to have suffered, too pure also to suspect the ugliness of life, had no sooner seen on the face of Beatrice the reflection of a beauty higher than all earthly beauty, than he discovered in himself and embraced with extraordinary ardour the vocation to the supernatural. From that time forward he received a permanent revelation from Beatrice living and Beatrice dead, and through the young girl miraculously conversed with God and the angels. At times, when the initiation struck him with too dazzling a light, he felt himself faint and about to die. Like all great mystics he experienced two contrary sentiments from his ecstasy : the beatific rapture in viewing the mystery, and a melancholy bitterness for earth and life, as soon as he lowered his eyes towards them. The world seemed to him to be covered with a mourning veil ; he imagined that the pilgrims who traversed "the city of woe" would break forth into sobs if they knew the reason of its suffering. Real objects lost their colour, real joys all savour, the body in which the soul was imprisoned perished. "I became in a short time so frail and feeble that the sight of me shocked my friends." In such a state of the conscience all the operations of the mind are disturbed; the conditions of the intellectual life are in some sort "transposed"; the moral fever that possesses the poet transforms every vision and every emotion; by a singular duplicating of the consciousness it is his own passion that he sees, under the form of an angelic figure, at the end of some path, and the sighs and plaints that the mysterious passer-by gives utterance to are only the echo of Dante's heart. If Beatrice appears to him and salutes him he faints as if overpowered by an infinite sweetness; it seems to him that his soul is nought but love; his senses die, and love alone lives in him and looks at Beatrice. "It often happened at that time that my body moved as a thing dead". At the same time symbolism became, as it were, the dominant category of his thought. All that he saw, all that he heard, had value only through a secret relation to the unseen and divine. The colour of Beatrice's garments was for him a mysterious language that he understood more clearly than any mortal tongue. Beatrice herself was transfigured, and, under the appearance of a Florentine virgin, theology or the eternal wisdom was to welcome Dante in the outer sanctuary of the heavenly Jerusalem. The aspects of nature, of sea and sky, the glittering of the stars "which seemed to weep", the movements of the wild beasts, the accidents of history, great minds, such as Virgil, great traitors, such as Judas and Brutus, were to serve him as means to decipher and translate a sublime Word.

By this first feature of his genius, then, he was attached to the mystic idealism of the Middle Ages, that manifested itself in manners so diverse,—in the sickly fancies of gothic sculpture, in the heraldry of the feudal age, in the very noble dreams of the best Christians, and in the transcendent Platonism of the greatest scholastics. But in his case the very child was father to the visionary. Imagine Dante's entering a cloister in his early youth, removed for ever from Italian life and sheltered from political storms, nurtured only upon the *Scriptures*, disdainful of ancient literature. As a poet he would resume the Franciscan tradition of Brother Pacifico and write pious lauds in imitation of Jacopone ; as a painter he would essay the mild and timid art of Frá Angelico ; as a popular preacher he would perhaps terrify the faithful by the apocalyptic images of a Savonarola ; as a teacher he would mount the pulpit of Bonaventura. He would be a monk, enlightened and passionate above all others, the greatest in the religious history of Italy, but still merely a monk.

## II

The very grief that he felt at the death of Beatrice restored Dante to the rational life. Among the books in which his master Brunetto Latini taught him to read, he chose the most serious, the philosophers, Aristotle, Cicero, and Seneca. "I began to read the book with which Boethius, when a prisoner and in exile, consoled himself. And, knowing that Cicero had written a book in which, treating of friendship, he had quoted the consoling words of Lælius, that excellent man, upon the death of Scipio, his friend, I began to read it. I penetrated as far as possible into the thought of these wise men, and like a man who, seeking silver, finds gold, I who sought only consolation, found not only a remedy for my tears, but also names of authors, sciences and books, and I considered that philosophy, which was the mistress of those authors, sciences and books, is a thing supreme. Then I began to go where that gentle lady truly showed herself, to the schools of the religious and the disputations of the philosophers, and in thirty months I felt so penetrated by her sweetness that her love drove out every other thought." (101)

The *Convito*, or the *Banquet*, the books of which were written at very different periods of Dante's life, contains in some sort the recollections of this pilgrimage in search of rational wisdom. But at Padua and Bologna, and perhaps at Paris, on the Mount of St. Geneviève, if he took part in the arguments concerning *Quolibet* and heard the *Book of Sentences* commented upon, if he studied the theology of Thomas of Aquinas and received the laborious culture of scholasticism, neither the teachers nor the doctrines could form him to that consoling philosophy to which his afflicted soul aspired. The philosophy that he desired was not merely an intellectual operation, the science of interpretation and reasoning, the art of treating by means of the syllogism all the notions of the human mind, all the facts of nature and all the data of sacred literature. It was above all else, through intercourse with the best philosophers and the purest poets, through the meditation of the conscience, a personal process, much more living than the discipline of the Rue du Fouarre, more generous than the logic and dialectic of the School ; it was the reason and the heart penetrating and completing each other in an excellent intimacy, and, to repeat the words that Dante himself addressed in the midst of hell to "the dear, kindly, and fatherly phantom" of Brunetto Latini, the science that teaches *come l' uom s' eterna*, how man makes himself eternal.

It was in fact with the lessons of Brunetto Latini that Dante's philosophical initiation had begun. Brunetto also had lived under the shadow of the French scholastic schools ; but he had taken thence to Italy a ray of pagan light. He was by no means, in his *Treasure*, the compiler of an encyclopædia, like Vincent of Beauvais, but a sage who, amid the promiscuous knowledge heaped up by the Middle Ages, had been able to attain to the great simple notions of which the ancients had the secret. The *Treasure* is sown with maxims that seem to proceed from the moralists of Greece or Rome. In it we find again the fundamental thought of the Socratic or Stoic morality, that science is nothing without conscience, and that virtue is the finest fruit of wisdom. 'A worthy thing it is that the words of a wise man should be believed when his deeds testify to his sayings". "To speak well and do ill is nothing less than to condemn oneself from one's own mouth". Latini was, according to Giovanni Villani, "a great philosopher, an eminent master of rhetoric, but a man of pleasure, *mondano homo*. He was "worthy of being placed among the best orators of antiquity", writes Filippo Villani, "of a cheerful disposition and amiable in his talk". He was also the master of the great poet Guido Cavalcanti, whose elegies were now pathetic and now sensual, one of the frankest unbelievers in the epicurean circle at Florence. By combining all these features we can reconstruct Brunetto's original figure. Even if we add the annoying mystery that Dante leaves regarding the memory of his master, we shall see in him a kind of forerunner of the humanists of the Renaissance, in whom character was not always as strong as intellect, but whose intellect, refined by classical literature and above all seduced by the oratorical beauty of the Latin writers, very unconstrained and much inclined to irony, was able to restore, without too much pedantry, along with the sonorous language of Rome, the rationalistic genius of antiquity to the Christian ages.

Undoubtedly all the lettered men of the Middle Ages read the Greek and Roman poets, historians and philosophers, whom Latini explained to Dante. But in this case a veritable novelty sprang up between the master and the pupil. The religious admiration that the master inspired in the pupil for the ancients called forth in the young man's soul a moral crisis very like that which Plato has described; in the impetus of his enthusiasm and the effort of his love, Dante tried to imitate those noble models, "to give birth himself", as Plato used to say, "to fine discourses." He was not content with venerating, at the entrance to hell, the school of his beloved Virgil, the majestic shades of Homer, Horace, Ovid, and Lucan ; with contemplating, in their garb of immortal light, Socrates, Plato, Diogenes, Anaxagoras, Zeno, Hippocrates, Cicero, Livy, and Seneca, "the philosophic family" all grouped around Aristotle the king of teachers,

*il maestro di color che sanno.*

In his turn he would enter the band of these sages, he would endeavour to stammer their language and find once more the age-long liberties of the conscience in the tradition of their doctrines.

## III

Dante's *Banquet* is in fact a work of free investigation. The scholastic and geometric apparatus, so rigorous in his treatise *On Monarchy,* there disappears behind moral empiricism, the discussion of possible objections, the testimony of ancient writers, of the doctors of the School or the Arabs, the discussion of popular prejudices, the observation of the manners of the age. Authority is to be found in it in the measure suitable to a free mind ; the Christian appeals in it at times to revelation upon obscure points where the reason and doctrine hesitate in uncertainty, for example, the question of the immortality of the soul. (102) The philosopher relates the opinions of his masters, but only after having explained his own, not to decide his belief, but to enlighten and to strengthen it. Interpretation in accordance with the syllogism is at last pressed into the service of rational research.

The whole of this philosophy proceeds from the idea that Dante had formed of the human reason. The reason, he says, is the chief nobility of man, it is his form, and it is from it that he derives his essential qualification ; for him to live is not to live merely by the senses, like the beasts, but also by the intellect. The lofty value of our reason, that ponders the eternal truths, lies in its relation to the thought of God, in which those verities reside. Our soul, which is aware of its affinity with the divine soul, tends to unite itself in the closest fashion with God by means of love ; despoiled of all matter it shines with divine light, like the soul of an angel ; man is thus, thanks to his rational soul, a divine animal. This reason is free, because it is in its own service only ; the senses and passion are servants to it. It is the mistress of man's entire person ; man becomes great by obeying it, and he who, endowed with a perverse nature, dominates his evil instincts, and by struggle attains to wisdom, is better than he whose virtue never fights an internal battle. The man who enjoys the plenitude of his rational life possesses at once wisdom and knowledge and receives the philosophic blessing, the measure of which is fixed by the limits of his philosophic desire. He does not wish to know things that are too sublime for his intellectual vision, such as the intimate nature of God and that of elementary matter ; consequently he will not suffer by being deprived of that knowledge. Dante affirms God's existence, but does not define Him ; no place is found in the *Convito* for the mystical process, the ascension of the soul towards the supernatural. Dante reserves infinite knowledge and happiness exclusively for the souls of the elect. (103)

Dante's peculiar views upon morality make all human life depend upon this theory of the reason. "To live without using the reason is to be dead". And is it not a renunciation of reason when a man does not reflect upon life and the way he ought to follow? The reason cannot alter the verities of the divine order or the geometric order ; nor can it change the conditions of the animal life or the laws of nature ; but it is sovereign for all the actions of the will, "such as the good or evil we do to others, courage in battle or flight, chastity or debauchery ". So it is the rule of manners, the living law to which all the works of life are subject, as in the political order every operation of public life is dependent upon the imperial authority. And this ever active primacy of the reason makes virtue a state or intelligent habit of man. Here Dante returns to the theory of the Peripatetic ethics, the distinction between the intellectual virtues, such as prudence, and the moral virtues, such as courage, liberality, magnanimity, and justice. The latter are essentially states or rational choices, based upon the mean, habits equally removed from the two contrary excesses, and this measure in virtue is for the soul at once a perfection and the cause of moral happiness. The felicity that results from the action is excellent, just as is the state of blessing that results from contemplation ; it is, moreover, common to a greater number of souls ; but, just as contemplative happiness was shown to us separated from all mysticism, so moral felicity, understood by Dante in the Aristotelian sense, requires none of the painful joys of asceticism, the monastic renunciation of the world, the heroic excesses of the saints and martyrs. (104)

Dante owed to this sentiment of moderation, that was one of the conditions of ancient wisdom, the tranquil optimism of his *Convito*. If man, by the constant operation of his reason, is, as the ancients thought, the architect of his own destiny, that destiny is easy and may be pleasant. He himself lightens the path on which he walks, without illumination coming from above or supernatural grace granted by God in answer to his prayers. It is not a valley of tears that he painfully passes through, but a peaceful region rendered lovely by his virtues. Adolescence, that ends at the twenty-fifth year, is a happy period, in which the soul receives all the germs of virtue ; it has its peculiar gifts, obedience, modesty, sweetness (*soavità*), the charm of face and body. Sweetness of manner, that will be necessary at the time when public life begins, gives adolescence the friendships without which there is no perfect life. Dante pauses complaisantly to consider the privileges and virtues of this age that, in his case, had been so gloomy ; the welcome that greets the adolescent upon all sides and that smiles in response to the courtesy of his words and his deeds ; the artless admiration he feels for things of which he knows nothing ; the modesty that keeps him free from all that is low, and as soon as a suspicion of sensual attraction creeps into his mind makes him blush or turn pale ; the shame (*verecundia*) that combines with the fright for the evil he has committed a bitterness of which the memory will prevent him from falling into the same fault again. Lastly, the beauty and nimble agility of the body (*snellezza*) " the sight of which causes a pleasure of admirable harmony ", the good health " that clothes the person with a colour pleasant to behold ", are a final effect of the interior beauty of the soul that takes pleasure in adorning and enlivening its own dwelling place. Dante has rediscovered the Socratic maxim, the soul artist that fashions the body and face of the man ; and his theory of adolescence, enlightened as it were by a reflection from Plato, once more conjures up before our mind's eye the elegant and slender young men of the Florentine schools of art, the supple and delicate bodies of Luca Signorelli, the modest dreaminess of the young figures of Luca della Robbia or Donatello.

To the qualities of adolescence, youth and man's estate add the rational government of the appetites or passions, fiery coursers that now rush onward, now pause and flee ; the good horseman who succeeds in mastering them checks them by the bit when they run too fast, chastens them with the spur when they rear or cowardly recoil ; the bit is temperance, the spur is magnanimity. Here again Dante is faithful to the doctrine of the Platonists or moderate Stoics. He is as far as possible removed from the monastic theory of the Middle Ages, the absolute renunciation of all earthly things, the death of the heart to every passion. For him man's merit consists in energy of mind regulating a nature enfeebled by no moral mutilation. And this long effort towards the good receives its reward in old age. The old man, tested by the storms of the world, sure of his virtue, may spread abroad the treasures of goodness slowly amassed in his conscience. He is, says Dante, " like a full blown rose, whose perfume is given to all alike ". He lavishes his prudence, derived from memory, for the past ; of right judgment, for the present ; of foresight, for the future. He lavishes his justice, and for the public good enters the councils of his city. He takes part with pleasure in conversations of an exquisite refinement. " The older I grow ", said Cato the Elder, " the more pleasure I find in conversing ". But the old man's great nobility lies in the nearness of God to Whom he is drawing closer, and the vision of death, that seems to him the eternal port that he is about to enter in peace, rejoicing at the good and prudent voyage of his life. Already the sails of the ship are furled, the oars are lowered and now only skim the tranquil water ; on the bank his fellow citizens and friends are assembling to welcome the pilgrim's return, the friends of the heavenly fatherland, the ancestors long since dead, the friends of God, by whom he is worthy to be received. Soon he will land from his vessel as one leaves a hostelry, and, blessing his past life, will return to his home.

It is the hour holy above all others, the hour that, consecrating the religion of the three ages of man, brings back the soul of the just man to the bosom of God. Here, on the last page of the *Convito*, Dante expresses for the first time his sentiments concerning the religious duty that unites man to God, and those sentiments correspond exactly to the rationalistic theory of the whole book. "It is an idle excuse", he says, "to blame the bonds of matrimony, in old age, if we are unable to return to religion, as do those who embrace the discipline and take the habit of Benedict, Augustine, Francis, or Dominic ; for a married man can return, even in the married state, to the good and true religion ; God in fact desires only our heart to be religious." *Iddio non vuole religioso di noi se non il cuore.* (105)

Was not the "religion of the heart" also that of the mystics of the Italian Middle Ages, and by means of that free religion, the work of individual faith, did not Dante's mysticism and rationalism become reconciled without discordance in the unity of a great conscience? The combination of spiritual faculties so diverse formed an admirable Christian, capable at once of pious exaltation and serene reason, a poet's soul, worthy of the most beautiful days of the revelation of Assisi, but tempered by the wisdom of ancient thought and by that exact sense of realities which the intellectual civilization of Sicily had restored to the Italy of Frederic II. Dante's moral character might have stopped short at the features we have just described ; a kind of Florentine Epictetus, often visited by visions of paradise. It needed the pontificate of Boniface VIII (1294–1303), the treason of the Holy See towards Florence and the flight of the papacy into France to complete the religious originality of this figure with the keenness of passion and the boldness of personal theology.

## IV

Boniface VIII was regarded by Dante as an actual antipope, because he had received the tiara in the lifetime of Celestine V; he was regarded as an apostate pontiff because of the excess of his simony, and as a bad Italian because of his political crimes. The poet firmly believed that the Holy Roman See, under the rule of Benedict Gaetani, had ruined the Church and separated itself from all genuine Christianity. "He was a pope of great boldness and lofty spirit", writes Dino Compagni, "who led the Church whither he would and who crushed all his adversaries". And Villani testifies that Boniface used to say that "everything was permissible that was in the interest of the Church". The fault of Boniface lay in the fact that, through pride, he misunderstood the real situation of the papacy and the actual relations of the Holy See at the end of the thirteenth century with Italy and Christendom. There were combined in him a Gregory VII and an Alexander VI who neutralized each other. He wished to be at once a pope of the eleventh century and an ecclesiastical king of the fifteenth. The contradiction between these two parts brought about the ruin of his work. While at Rome he was fighting for the greatness of the Orsini, the secular fortune of his nephews, and the absolute authority of the pontifical monarchy, he was trying to resume the mystical primacy of the past and the right to regulate in the name of God the affairs of princes and republics. The lofty majesty of his bulls reminds us of the claims advanced of the quarrel about investiture. "Every human creature is necessarily subject to the Roman pontiff. For the pope is the spiritual power who institutes all earthly power and judges it if it be not good. God has set up the Apostolic See above kings and kingdoms, and every soul ought to obey that supreme master through whom princes receive their authority ".

But this great theory was repudiated by the France of Philip the Fair (1285–1314); as to Italy and Germany, they deemed it too sublime for the conscience of the pontiff whom his contemporaries called *magnanimus peccator*. Gregory VII and Innocent III could speak in this tone because Christendom saw God by their side. But Boniface, owing to the selfishness, knavery, and even cruelty, that characterized all the actions of his public life, was no more than an ambitious and greedy-minded pope, after the manner of his successors in the fifteenth century. Not content with lavishing fiefs, bishoprics, and red hats, upon his friends, he bought them signorial domains in Latium, contrary to the bulls of Martin IV (1281–1285) and Nicholas IV (1288–1292); for Pietro Gaetani he formed, by traffic or violent confiscation from the Colonna, a principality extending from Sulmona to Terracina. He spent the treasures of the Church without scruple for these acts of liberality towards his family. In the Jubilee of 1300, to which the Christian world hastened with the faith of ancient days, there were seen, wrote a pilgrim, "night and day two clerics standing near the altar of the apostle Paul with rakes in their hands gathering the piles of money ".

One after the other Boniface cast down all the secular supports of the Holy See. He isolated himself from the Roman communes by taking part in the quarrels of feudal families; he isolated himself from the Guelfs of Italy by calling in the brother of Philip the Fair, Charles of Valois, and handing over to him the White Guelfs of Florence. He profited by the weakness of the empire in his desire to restore, in a theoretical manner, the œcumenical power of the emperor to the papacy. He was suzerain of the

Angevins of Naples, and he wished to drive the Aragonese from Sicily or to impose upon them political obedience to the Holy See. He drenched Latium with blood. He understood nothing of the strength of the French royalty; he did not know that it was upheld by the *parlement*, the university, the clergy, and the estates; he believed that three or four haughty bulls would suffice to render Rome mistress of the public law of Church and state in France. Philip had the bull *Ausculta fili* burnt before Notre-Dame; the *parlement* declared the pontiff a heretic; and Nogaret, a royal legist, together with Sciarra Colonna, were sent into Italy. All the malcontents of the peninsula, the barons of the Roman campagna, the clients of the Colonna, hastened to the legates of the French king and went with them to assault Anagni, where Boniface, seated on the throne, with the tiara on his brow, underwent the cruellest affront a pope has ever endured. After three days of horrible scenes, the people and the Guelfic cardinals rescued the pontiff and took him back to Rome half mad with rage. There he refused all food, beat his head against the walls, and wept with fury at his impotence. He died at the end of 1303, at the age of eighty-six. With him disappeared the feudal papacy and the pontifical Middle Ages. The Roman Church, exiled on the Rhone, began slowly to prepare for its evolution into the tyrannical or monarchical state to which almost all Italy submitted in the course of the fourteenth century.

Dante was for a moment moved with pity by this unheard-of fall. "Christ was captive", he said, "in the person of His vicar". But it was the outrage inflicted upon the Christian pontiff, upon the august head of the Church, and it was also the insolence of the *fleur de lis* entering Anagni, that he resented. For the person of Boniface he never felt anything but implacable hatred. He could not forget that he owed his exile to the duplicity of the pope who, in 1302, had detained the Florentine embassy, of which he was a member, at Rome long enough to complete the ruin of the moderate Guelfs of Florence. He could not forgive him the brutality of his legate Charles of Valois, and the strange manner in which that pacifier had appeased Florence by pillaging and burning it. He deemed that this pope, by reversing the national tradition of the Holy See towards the Italian cities, had put the coping stone to the attempts of the Papacy against the liberties of Italy. He thought himself thenceforth absolved from loyalty to the visible Church of Rome, in the very name of his love for the eternal and mystical Church of Jesus. And, as he was at once a humanist and a visionary, a *Fraticello* enlightened by communion with the ancients, he was able, in his *Divine Comedy* to manifest a wholly revolutionary Christianity, strangely personal, but very logical, combined of ecstasy and rationalism, the last originality of the religious invention of Italy.

## V

The *Divine Comedy* is, in the greatest part of its development, a political pamphlet directed against the Holy See. In order to shut up a pope in the burning tombs of the heresiarchs, Dante confuses pope Anastasius II with the emperor Anastasius who was led astray by Photius. In the circle of the simoniacs, in which the damned are plunged head downwards in flaming pits, he meets Nicholas III who cries to him: "You already, and still erect, still erect, Boniface? Prophecy then has deceived me by several years?" Then, after having thus greeted the approaching coming of Boniface VIII, the Orsini pope announces that of Clement V, the first Avignon pontiff, "a pastor without authority, who will come from the west and cover Boniface and me". And in his anger Dante questions the greedy pontiff: "Tell me what treasure was it that Our Lord asked of St. Peter before entrusting the keys to him? He asked nothing of him, but said 'Follow me. . . ." It is your avarice that desolates the world, your avarice that tramples the good under foot and exalts the wicked. It is you, the pastors, whom the evangelist saw when he beheld the woman sitting on the waters prostitute herself with the kings. . . . You have made a god of gold and silver". (106) He consents to punish merely with purgatory pope Adrian V, who, with his neck twisted round, thus makes his confession! "See to what a degree, through my avarice, my soul was miserable and abandoned by God!" But in the midst of paradise he lends these terrible words of St. Peter himself! "He who upon earth usurps my seat, my seat vacant in the sight of God, has made of my tomb a sink of blood and corruption!" (107)

Inexpiable political rancour is not sufficient to explain such a passion. This severe Christian, in order to reassure his conscience and justify his hatred, possessed in fact a dogmatic theory that seemed like good orthodoxy to him. The last word of his belief, that "religion of the heart" of which he spoke in the *Convito,* is contained in the twenty-fourth canto of the *Paradise,* and it is to Peter himself that he makes his confession of it. He has come back to the very simple creed of Paul, faith, hope, and love. For him, as for the apostle, faith itself at bottom is nothing but hope, *fides sperandarum substantia rerum.* And when the first of the popes asks him to affirm more explicitly the object of his faith, he replies: *Credo in uno Dio solo ed eterno.* He believes in the name of Moses, the prophets, the Gospel, and in the name of the doctors of the Church. He believes in the Trinity: *E credo in tre Persone eterne.*

And this is the essential of Christianity, the initial

belief of the Christian family between the Apostles' Creed and the metaphysical Nicene Creed. To believe, to hope, to love,—what else is this than the reasoned adhesion of the heart to the truths "which are not visible to the reason?" is the repeated question of Dante. (108) And if faith, hope, and love are the triple source of all religious life in the human soul, if on this earth and beyond the grave these three virtues raise men to the rank of the elect and justify them, what becomes of "works",—of prayer, of penance, of the observance of the Christian who trembles before the Church, of the bloody labour at the price of which he believes he can redeem his sins and win paradise? Is it not upon the jurisdiction of this inner Church, built, in freedom, in every man's conscience, that each one of us depends, and does not the beauty of this hierarchy in which there are only two degrees, the soul and God, cast into the shade the splendour of the ecclesiastical hierarchy, of which the visible summit is the bishop of Rome?

Thus the capital point in the *Divine Comedy* is a latent doctrine that reveals itself in a thousand ways, a doctrine that concerns at once the dogma of sin and the part played by the Church in the religious life of every soul. "You must know", wrote Dante to Can Grande della Scala, when he dedicated the *Paradise* to him, "that the meaning of this work is not simple but manifold. The first meaning is that which appears from the written words, the second is that which is hidden beneath the things enunciated by the words; the first is called the literal meaning, the second the allegorical or moral." The first meaning in fact is quite literal, consisting of a return to the most canonical traditions of the Middle Ages, traditions theological, poetical, and scholastic. That picture of the three regions of the other world is derived from a hundred edifying poems and a multitude of legends that proceeded from the Celtic world of Patrick and

Brandan, the *Dialogues* of Gregory the Great, the visions of Paul, the vision of Brother Alberic, a monk of Monte Cassino in the twelfth century, and the *Fioretti* of Francis of Assisi. But what seems to dominate in the *Hell* is the doctrine of Satan as it had been understood since the *Apocalypse*, Satan, the enemy of God, who at times and for a few short hours is stronger than God. All the ontological and cosmological apparatus, the theory of the capital sins, the manner of analysing the play of the soul's passions, the movements of the heavens and the harmony of the world, come from his masters, Albertus Magnus and Thomas of Aquinas, the two angels of light whom he meets one after the other at the head of the group of great teachers, in the tenth canto of the *Paradise;* it is from them that he received the method and treasures of the scholastic science. As in the treatise *On Monarchy* and the dissertation upon *Land and Water*, he is, for all that escapes the jurisdiction of the individual conscience, the exact and scrupulous disciple of traditional Christianity and the School.

But the intimate and personal thought of the mystic and the rationalist is hidden behind the veil of tradition. We may put that veil aside and see Dante's true religion. Undoubtedly, as Ozanam showed, there is no belief and no sacrament of the Church that he does not dutifully accept. But the poet's originality lies in the agreement of this regular faith with the views peculiar to himself of justification, salvation, and damnation. Tradition gave him hell ; he adds to it the almost happy region to which are relegated the shades of the ancient sages, the pleasant meadow where the great pagan souls, and with them the anti-christ Averoees, converse in everlasting peace. Tradition gave him purgatory ; and it is Cato, again a pagan, a Stoic, who killed himself with his own hand, who is made the guardian of it. Tradition gave him paradise ; he places in it Ripheus, the Trojan who died for his country, and the good emperor Trajan. With him the supreme sin, that which he punishes with crushing contempt, is not heresy, nor unbelief, which he has shown, by the very disdain and lofty countenance of the damned, to be superior to hell ; it is *viltà,* the timid renunciation of active duty, devotion, and life, the cowardice of pope Celestine, more criminal than the treason of Judas. And yet it is not among the mortal sins or the venial, and it greatly resembles the humility of the ascetics, the fearful egotism of the monks. For these "vile" he creates the *Preinferno*, the lamentable vestibule where languish "those who were for themselves". You will seek in vain in the *Inferno* for the place where the souls of irregular Christians suffer, I mean those who failed in the duties of devotion, sacramental assiduity and the pious works prescribed by the Church ; all the lukewarm, the indifferent, those who wait till the last hour to make their peace with God, Statius, who from fear hid his baptism and faith, and was *per paura chiuso cristian,* are sent by Dante to purgatory, and that purgatory is very mild, in full sunshine, visited again and again by the angels with their songs. The poet's reason has freely revised the ecclesiastical theory of salvation.

## VI

The personal doctrine of Dante regarding justification is manifested in a very daring manner by the way in which he placed one soul, that of Siger de Brabant, in paradise, and another soul, that of king Manfred, in purgatory. Master Siger, a professor in the University of Paris in the latter part of the thirteenth century, had been condemned in 1270 by bishop Etienne on account of thirteen heretical opinions tainted with the philosophy of Averoees and that of

Aristotle. (109) Yet for seven years he continued to preach from his academic chair these doctrines of incredulity. On January 12, 1277, John XXI (1276–1277) wrote from Viterbo to bishop Etienne ordering him to condemn before his episcopal court the errors that were again swarming in the University, the pope's attention having undoubtedly been called to them by the great inquisitor for France, the Dominican Simon du Val. On March 7 the bishop of Paris, after having consulted the teachers of the *Scriptures*, denounced and condemned two hundred and nineteen propositions detected in the books and teachings of several doctors as contrary to the Catholic faith, among others those of Siger de Brabant and Boëce of Denmark. (110) Here again the offensive doctrines, that separated God from the world and the human soul from God by an unfathomable abyss, had come either from the Arabic science or from the excessive peripateticism of the University. Siger and his accomplices denied the substantial unity of the Trinity; and they also declared themselves unable to believe in Providence, creation, miracles, and the possibility of God's knowing anything beyond himself. They recognized the eternity of celestial matter, of the world of motion, and of the human race. They denied Adam, and also the fall of man, which is the starting point of the doctrine of redemption; they proclaimed the necessity of all existing things, the powerlessness of God to modify the order of the forms of life decreed by fate, of the earthly soul and the heavenly soul, and of the souls of the celestial bodies; they insisted that man's soul is inseparable from the body and dies of the same death; impersonal reason was the only thing they deemed to be immortal; the celestial bodies they declared to be masters of our will; they preached the nothingness of theology, the vanity of continence, and of humility and prayer; only earthly happiness is real, they asserted, death being the last term of human terror beyond which there is neither paradise nor hell ; and, finally, they contended that Christianity and its fables form an insurmountable obstacle to perfect science.

The theological edifice was thus overthrown in its entirety. Dogma and morals, the *New Testament* and the *Old Testament*, the Church and the University, were thus destroyed from top to bottom. And in order to show better the truly devilish character of these prodigious errors the bishop of Paris by the same sentence prescribed books of necromancy, sorcery, conjurations, and diabolical invocations, the painful religion of Satan which in France had preceded and survived the Albigensian heresy. Those who persisted in retaining these books were in their turn threatened with the condemnation of the Church and the punishment of the secular power. Master Siger was expelled from his chair and driven out of the kingdom. We know from a triplet of the *Fiore*, which is the Italian *Roman de la Rose*, how he ended. "Master Siger was not very happy," says False-Seeming ; "I made him die in poverty, in bitter anguish, at the court of Rome, at Orvieto".

*Mastro Sighier non̄ andò guari lieto,*
*A ghiado il fe' morire a gran dolore,*
*Nella corte di Roma, ad Orbivieto.* (111)

Dante as a child may have seen the exile pass through Florence. He may also have heard the echo of these strange doctrines either in Paris, or from the lips of Brunetto Latini, or from the Epicureans of Tuscany. It is then with a very clear understanding of the doctrinal misadventures of Siger that he dared to place the old master in paradise, in the sphere reserved to the greatest doctors of the Church, amongst the companions of St. Thomas Aquinas. "Here is the eternal light [the soul] of Siger, who, reading in the University, proved by syllogisms truths that excited the malice of the envious ".

*Essa è la luce eterna di Sigieri,*
*Che, leggendò nel vico degli Strami,*
*Sillogizzó invidiosi veri.* (112)

Here we certainly find a very curious mystery. It is impossible to admit, in spite of the last line of this triplet, that Dante had accepted as truths the condemned propositions of the Parisian teacher. And it would be very hard to think that, blinded by his passion against the Holy See, he would have deliberately introduced into such an august place, into the very radiance of God, an impertinent heresiarch. The explanation that was then made of Siger's opinions, that is that as a philosopher he thought differently than he did as a Christian, is absurd, especially for a mediæval conscience, and therefore it serves only to becloud a subject already obscure. Finally, the hatred displayed by the Dominicans, and consequently by the Inquisition, against the University and Siger could not justify such a multitude of accusations, such an abundant harvest of religious negatives. The calumny would be really excessive, even for the period of narrow discipline imposed by the popes upon the University which lasted until the reign of Philip the Fair. One answer alone remains, the expiation of the doctor, the great misery, to which the *Fiore* testifies, when he languished between the walls of gloomy Orvieto, perhaps, also, the tortures and the violence that shortened his life. (113) "Death", says Dante, "had seemed to him very slow in coming ".

Hence, according to the poet, the supreme moment, the last breath of life, the expiring light of conscience, belong to God and to God alone. The entire work of salvation is contained in that moment, quick as lightning, when through the lips of the dying man the soul exhales itself, far from the priest, without any sacramental formula. Buonconte di Montefeltro, the Ghibeline captain, when wounded at Campaldino, expired alone, without confession, on the bank of the river Ermo ; but as he died he murmured the name of the Virgin Mary, and God, despite the crimes of his life, received him into purgatory. "The angel of God took me and the angel of hell cried out : O Thou Who cometh from heaven, why dost Thou snatch him from me and carry off his eternal soul? Why should a little tear rob me of my prey?" *Per una lagrimetta che' l mi toglie.* (114) That "little tear", whose secret is known only to God, was without doubt sufficient for the perfect redemption of Master Siger, the woes of exile and the malice of the papal court having already paid his debt to purgatory.

On this mountain of expiation Dante meets a very unexpected person, Manfred, son of Frederic II, for whom the Church of Rome had not thunderbolts sufficient. "He was fair and beautiful and of noble aspect, but one of his eyebrows was cut by a wound". And Manfred smilingly shows the poet a second wound near his heart. The vanquished of Ceperano, the heir of the great designs of the Suabian emperor, says to Dante : "When my life was reft by two mortal blows, I resigned myself with tears to Him who willingly pardons. My sins were horrible, but the infinite goodness has arms so wide that it receives all who turn to it. If the bishop of Cosenza, whom pope Clement sent in pursuit of my body, had understood that truth, my bones would still be at the head of the bridge near Benevento, guarded beneath a heap of stones ; now they are bathed by the rain and tossed by the winds, outside of my kingdom, near the banks of the Verde, where the bishop took and cast them with extinguished torches. But no, their malediction cannot damn us or prevent us from finding eternal love as long as a single flower of hope blooms in our heart".

> *Per lor maledizion si non si perde,*
> *Che non possa tornar l' eterno amore,*
> *Mentre che la speranza ha fior del verde.* (115)

It was the cry afterwards uttered by Savonarola to the bishop who degraded him, in the presence of the executioner, of his dignity as priest and friar. "It is in your power to cut me off from the Church militant, but not from the Church triumphant!" The Church disarmed, priests and bishops and even the pontiff rendered powerless to change the sentence of God,—every time the Italian mystics disclose the inmost recesses of their heart that is the doctrine and the hope to which they bear testimony.

It needed long misery, immeasurable rancour and the shipwreck of his earthly fatherland to make Dante confess, with so rough a frankness, his opinion about Rome and the Church. It will cause no astonishment that he undoubtedly placed in paradise only the martyr popes, the first successors of Peter, and Gregory the Great, the apostolic pope whose figure I have placed on the first pages of this history. But it was in the name of the inner religion that he could thus protest against the priesthood; and that religion, that went back to the *Gospel*, to John and Paul, that creed of a faith certainly eternal since it answers to all that is excellent in the human heart, had been for a century and a half the fruitful work of Italy and, as it were, the original function of the peninsula in the historical destiny of Christianity.

# NOTES

1. For all that precedes see Ferdinand Gregorovius, *Geschichte der Stadt Rom im Mittelalter*. Vols. 1–4. Stuttgart. 1872. There is an English translation of this work. London. 1894–1906.

2. George Heinrich Pertz. *Editor*. *Monumenta Germaniæ Historica*. 5 : 43–45. Hanover. 1839.

3. Vincenzo di Giovanni. *Filologia e Letteratura Siciliana*. Palermo. 1871. Page 129.

4. Felice Tocco. *L' Eresia nel Medio Evo*. Florence. 1884. Pages 387 ff. See also François Lenormant. *La Grande Grèce : paysages et histoire*. Paris. 1881–84. Vol. 1, chap. 6.

5. The conflict between Venice and Pisa over the relics of St. Nicholas is to be found in Marino Sanuto's *Vitæ Ducum Venetorum*. These biographies of the Venetian doges are to be found in Vol. 22 of Muratori's *Rerum Italicarum Scriptores*, Milan, 1750 ; and also in Parts 3–5 of the new edition of Muratori. Sanuto's works have been edited by G. Monticolo. Città di Castello. 1900.

6. Gabriele Rosa. *I Feudi ed i Communi della Lombardia*. Bergamo. 1854.

7. Benvenuto d' Imola. *Benvenuti de Rambaldi de Imola Comentum super Dantis Aldigherii Comoldiam*. Florence. 1887.

8. *Arnulfi gesta archiepiscoporum Mediolanensium*. To be found in Muratori, 4 : 20. Also in Migne, 147 : 39. And in Pertz, 3 : 17.

9. Ludovico Antonio Muratori. " *Vilium personarum congeriem, ac deinde seditionem abjectorum artificum*."

10. *Archivio Storico Italiano*. Florence. 1842, etc. Vol. 6 ; series 3. Muratori. *Antiquitates Italiæ Medii Aevi*. Vol. 5, division 60. Milan. 1738–42. Tocco. *Ibidem*. Page 207.

11. Charles Guillaume Adolphe Schmidt. *Histoire et Doctrine de la Secte des Cathares ou Albigeois*. Paris. 1849. See also the *Liber Inquisit. Tholos*. Pages 33, 174, and 204.

12. Charles du Plessis d' Argentré. *Collectio Judiciorum de novis Erroribus*. Paris. 1755. See the *annales* for the year 1180.

13. Victor Cousin. *Editor*. *Abælardi Omnia Opera*. Paris. 1849. 2 : 646.

14. *Theologia Christiana*. Page 456. To be found in Cousin's collection of Abelard's works.

15. "*Non fuisse necessarium in mundo Christi adventum.*" See Jacques Paul Migne. *Patrologiæ Cursus Completus.* Latin series. 108 : 269. Paris. 1844, etc. Also Martin Bouquet and others. *Editors. Recueil des Histoires des Gaules et de la France.* 14 : 370. Paris. 1738–1906.

16. Bernard of Clairvaux. *Epistolæ* 195. To be found in Migne's *Patrologia.* Bernard's complete works have been translated by the Abbé Charpentier into French. Paris. 1873.

17. Bernard of Clairvaux. *De Consideratione.* 4 : 3. See also his *Epistolæ,* 256.

18. For this entire chapter see the following works. Heinrich Suso Denifle and Franz Ehrle. *Archiv fur Litteratur- und Kirchengeschichte des Mittelalters.* Berlin. 1885, etc. Volume 1, No. 1. Herman Ferdinand Reuter. *Geschichte der Religiösen Aufklarung im Mittelalter.* Berlin. 1875–77. Dom de Riso. *Della Vita e delle Opere dell' Abbate Gioachino.* Joseph Ernest Renan. *Nouvelles Études d' Histoire Religieuse.* Paris. 1884. John Boland and others. *Editors. Acta Sanctorum.* Three editions. Antwerp—Tongerloo—Brussels; 1643–1902. Venice; 1734–70. Paris; 1863–83. See Volume 7 for May.

19. Joachim of Flora. *Divini Vatis Abbatis Joachim Liber Concordia novi ae veteris Testamenti.* Venice. 1519. *Expositio magni Prophetæ Abbatis Joachim in Apocalypsin. Psalterium decem Chordarum.* Venice. 1527. For a list of the unedited works of Joachim see Denifle and Ehrle as cited in note 18.

20. Augustine. *De Civitate Dei.* Chapters 20 and 22. *In Joannis Evangelium Tractatus.* Pages 36 and 124. Both these works, with Augustine's other writings, are to be found in Migne's *Patrologie.* Latin Series. Volumes 32–47. Nearly all Augustine's writings have been translated into English. They are to be found in the "Nicene and Post-Nicene Fathers." Buffalo. 1886, etc.

21. Joannes Scotus Erigena. *Expositiones super Hierarchias Sancti Dionysii.* Book 2. To be found in Migne's *Patrologia Latina.* 122 : 39. Erigena's *Commentary upon the Fourth Gospel* is to be found in the same volume of Migne, page 308.

22. D'Argentré (as cited in note 12). See the *annales* for the years 1204–10. Nicolaus Eymeric. *Directorium Inquisitorium.* Rome. 1578.

23. Joachim of Flora. *Expositis in Apocalypsin.* Pages 80 and 3. See note 19.

24. Joachim of Flora. *Concordia.* Book 5, division 84. See note 19.

25. *Ibidem.* Book 5, divisions 116, 117, and 119. See note 19.

26. *Ibidem.* Book 1, division 8.

27. *Ibidem.* Book 5, division 57.

28. For the biography of Francis of Assisi see the following

works. *Acta Sanctorum*, volume 2 for October, where are to be found the two *Lives* by Thomas of Celano (translated into English by A. G. Ferrers Howell. New York. 1908), the so-called *Legenda Trium Sociorum*, finished in 1246, and the *Legend* of Bonaventura, finished in 1263. Lucas Wadding. *Annales Minorum seu Trium Ordinum a S. Francisco Institutorum*. Rome. 1731, etc. For the intimate character of the saint one should read the *Fioretti*, the popular gospel of Franciscanism in the fourteenth century. There are several translations into English of *The Little Flowers of St. Francis*. The *Liber Conformitatum*, upon which Brother Bartolommeo, beginning in 1385, spent more than fifteen years, displays, with subtle analysis, the resemblance, feature by feature, of Francis to Jesus. Milan. 1510. For the first apostolate one should read the *Chronica Fratis Jordani a Giano*. Leipsic. 1870. A second edition is to be found in the *Analecta Franciscana*. Quaracchi. 1885, etc. For the crisis that occurred immediately after the death of Francis recourse should be had to the *Historia Septem Tribulationum*. The text of this *Chronicle of the Tribulations* by Angelo Clareno is to be found, though not in its entirety, in the second volume of the *Archiv für Litteratur und Kirchengeschichte des Mittelalters* (see note 18). For the influence of Francis upon poetry and art in Italy see Henry Thode's *Franz von Assisi und die Anfänge der Kunst der Renaissance in Italien*. Berlin. 1885. And for information regarding the works and the spirit of Francis the following books should be consulted. Karl Hase. *Franz von Assisi: Ein Heiligenbild*. Leipsic. 1856. Renan. *Nouvelle Études d' Histoire Religieuse*. Antoine Fréderic Ozanam. *Les Poëtes Franciscains en Italie au Trezième Siècle*. Paris. 1852. Johann Görres. *Der Heilige Franciskus von Assisi, ein Troubadour*. Strassburg. 1826. To these references cited by Gebhart there should be added, for general information regarding Saint Francis, Paul Sabatier's *Life of St. Francis of Assisi*. London. 1907. And for further information regarding the early Franciscan literature one should see W. Goetz's *Die Quellen qur Geschichte des hl. Franz von Assisi*. 1904.

29. This rule of 1209, now lost, has been restored with a great degree of probability, by Karl Müller, in his *Die Anfänge des Minoriten Ordens und der Bussbruderschaften*. Freiburg-in-Breisgau 1885. It ought to be substituted for the first traditional Rule, which belongs to 1221.

30. Bartolomæus of Pisa. *Liber Conformitatum*. Bologna. 1590. Page 185.

31. See the *Legend of the Three Companions* in note 28.

32. See *The Little Flowers of Saint Francis*, division 26. See also the Rule of 1221, division 7: *Et quicumque ad eos venerint, amicus vel adversarius, fur vel latro, benigne recipiatur*.

33. *Acta Sanctorum.* October. 2 : 757.

34. *Liber Conformitatum.* Edition of 1590. Page 178 and 262

35. Rule of 1221. Division 20.

36. *Liber Conformitatum.* Edition of 1590. Page 243.

37. *Ibidem.* Page 244.

38. Wadding. *Annals Minorum.* 1 : 61. See note 28. The *Liber Conformitatum* omits the entire passage relating to the rich. See page 146 of the 1590 edition.

39. Lapo Mazzei. *Lettere di un Notaro a un Mercante del seccolo XIV.* Florence. 1880.

40. *Epistolarum Petri de Vineis.* Basel. 1566.

41. Jean François Michaud. *Histoire des Croisades.* Volume 2, book 32, chapter 15. Paris. 1857. *L'Estoire des Eracles Empereur et la Conquest de la Terre d'Outremer.* Book 32 ; chapter 15. Paris. 1841, etc.

42. Machiavelli's *Discorsi sopra la Prima Deca di Tito Livio* is to be found in his *Opere Complete,* published at Florence in 1843. There are several English translations. The present quotation is to be found in book 3, division 1. Machiavelli saw Dominic through the eyes of Savonarola. The Florentine reformer had listened with eagerness to Dominic. But had Savonarola lived in the thirteenth century he would undoubtedly have been much more of a Franciscan than a Dominican.

43. Jean Louis Huillard-Bréholles. *Historia Diplomatica Frederici Secundi.* 2 : 2 and 6 : 257. Paris. 1852–61. Jules Zeller. *Histoire d' Allemagne.* Passim. Paris. 1872–91.

44. *Cento Novelle Antiche.* No. 52. Naples. 1879.

45. Muratori. *Rerum Italicarum Scriptores.* 3 : 585.

46. Huillard-Bréholles. *Vie et Correspondence de Pierre de la Vigne.* Page 196. Paris. 1864.

47. Huillard-Bréholles. *Historia Diplomatica.* 6 : 326, 614, 618, and 676.

48. *Ibidem.* Introduction.

49. *Ibidem.* 6 : 336, 473, and 811.

50. *Ibidem.* 6 : 176.

51. *Ibidem.* 4 : 910. 6 : 391.

52. *Ibidem.* 6 : 685.

53. *Ibidem.* 6 : 391.

54. *Cento Novelle Antiche.* No. 139.

55. *Ibidem.* No. 71.

56. *Ibidem.* No. 112.

57. *Historia Diplomatica.* 5 : 339.

58. Renan. *Averroès et l' Averroisme.* Second edition. Page 167. Paris.

59. *Ibidem.* Chapter 2.

60. *Ibidem.* See also an article by Michele Amari in the *Journal*

*Asiatique.* 1853. Page 240. Vincenzo di Giovanni. *Storia della Filosfia in Sicilia.* 1 : 124. 1873.

61. Benvenuto d' Imola. See note 7. *Comm. ad Inferno.* 10.

62. Giovanni Boccaccio. *Il Decamerone.* VI, 9. Included in his *Opere.* Florence 1723–24. There are a number of English translations of *Il Decamerone.*

63. Dante. *Inferno.* X. 35. For the original see *Tutte le Opere di Dante Alighieri.* E. Moore. Editor. Oxford University Press. 1904. Charles Eliot Norton's prose translation of the *Commedia* is recommended. Of the renderings into English verse that by Longfellow is the best known and that by Melville Best Anderson the most scholarly.

64. Frà Salimbene. *Chronicle.* All the editions of this work are defective. The best is probably that of the Franciscans of Quaracchi. It is to be found in the *Analecta Franciscana.* The translator does not know what edition was used by Gebhart. The citations to pages of the *Chronicle* in the original of *Mystic Italy* are therefore omitted in the translation.

65. Adolf Gaspary. *Die Sicilianische Dichterschule des Dreizenhten Jahrhunderts.* Chapter 2. Berlin. 1870.

66. Émile Gebhart. *Les Origines de la Renaissance en Italie.* Chapter 6. Paris. 1879.

67. Allesandro d' Ancona. Domenico Comparetti, Editor. *Le Antiche Rima Volgari.* 1 : 51, 17, 38, 21, 74, and 75.

68. *Bibliothèque de l' Ecole des Chartes.* A periodical publication of the *École Impériale des Chartes.* See the thesis by M. L. Richard, entitled *Jean XXII et les Franciscans,* which appeared in 1886. See also in the *Archiv für Litteratur- und Kirchengeschichte des Mittelalters,* Volume 3, No. 1, an article by Ehrle entitled *Zur Vorgeschichte des Concils von Vienne.*

69. See in the *Archiv für Litteratur- und Kirchengeschichte des Mittelalters,* Volume 1, No. 4, an article by Ehrle entitled *Die Spiritualen, ihr Verhältniss zum Franciscanerorden und zu den Fraticellen.* See also Volume 2, No. 2 for *The Chronicle of the Tribulations.* And see Felice Tocco's article *Docum. Franciscani* in the *Archivio Storico Italiano* for 1886, Disp. V.

70. The first chronicles do not agree as to the time he was elected general, nor are they in accord as to the number of times he held that office.

71. Antony of Padua's works are to be found in Migne's *Patrologia Latina.* 6 : 1206.

72. See *The Chronicle of the Tribulations* in the *Archiv für Litteratur- und Kirchengesch des Mittelalters.* 2 : 256.

73. *Archiv für Litteratur- und Kirchengeschichte des Mittelalters.* 2 : 259–63. *Bene et opportune venisti, sed venisti tarde.*

74. *Histoire Littéraire de la France.* Begun by the Benedictines

us down in the snow, and if we bear all this thinking of the sufferings of the Blessed Jesus, Brother Leo, that verily is perfect joy."

This religious gaiety was one of the forces of the apostolate of Francis. He charmed his brethren, and they in their turn charmed Italy, by the smiling serenity with which they welcomed great misery and the little distresses and humble joys of life. Once upon a time he, being of mean appearance, received only a few crusts of dry bread in a village, while Frà Masseo, who was, the *Fioretti* tells us, "tall and comely in person," was given generous pieces of fresh bread. They spread out their takings on a large white stone, near a clear spring, in the sunshine, and Francis was amazed at the beauty of the feast. "But, father," said Masseo, "we have neither cloth, nor knife, nor plate, nor table, nor house, nor man servant, nor maid servant." "And for what then," replied Francis, "do you take this fine stone, this limpid water, and these pieces of bread?" As he had always a merry heart he did not like to have about him any but good-humoured faces, and did not allow the mournful pre-occupation of *mea culpa* to be brought into the cheerful chapter of his Minorites. He used to say to a novice: "My brother, why this sad face? Hast thou committed some sin? That concerns God and thee alone. Before me and my brethren keep always a look of holy joy; for it is not seemly, when one is in the service of God, to show a gloomy and frowning air." (30) And in the Rule of 1221 he made joy a canonical obligation, together with chastity and obedience. The true Franciscans must always be *guadentes in Domino,* "merry and of good courage." There is no valley of tears in the Holy Land of Umbria.

Yet the Franciscans were very poor; every day they held out their hands at the doors of houses and churches; to shelter them they had but a few huts made of rushes near Assisi. Communal Italy, the

97. Allessandro d' Ancona. *Origini del Teatro in Italia.* Volume 1, pages 117 and following. Florence. 1877.

98. *Offices Dramatiques des Penitents de l' Ombrie.* Published by Monaci. Imola. 1874.

99. D' Ancona. 1 : 189. See note 97.

100. Eugène Müntz. *Histoire de l' Art pendent la Renaissance.* 1 : 285. Paris. 1889–95.

101. *Convito.* 11 and 13.

102. *Ibidem.* 11, 9.

103. *Ibidem.* II, 8 and III, 14–15.

104. *Ibidem.* IV, 17.

105. *Ibidem.* IV, 27–28.

106. *Inferno.* XIX.

107. *Paradiso.* XXVII, 22.

108. *Ibidem.* XXIV, 65.

109. *Chartularium Universit. Parisiens.* Volume 1, No. 432.

110. *Ibidem.* Volume 1, No. 473.

111. *Roman de la Rose.* XCII.

112. *Paradiso.* X, 136.

113. See an article by Hauréau in the *Journal des Savants* for April, 1890.

114. *Purgatorio.* V, 107.

115. *Ibidem.* III, 133–35.

# A LIST OF BOOKS BY ÉMILE GEBHART

| YEAR. | TITLE. | PUBLISHER. |
|---|---|---|
| 1860. | De Varia Ulyssis apud Veteres Poetas Persona. | *Durand.* |
| 1860. | Histoire du Sentiment Poétique de la Nature dans l' Antiquité Grecque et Romaine. | *Durand.* |
| 1864. | Praxitèle ; Essai sur l' Histoire de l' Art et du Génie Grecs, de Péricles à Alexandre. | *Tandou.* |
| 1869. | Essai sur la Peinture de Genre dans l' Antiqué. | *Thorin.* |
| 1876. | De l' Italie ; Essais de Critique et d' Histoire. | *Hachette.* |
| 1877. | Rabelais ; la Renaissance et la Réforme. | *Hachette.* |
| 1879. | Les Origines de la Renaissance en Italie. | *Hachette.* |
| 1884. | Introduction à l' Histoire du Sentiment Religieuse en Italie depuis la fin du Douzième Siècle au Concile de Trente. | *Berger-Levrault.* |
| 1887. | Études Méridionales ; La Renaissance Italienne et la Philosophie de l' Histoire. | *Cerf.* |
| 1890. | L'Italie Mystique ; Histoire de la Renaissance Religieuse au Moyen Âge. | *Hachette.* |
| 1893. | Autour d' une Tiare. | *Colin.* |
| 1895. | Rabelais. | *Lecene et Oudin.* |
| 1896. | Moines et Papes ; Essais de Psychologie Historique. | *Hachette.* |
| 1897. | Au Son des Cloches ; Contes et Légendes. | *Hachette.* |
| 1899. | La Baccalauréat et les Études Classiques. | *Hachette.* |
| 1900. | Cloches de Noël et de Pâques. This is merely a reprint of three stories from Au Son des Cloches with the addition of illustrations and decorations. | *Piazza.* |
| 1901. | Conteurs Florentines du Moyen Âge. | *Hachette.* |
| 1902. | D' Ulysse à Panurge. | *Hachette.* |
| 1905. | L' Ulysse à Panurge ; Contes Héroï-Comiques. | *Hachette.* |
| 1907. | Sandro Botticelli. | *Goupil.* |
| 1907. | Petite Legende Dorée. | *Bloud et Gay.* |
| 1908. | Rome et Italie. | *Bloud et Gay.* |
| 1908. | Michel-Ange ; Sculpteur et Peintre. | *Manzi et Joyant.* |
| 1910. | La Vieille Église. | *Bloud et Gay.* |
| 1911. | Les Jardins de l' Histoire. | *Bloud et Gay.* |
| 1911. | Souvenirs d' un Vieil Athénien. | *Bloud et Gay.* |

| YEAR. | TITLE. | PUBLISHER |
|---|---|---|
| 1911. | De Panurge à Sancho Pança ; Mélanges de Littérature Européenne. | *Bloud et Gay.* |
| 1912. | Petits Mémoires. | *Bloud et Gay.* |
| 1913. | Les Siècles de Bronze. | *Bloud et Gay.* |
| 1914. | L'Age d'Or. | *Bloud et Gay.* |

The last seven books, made up of contributions to periodicals, were all published posthumously. One other, *Alma Mater*, was announced, but its publication is doubtful. The *Botticelli*, as first published, was, like the *Michel-Ange*, a richly illustrated and expensive book. A cheap edition of the text was published in 1908 by Hachette.

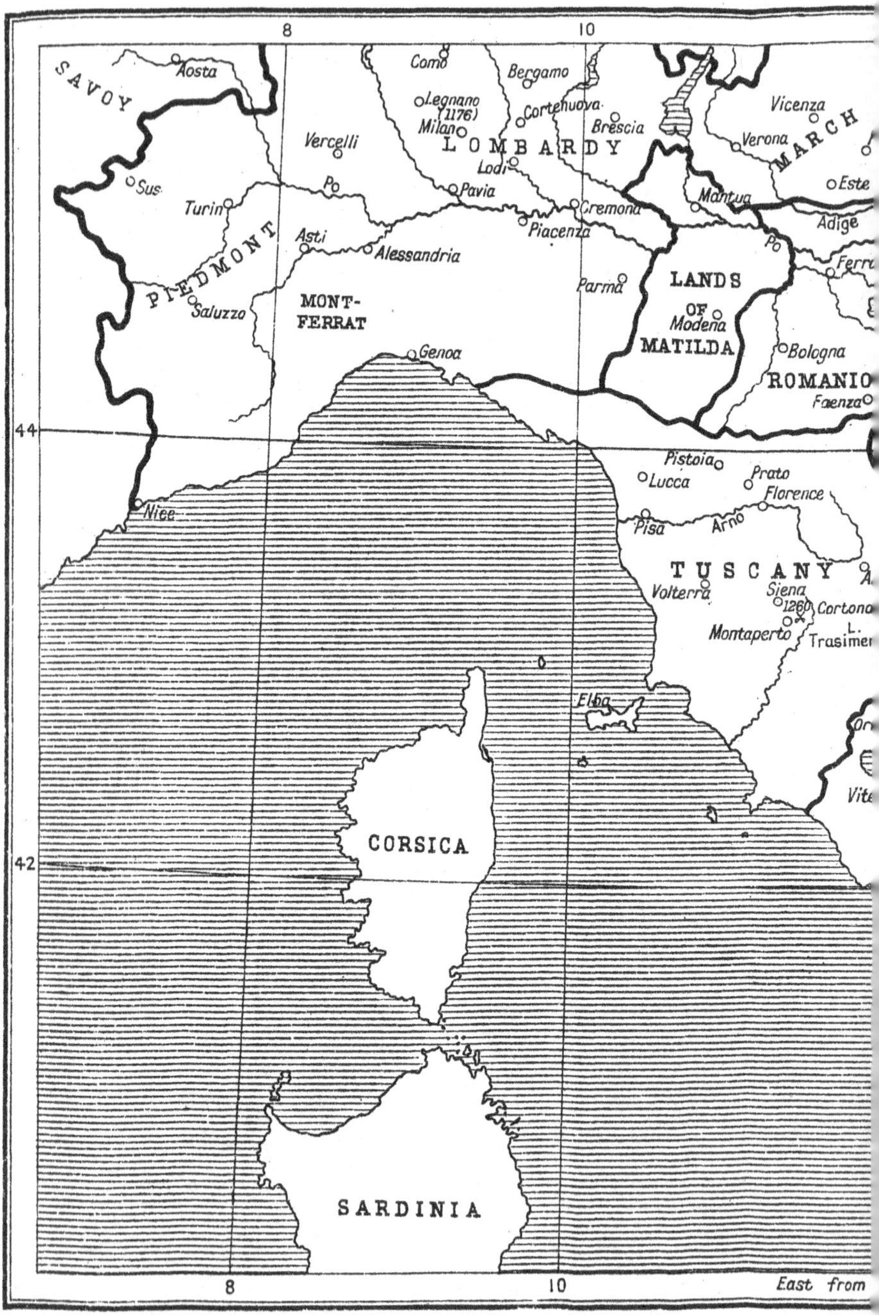
SAVOY
Aosta
Sus
Turin
PIEDMONT
Saluzzo
Vercelli
Po
Asti
Alessandria
MONT-
FERRAT
Genoa
Nice
Como
Legnano
(1176)
Milano
LOMBARDY
Bergamo
Cortenuova
Brescia
Lodi
Pavia
Cremona
Piacenza
Parma
LANDS
OF
Modena
MATILDA
Vicenza
Verona
MARCH
Este
Mantua
Adige
Bologna
ROMANIO
Faenza
Pistoia
Lucca
Prato
Florence
Pisa
Arno
TUSCANY
Volterra
Siena
1260
Montaperto
Cortona
L.
Elba
CORSICA
SARDINIA
8
10
44
42
East from

George Philip & Son, Ltd.

# INDEX

*Printed in Great Britain by*
UNWIN BROTHERS, LIMITED
LONDON AND WOKING